CU00940472

'I've been privileged to have had
George and Helen over the past 2
feels like those warm, hospitable
honest, personal experiences and concepts to take away and ponder at
leisure. I'm glad to have read it while it's still summer for me, so there's time
for the rich choice of ideas and wisdom to take root for my own autumn.'
**Lucy Moore, founder of Messy Church and head of the
Growing Faith Foundation**

'George Lings has written the book I should have read ten years ago when
I was entering the third age of autumn. He makes a wonderfully readable
companion to this important phase of life, giving us rich images and meta-
phors to help us value these special years as ones of both autumnal glory
and inevitable loss, of adventure and letting go. *Living the Autumn of Life* is
packed with wisdom and humanity. It reveals an author with a well-stocked
mind, a memory full of rich experience and a spirit full of desire to live autumn
well and to commend its fruit to others. I loved it.'
John Pritchard, former Bishop of Oxford

'We live in a time of gifts, not least the gift of age. But the journey needs
guidance. Out of his experience and rooted in scripture, George has given
us a guide to these later seasons, which can be long and fruitful. Reading
it I found myself better equipped to use the God-given time, and I believe
this will be true for you too. Highly recommended!'
Paul Bayes, former Bishop of Liverpool

'It is tempting to underline so many passages of this book. Drawing on an
impressively wide range of authors, Lings has blended his own personal
observations of living the autumn of life with those of carefully questioned
interviewees. I valued his insights, especially, when it comes to living with
regret, describing a significant early childhood bereavement as "one of the
negative cards I am likely to have to hold". It is an approach encapsulated in
his invitation: "So, tread with me some sort of middle ground to hold these
two themes – glory and loss – in tension with one another."'
Debbie Thrower, founder of Anna Chaplaincy

'I can't remember the last time I read a book that brought tears to my eyes or a smile to my lips more often than this one. I have read other books about "the autumn of life"; this is by far the best I have read, not least for the sane, wise, warm, balanced approach George Lings takes. I have a long (and growing) list of friends around my age to whom I am going to recommend – and if necessary give – this book!'
John Bowen, emeritus professor of evangelism, Wycliffe College, University of Toronto

'One of the many good things about the book which George Lings has produced is the way in which it – or rather he – invites the reader into a conversation with him. In spite of its deeply theological core, it is nevertheless less of a treatise, more a meditation; not a series of essays but a reflection, a ruminative process which draws the reader in and invites response.'
The Revd Canon Sue Hope, priest, author, tertiary of the Order of the Holy Paraclete

'George Lings helps us to be realistic about retirement with its challenges and opportunities. It is an easy read and well worth the time. It will help the reader approach retirement or continue living in retirement with a sense of realism, opportunity, and hopefully happiness and fulfilment. Each section of the book ends with a page of application points which are very helpful pointers for reflection and a guide on the way forward.'
Philip Johanson OBE, chief secretary of Church Army, 1990–2006

'This remarkable book is among the most informative and inspirational books I've ever read. It deals with a consequential but often overlooked aspect of our daily lives – old age! Wide-ranging in its scope, covering the different phases of living the autumn years, it is packed full of wisdom and spiritual insight, each of which is full of honesty, humility and humour. It is autobiographical in parts, covering issues of sociology, theology, ecology and urology! A book to read and re-read, so as to learn the art of living the autumn of life, walking through retirement with gratitude and trust, courage and hope. Highly recommended.'
Trevor Miller, former abbot of the Northumbria Community

'This book is written with disarming honesty and compassion, releasing us to reflect on our own autumn journey. With breadth and clarity it gives us both the wisdom we need to embrace the opportunities of this life season, and also spiritual insights to help us walk with God through its losses, in gratitude and trust. The questions offered at the close of each chapter make this a very useful resource for those involved in spiritual accompaniment and for small groups.'
Jenny Hellyer, spiritual director

'Once on holiday to France I stopped the car to stare at a field of sunflowers. They were sunflowers as I'd never seen them before: brown, dry, their heads drooping. I later did an online search for sunflowers. Sure enough, all the images that appeared were yellow and perky, their faces towards the sun. Then it struck me. This was simply a different season for the sunflower. This was when they were at their most fruitful, just before harvest. This season was why they were planted in the first place. The drooping sunflowers were not an image of loss or failure, but fulfilment and maturity. George Lings reflects on the autumn of life with characteristic insight, candour and spiritual wisdom. As I begin to see the leaves in my own life turn yellow, red and brown, and as I become a grandparent myself, I'm grateful to George and his cast of companions for these moving missives from the season of mists.'
Mike Starkey, writer and Anglican priest

 Ministries

15 The Chambers, Vineyard
Abingdon OX14 3FE
+44 (0)1865 319700 | brf.org.uk

Bible Reading Fellowship (BRF) is a charity (233280)
and company limited by guarantee (301324),
registered in England and Wales

ISBN 978 1 80039 281 6
First published 2024
10 9 8 7 6 5 4 3 2 1 0
All rights reserved

Living the
Autumn of Life

Walking through retirement
beginnings and endings

George Lings

BRF
Ministries

With thanks to Paul Tournier
and all my third-age friends

Contents

Acknowledgements

I am grateful to all those who gave me hours of their time in 16 interviews. Thank you Alec, Bill, Brian, Christina, both Christines, David, Helen, Jonathan, Michael, Mike, Paul, Sue, Susan, Tim and Vicky. You were so patient with my 25 questions! You even let me dig deeper into your initial answers when I needed to. You gave me well-tried advice as well as perceptive fresh questions. You were sources of new insights and also fortified some of my existing perceptions. Crucially you helped me believe that I wasn't the only one mad enough to think that trying to describe a conscious living of the autumn of our lives was a worthwhile pursuit.

My thanks also go to other anonymous characters. Some of you, by a chance remark, unwittingly opened a whole line of thought. Many more of you by your warm response to the initial theme of the book encouraged me to believe it was timely and needed.

Thank you Paddy McGlinchey, for steering me through the theological minefields of chapter 8 and heading off my more obvious over-simplifications.

My special thanks to my wife Helen, who contributed images and stories at various points. What you won't know was her encouragement when I couldn't find a word or, worse, got stuck or, worst of all, lost belief that I could do this at all and contemplated deleting all I had written. Thank you for always being there for me.

Introduction

Welcome to my world

Why this book?

I was drawn to write this book because I wanted to make sense of the stage of life that I am still living through. I realise that I began to be aware of something profoundly changing way back in 2011, when our youngest son left home. We drove him to start his first graduate job in the south of England and then had to drive back without him. It was the beginning of empty nesting and certainly a new stage of life. We drove north with a glowing setting sun in the west. I can still recall the feeling that I was seeing something special – the brighter colours together with the longer shadows and sharper contrasts.

I was 62 and, having passed 60, the question of when to retire had begun to raise its head. Work no longer stretched to an infinite horizon. I wondered then whether I was seeing the colours and perspectives of the evening of life. However, the longer I have lived since then, I realise that the time frame of the evening image is not really right. Even on a September evening in the UK, the night is not far away. And already a decade since my being 62 has come and gone. This metaphor of evening implies far too short a time frame. So at that point I didn't have a controlling metaphor to explore this shift, nor was it clear to me whether this transition was best understood as just being my age or was it something else?

During this period I began to notice that there didn't seem to be much written by Christians about this stage of life, which could be called being 'active elderly' or 'young-old'. Nor did it seem high on the list of church priorities. Understandably, in view of the declining proportion of young people in churches, the focus of books written and money spent is on reaching and then keeping children, youth, young adults and young families. The growth of Messy Church, school-based church and youth congregations are examples of this priority. There is, rightly, a humane emphasis on the spiritual care of the dependent elderly.[1] And there is also material on making thoughtful, caring, architectural provision for those older people still able to get to church, and recognising these people still have ministries to offer; they are not just recipients.

But what is written for people learning how to be retired, stretched by commitments to their wider family, some of whom may be far away, living with more in the diary than they expected, maybe looking for fresh outlets but not necessarily propping up existing ones any longer?

The little that I read at the start quickly convinced me that, whatever I called what was happening to me, it was not mainly about chronological age. Nor did everyone remotely fit into one neat box if you just define this stage of life by health. Sadly, I have known those who are chronically sick and those who died, in both youth and the so-called middle years. They and their relatives deserve our care and compassion. Conversely it is also a source of hope that there are those people who are remarkably fit in their 90s. I have been inspired and encouraged by the lives of people like Queen Elizabeth II, Captain Sir Tom Moore and Sir David Attenborough. They provide testimony that the role of attitude and the gift of enduring energy are crucial factors during this season of life. I have concluded that this stage is more defined by other factors than by the number of birthdays we have had. Bear in mind, too, that health has both physical and mental components. But the physical and mental health aspects will be the primary ones by which the ability for continued independent living is assessed, however positive and vibrant a person's inner attitude may be. When I first started thinking about this topic and reflected on my own state of health, I toyed with calling the book *Creaky But Feisty* and started to make a mind map around it. That title may amuse, and it has been my lot to embody it, but it doesn't go wide enough.

It also isn't an image, and I was looking for one. During my 20-year research life working for Church Army, and trying to communicate what I was finding, I noticed that stating a principle tends to stifle engagement and conversation. Any responses tended to be binary – either approval or disagreement. Throwing out an image, on the other hand, tended to open conversation; people sensed themselves free to play with the picture or metaphor and apply it in unexpected directions. The result is richer, and the learning is deeper.

So this book deliberately brings to its readers a number of images. I doubt that the list of images is closed; I can't even know if my preferred is the best. But if a creative conversation follows, then I will be content. The book title tells you which one I chose. The season of autumn is a feature of the year that everybody knows; some may be especially drawn to it and call it their favourite one. It contains the glories of fruitful harvests, changing leaf colours and opening vistas, but it is also characterised by the loss of leaves, temperatures drifting downwards and less hours of light. It is those two intertwined themes of glory and loss that have dominated my perceptions. This book tries to unpack the contours of both realities and to insist that neither eclipses the other.

When is life's autumn?

Autumn marks an untidy end to summer. Those years which also contain an Indian summer make it especially hard to say when it actually starts; that warmth of the sun induces hope of an extended summer. By contrast, in 2022 I noted that the leaves were falling off the silver birches and chestnut trees as early as 24 July. Yet we can determine the calendar beginning of autumn, and I will give my understanding of that in this book.

It is equally true that autumn isn't dishonest about winter coming, and yet it celebrates its own distinct character. All this takes a fair time. In the annual calendar, it is no less than 13 weeks or 91 days. Maybe so it is in life. I am not what I was in the spring and summer of my life, nor mercifully am I in the state of physical dependence on others or of mental incompetence (though at times I wonder). Certainly I am not yet all that I shall be, when my winter is past, heaven's morning breaks and celestial spring has blossomed.

What then are the markers or borders of this autumnal stage of life? I have worked with these two markers: it begins with a person being aware that retirement is about to start, and it ends with realising that it won't be long before that person is no longer able to live independently. I know too that such an autumn, in the life of a given individual, might be only a few years or it could take several decades.

This is not a formally researched book. It's more like a bit of extended journalism in which I happen to be living out some of the story and watching others do the same. I freely admit that the story snippets this book contains, and the quotes from among those 16 I have interviewed, tend to be from reflective, candid and perceptive people. These are qualities I have especially valued. However, perhaps less helpfully, these folk were white British, middle class, middle income, existing Christians. One was ex-Catholic, one a Northumbria Community companion, three were Free Church and the rest Anglicans, as that's where most of my network of friends has fallen. I did achieve nearly equal numbers of women and men, and the length of their retirement varied from less than one year to over a quarter of a century. Their ages range from 63 to 87.

The least representative element was the disproportionate number of retired clergy, of whom I am one, not to mention a few recognised lay ministers. But at least the lay people outnumbered the clergy. What they all had in common was that they are among friends of whom I could ask a favour; namely two hours of their time to talk about their experiences, faced with 25 questions (found in the appendix). I realise these are people whom life has treated fairly well, but I am certain their lives have not been all sunshine. Some readers may either think that this selection is too monochrome or that their own story is too different.

Also the book's content is somewhat narrow. I am aware that there are very deep transitions demanded of those who find they are now living alone. That might be either by their choice, by the force of unchosen circumstance or through bereavement. Neither does this book address the specific issues faced by the single person, the divorced or those living within emotionally dead marriages. It is not designed to offer wisdom to those living with a major tragedy, a life-threatening illness or in grinding poverty. There are specialist landmark books on some of these topics. What is common to all those human experiences is an experience of bereavement. It deserves literature of its own.

Who then is this book for?

As this book explores the beauty and fruits of autumn while noticing the leaves are falling, I doubt if it can be of much value for those people who are totally assured, who brim with self-confidence and seem to live full of trust and hope for the future. But I say to them – don't you notice that the leaves are falling? What do you make of that? Nor can I offer much help to those who are convinced the future is without hope, who believe that everything is dreadful and who may even wish they could end it all. I dare to say to them, would your friends say that your life has been totally without fruit? Are you of no value in yourself? Might God surprise you by the value in which he holds you? So tread with me some sort of middle ground to hold these two themes – glory and loss – in tension with one another.

I mention these two groups that I doubt I can write for, because I confess that I myself don't do well living with those people whom I find to be exhaustingly and indefatigably positive. Even the advent of a death, tragedy or disaster is met with a smiling face and cheerful words. Don't they hurt and suffer too? Are they immune to bereavement?

I ask myself whether they are truly heroic, yet wonder if it could be denial? Too often I come away from being with them not lifted up. Rather, I struggle with a sense of guilt that I can't be like them, and yet at the same time I remain unconvinced that they are being honest about living through hard realities.

So I was intrigued to find, quite by accident, at least one writer who thinks there is a cultural backdrop to what I saw as my own private struggle. Katherine May has been a university lecturer and is now an author and a podcaster. In her 2020 book *Wintering*, she comments on the prevalence of bland but positive social media posts supposedly sent to encourage people facing crises, such as 'Hang on in there' and 'You are stronger than you know'. I have met something similar in those people who describe their own profound discouragements and personal disasters as nothing but 'challenges', as though that word was all that needed to be said about how they felt and thought. May reflects: 'This is where we are now: endlessly cheerleading ourselves into positivity, while erasing the dirty underside of real life.' She asserts that this pressure urges that 'misery is not an option. We must continue looking jolly for the sake of the crowd.'[2] She then goes on to argue that unless we are honest about loss and sadness, we miss an important cue to adapt.

I meet this questionable ultra-positivity in two ways. I notice that funerals now have an enforced positivity by an exclusive focus on the celebration of the person's life, such that proper lament is excluded and lost. I meet it, too, in some younger adults and among those whom, in their onward and upward journey, have not yet met tragedy or profound disappointment. Nor, tellingly, have they hit the limits of what they are able to do. Looking back at my own springtime of life, I realise now that I had almost no idea what my own autumn would be like, and I regret how inwardly impatient I could be with my own much older family relatives.

I also struggle if I have too much contact with those unfortunate people for whom the glass is not merely half empty, but they are quite sure that someone is drilling through the bottom of it. I find being with them is like being attached to a vacuum cleaner pipe that is never turned off, constantly sucking up everything that might be encouraging or transformative. In the end they drain the life out of me. Of course, they aren't manifestations of J.K. Rowling's dementors, who intentionally suck happiness out of all they meet, but you may know what I mean. I simply don't know what would help them enough to escape the prison they occupy. Meeting them, I am reminded of Jesus' penetrating question to the man lying for 38 years by the pool of Siloam: 'Do you want to get well?' (John 5:6).

This book, then, is for those who, like me, are themselves wandering through this autumn stage, wondering whether anyone else is being truly honest about what it is like. It may speak to those able to be glad of the highs, the satisfaction, the fulfilment and the freedom. Yet they are also those who are able to mourn the losses, notice the waning of powers, finding they are in a place they haven't been before. Perhaps worst of all, their previous stages of life have not prepared them much for this one. They know the leaves are falling off the trees. If you, like me, waver between hope and fear, and you know both doubt and trust, then let this book open an honest conversation between those of us who are living this stage, so that we notice and draw upon its glory with gratitude and wonder. And we face the realism – of watching falling leaves, of us living through it being our autumn, which will end sooner or much later in the season of winter. I hope it might also be read by those now old enough that they see their parents and relatives living through autumn. I wish I had understood more of this when I was in my 40s.

A curious coincidence

I write also to pay a debt. Retirement is a great time to re-read your favourite authors. I have long been a fan of Paul Tournier's many books. He was a Swiss doctor, based in Geneva, who also took psychiatric training, knowing his patients needed help that went deeper than

medicines or surgery. He was for many years influential in the movement for 'the medicine of the whole person', being the cofounder of its
annual conference. Imagine then my surprise and pleasure to find he
wrote his book about learning to grow old when he was aged 73, the
same age as me. Similarly, at that age we both could describe ourselves
as semi-retired or, to borrow his language, we found ourselves on a
kind of second career, but one less professional and more personal,
which in both our cases includes writing.

Yet more personally, we both rejoice in being reflective, yet admit to
vulnerabilities, both of us having lost parents during our childhoods.
Like me he too admits to being anxious by nature. I was relieved he
also thought of himself as an amateur in life, struggling with feelings of
inferiority and a lack of confidence.[3] His autobiographical comments
even gave me precedent and permission to re-read my favourite books
and spend pleasurable time playing games of patience. That I needed
his permission to so indulge – and even my use here of that word
'indulge' – tells me a lot about how I have valued my work more highly
than my leisure. I need to unlearn that distortion. I wish I had met him,
to tell him that my own autumn of life has been enriched by at least
two of his books: *The Adventure of Living* (first published in 1965) and
Learning to Grow Old (1971). He would have listened to me as a person,
for like me he was always interested in other people's occupations. His
two books are not opposites, seeing the first as upbeat and the second
as an inexorable descent. No, I found they complement one another.
In view of his two titles, I want to say that autumn has its adventures,
but it does also involve endings. We need to face both with open eyes
and not knowing the future timetable. Tournier himself lived another
15 years, until 7 October 1986.

Two halves or four seasons?

I also write about autumn to suggest that working with a four-fold image
of life, provided by the four seasons, may offer us more than the view
that there are two halves to life. Evidence that others, such as author

Tina English, see life as consisting of four stages is the very terminology 'third age', for the active retired, and 'fourth age', for those who have become dependent. Presumably, the prior two ages are youth and middle age. Kathleen Fischer's book *Autumn Gospel* implies a fourfold view. It begins with the account of two women watching leaves, both those lush and green and those that are dry and falling. They sensed too how autumnal light differs from that of a spring morning and of high summer.[4]

Even my hero Tournier, in *Learning to Grow Old*, writes of three stages: 'There are, in fact, two great turning points in life: the passage from childhood to adulthood and from adulthood to old age.' Moreover, every so often he differentiates between living a summer of life and living its autumn. He makes a case that Freud helpfully unpacked psychological laws that govern that first passage or half of life, whereas it is Jung who is a better guide to the second half of life. Tournier continues: 'The first is an advance to maturity, the second is an advance into a new fulfilment… the first is orientated towards production, the second is more meditative.'[5] Even the familiar terminology of middle age, a period often vigorously denied by those chronologically living through it, conveys the implication of life being made of two halves and also a middle, which is not a mere point along a line but a stage in itself.

So do we do better to think of four stages rather than two? Recently I have begun to read Richard Rohr and confess to finding myself both illuminated and frustrated. *Falling Upwards* opens as follows: 'A journey into the second half of our own lives awaits us all.' Early on he contrasts the two halves in a variety of images: as raft and shore; as there being a new map for a further journey, of discovering our identity and living our destiny, all of which require unlearning; discovering the script and then writing and owning it. The twofold image he works with most is that 'the first task is to build a strong "container" or identity; the second is to find the contents that the container was meant to hold.'[6] Even more salutary is Rohr's argument that we can only see and understand the earlier stage from the wider perspective of the later one.

I concur with the advice from those writers who urge younger (middle-aged?) readers to engage with this second-half-of-life material now. But I am amused that the cover of my copy of Rohr's *Falling Upwards* is an autumnal scene of trees ringing a small lake. My present understanding is that there may be two halves to life, both chronologically and psychologically, but nevertheless the motif of autumn offers us sight of two different and equally important stages in that second half – autumn and winter. Nor is autumn just the changing room for winter. It has its own character and purpose. One of which is to be honest about the transition from summer to autumn. That matters, for I judge that we live in an age and culture of fostering apparent permanent youth, which in the end is delusional. Cliff Richard, Paul McCartney and the Rolling Stones still sing their songs and have their fans, but I insist they also show their age. High summer is past, and the occasional autumnal sunny day is to be enjoyed, not to be mistaken for it.

I don't even remember when my chosen book title floated into my mind. I do know that when I retired in 2017, I wondered about starting some sort of record, in a scruffy school exercise book, of what I called 'God thoughts'. I never kept it up, as life intervened. But curiously I picked it up in the winter of 2022 and read to myself the October 2017 jotting. 'The Autumn of Life – what parallels are there to the physical autumn? Fruitful time, beauty in colours, falling leaves.' I hadn't realised the seed had been sown so long before. Yet it was some months later that I was prompted to notice not the word 'autumn', but a further word: 'living'. Because the leaves are falling it is not difficult to shrink 'living' down to a state of merely resignedly existing through a period of unremitting decline.

To help resist this resignation, among the gifts to the Christian is the conviction that, because God called all existence into being, life has a purpose. Moreover, each of us has been called by name by Christ; we can believe that we are meant to exist. We do not just believe; we belong. And we believe that by the work of the Holy Spirit within us, as we relate with God, the trajectory is for us to be changed from one degree of glory to another (2 Corinthians 3:18). Such foundations mean that we can do more than merely exist, we are to *live* – with the adventures of autumn and with its losses; the fruit and the falling leaves. This book explores those two sub themes within autumn and insists that they are a complementary, if an uncomfortable and unfamiliar pair.

You will find three voices in what follows. First, there is contemporary experience – my own and that of my 16 interviewees. Second, there is the wisdom I have mined from authors more expert than myself, deliberately choosing both those who wrote over 50 years ago and those writing recently. The third voice is the Bible, or rather, what I understand it to be saying. Classic seafaring navigation taught that bearings taken from three separate sources gave the sailor a reasonable basis for knowing where his ship was and was heading. I hope that may be true here too.

Application questions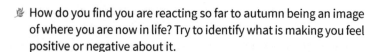

🌿 How do you find you are reacting so far to autumn being an image of where you are now in life? Try to identify what is making you feel positive or negative about it.

🌿 Whose life and attitudes have inspired you for this stage of life? Jot down what they taught you.

🌿 How full or empty is your 'glass'? How do you best deal with those who see the glass differently?

🌿 Picking up Rohr's viewpoint (p. 17), how is it going identifying the 'second half content' to put in the 'first half container' you have built?

I

When is autumn and what are its harvest gifts?

Sorting out some dates

When does the season in the calendar that we call 'autumn' start and stop? What follows here is a northern hemisphere perspective. Readers from the southern hemisphere will know which opposites apply. Setting that aside, the answer is complicated by whose view you take, and maybe it matters which of the two views you adopt. Type into the internet words like 'equinox' or 'solstice' and you'll find many sites that say summer begins with the June solstice; that is, it starts 20–22 June. Then, in this view, summer ends and autumn begins around 23 September, and autumn in turn runs on to 20–23 December, which is the date range of the winter solstice. That's one view.

I find this view unconvincing for a number of reasons. For a start, in years past, I have got sunburnt in May, and it feels like summer to see allotment plants going to seed in the garden or to behold crops in the fields maturing well before 21 June. Moreover, I have needed to put my winter clothes on way before 21 December. In my hometown of Sheffield, we can have snow well before then. It makes more sense to me that, because there are equal hours of daylight on either side of the summer solstice, the period of summer is just over six weeks that fall either side of 21 June. Similarly, we live through shortest days both sides of 21 December, as anyone who suffers from seasonal affective disorder knows only too well.

Maybe many have been seduced into the unrealistic view that summer runs from 21 June to 23 September by the phrase 'the summer holidays' for periods in August. In contrast, the pagan view of the year consists of a wheel with eight segments. In this view, summer runs from Beltane (30 April–1 May) through the summer solstice to Lammas (31 July–1 August), which marks the start of autumn. Autumn runs through the equinox of 23 September to Samhain (31 October–1 November) and the arrival of winter. Michael Mitton in his book *Seasoned by Seasons* concurs with this timing, which he claims is Celtic.[1] So I put the case that August marks early autumn, not late summer, despite the inducements from the sunny days that happen often in that month or our longing that summer will go on longer.

This view is furthermore grounded in the hard facts of the length of days from sunrise to sunset. It helps living in sympathy with the seasons and what can be observed in them. I noticed that the leaves on the trees in August 2022 began to look tired and lacked the lustre they sported in April and May. Water levels in our reservoirs too were low. I saw harvests being taken in as marking the end of a cycle of production. I noticed how few further flowers there were. The shortening of the days started to make a practical difference. I began keeping a diary in July 2022 and across the following autumn. On 24 July in Sheffield, sunrise was at 5.09 and sunset 21.15. By 25 August sunrise was 6.02 and sunset 20.13 – over two hours of daylight lost. By 25 September, the times were 6.56 and 18.58; the hours of daylight and darkness were now all but even. By the changing of the clocks, the Sheffield sunrise was 7.00 and sunset 16.38. By 22 December those figures had shrunk the hours of sunlight further, from 8.20 to 15.49. By then every day we were getting out of bed while it was still dark outside. Across those days the leaves fell in increasing numbers. (It is no accident that in North America the season is called fall, as the leaves change colour prior to their fluttering descent.)

Another change is the uneven but overall gradual lowering of the temperature and the rise of wind strength and rainfall. My 2022 diary tells me that, even by mid-September, I needed to wear a pullover. By that month's end, out came the vest and the thicker trousers. It was also time to activate the central heating and find the hot water bottles. My 30 September diary entry reads: 'Early autumn is now over. More blue skies will be an occasional gift, not an expected occurrence.'

This book adopts this second view of the dates of the seasons. By autumn I mean roughly the period from 1 August to 31 October. I don't set much store by assigning a specific calendar date, for that gives the false feeling that the borders between the seasons are sharp and marked by obvious changes. Watching the autumn of 2022 unfold, I knew first hand it's not like that and the difference in the weather between one day and the next in August may be imperceptible.

Among my friends are both those who approve of August being deemed the start of autumn, because they enjoy its glorious colours, welcome its cooler days and rejoice in its harvest, and those who repudiate that thought, because they find the end of summer and the onset of winter depressing. In both cases these judgements reflect underlying attitudes not just about the varying seasons, but also about the very onset of the autumn of life. For some it is a release or even an adventure, while for others it is more like a closing door.

In spiritual and emotional terms what are the parallels to autumn in the stages of our lives? What are the differences too? What is it like to live through a spiritual and an emotional autumn of life, related to being in retirement and being over 67, the UK male pensionable age? How do we know that a spiritual summer has gone?

My wife Helen recalls a clear marker that came unbidden to her.

Helen walks among falling leaves

It was 2017. George was newly retired, aged 68, and we were lucky enough to celebrate it by spending three weeks in southern Switzerland, where our younger son Julian lives. I was 66, and had been already retired from teaching for a few years.

It was autumn; glorious in its golden colours and still with the sunshine that is more certain in central Europe. After enjoying the mountains and lakes, one day we were walking in familiar hillside woods just behind our son's village of Stabio in the Italian-speaking Swiss canton of Ticino. As we walked, occasionally leaves just detached from the trees and floated slowly down towards the forest floor. There was nothing dramatic, there was no swirl of gusty wind; the leaves slowly, gracefully, twirled and parachuted to the ground. They fell.

I began to think: 'Ah, now it's the end of life! Like them, we will one day just detach from daily life and die.' Of course, as a good Christian, and wife of a clergyman to boot, I reminded myself of the positive – 'and be raised to new life in Christ.'

Then a new train of thought chugged clearly into my mind: 'No. What you've just said to yourself, well that's winter – when life is over. Then the leaf is shrivelled and dies. You, Helen and George, you are in autumn. It's the season of fruitful harvesting. This is not the end, though it is a season of preparing for the end, just as trees prepare for winter by losing their leaves. Yes, there will be losses, but it's the time of harvesting the fruit. How about all that you have put your lives into: careers, family, reading, writing, praying, experience. It is bearing its fruit now. Don't disregard all that industry that went into spring sowing, then summer growing, and miss the harvest.'

When Helen showed me this reflection, I instantly remembered from school days the contribution of a defter wordsmith than me who saw autumn as a specific, plentiful, exuberant season of maximum fruitfulness. It was 19 September 1819, and Keats (1795–1821) wrote of autumn:

Season of mists and mellow fruitfulness,
  Close bosom-friend of the maturing sun;
Conspiring with him how to load and bless
  With fruit the vines that round the thatch-eves run;
To bend with apples the moss'd cottage-trees,
  And fill all fruit with ripeness to the core;
    To swell the gourd, and plump the hazel shells
  With a sweet kernel; to set budding more,
And still more, later flowers for the bees,
Until they think warm days will never cease,
  For summer has o'er-brimm'd their clammy cells.
'To Autumn', by John Keats

Both summer and spring will have their fan clubs. They might be larger than those whose shout would be for autumn. It's easy to prize spring and its alluring promise: the enthralling awakening from the apparent deadness of winter, the bright, freshly painted flower colours, the lengthening of the days, the sun climbing higher in the sky, watching elastic-heeled newborn lambs, seeing the arrival of swooping swallows or hearing the first cuckoo. All these are verdant signs of hope and the promise of a fuller future.

Summer promises ease and entertainment. It gives you the full whack of vitamin D, it ushers in Wimbledon and strawberries, cricket and the clunk of willow on leather, the freedom of sailing or swimming without a wet suit, and seaside holidays at home or abroad. We hope for lazy days in the garden, even barbecues if the rain doesn't sneak in to fool the weather forecasters. It means the exams are over and it's the end of term. And it's the main break from a working life and the job.

So Keats is at pains to remind us that autumn need feel no compulsion to compete with either summer or spring. As his third verse begins:

Where are the songs of Spring? Ay, where are they?
  Think not of them, thou hast thy music too.

The words given to Helen in 2017 outside the village of Stabio open that door. Let me unpack what I see on this heart-warming, life-enhancing view that makes visible the relational and spiritual fruitfulness in the autumnal stage of life. What is to be celebrated in song? What harvest is there to notice? Here's an entrancing introduction to that abundant season, from Tournier: 'A beautiful old age... is a fruitful old age, open to the world, attentive to people... ardent as well as serene.'[2]

Fruit from family and our working lives

Children as fruit

There is a background factor here. In my 2017 book *Reproducing Churches*, I argued that an integral part of being human and being made in God's image, as disclosed in the early chapters of Genesis, is our capacity to reproduce. There I pointed out that it is striking that the very first command to Adam and Eve is to be fruitful and multiply (Genesis 1:28), although today more notice is taken of, and more commentary written about, the ecological responsibility that follows. But without having successors, that responsible caring task cannot be fulfilled.[3]

The outworking of this is that, well before our autumn of life and during our springs or summers, many of us, but not all, have reproduced and welcomed daughters and sons. For those for whom it happens this is an elemental moment. As I write this, I have been struck once more by the wonder and joy of the arrival of a first child; I watched these very reactions on the faces of our youngest son Julian and his wife Hortense, at the arrival of their baby boy Sebastian. There is a sense in which we suddenly find this is a deep part of what we exist for. Commentators like David Attenborough and Chris Packham talk about an animal's instinct to pass on its genes. I have never met an animal that even knows it has genes. It's deeper and more basic than that. I think our joy and wonder at such birth moments draws on that deep surpassing instinct for reproducing something of ourselves. In the horticultural world that reproduction happens by fruits and seeds.

Both the Old and the New Testament pick up the latter imagery and refer to spiritual descendants as Abraham's 'seed'. The longer story, from birth onwards is seeing one's children develop, grow, mature, become settled and in many cases find a life partner and a purposeful career. But that's not the end of this story.

There is something deeper going on, behind this first generation of such tangible, delightful and immediate fruits. Simon Barnes, the retired sports writer and now keen environmentalist and self-described 'bad birdwatcher', writes:

> The aim of every living thing is to become an ancestor; that is what evolution means. If you have bred things that will survive and breed in their turn you have made your mark… That is why there is joy unconfined for every human being who becomes a grandparent.[4]

I concur. There is a sense that because I now see three generations in my own family, I know that I have played my part in the big ongoing story. I have had my day in the sun or on the stage and ensured that life will go on, to which I have made a unique contribution. Without surrendering for one moment to the obsession of the necessity for male succession that plagued Henry VIII and created mayhem in the lives of six women, it is curiously reassuring to me that the endangered species with the rather rare surname 'Lings', which I inherited from my father, with all its linked history, traceable back to another George Lings (1775–1847), will now live on longer.

The joys of having grandchildren and relating to them

I deeply enjoy being a grandparent. I've had many happy hours with my grandchildren, absorbed in their games, freed from the cares of this world, entertained by the surprising connections they make and prizing the pearls they come out with. Young children restore to adults the gift of play. It legitimates my aphorism that I sometimes trot out on my own play-days with them: 'Growing up is greatly overrated.' So I was relieved and heartened that Fischer spots that through play: 'Ageing can bring a return to the awe and enjoyment we knew as children.'[5] I do agree and was intrigued that this quote came from a section where she explores the gift of imagination as one way to gain inner personal wisdom in the autumn of life.

Professor Debora Price of the British Society of Gerontology held an international photography competition in 2016 called 'Ageing: the bigger picture'.[6] Photographers were invited to portray the joys of ageing. One of the substantial themes Price noted among the entries was the joy associated with social connection.

It is held that there is a special relationship between grandparents and grandchildren. I invited my wife Helen to add her own take on that.

Helen tells her tale as a grandmother

On the day George asked me to write this, I set aside a morning to do so, only to get a phone call asking us to do some care of grandchildren as the school teachers were on strike. I had to smile! For that is partly what the special relationship is about.

It's being available, at a moment's notice, to step back into those well-worn parenting shoes, moulded over 20 years of bringing up a family in our own house. Even though two of our children are over 40 now, we still feel that we are holding their hands, albeit remotely. What a privilege! It says that none of that experience, hard-won yet so enjoyable, is wasted.

So, here I am, once more trying to write. It's the day after King Charles III's coronation, a remarkable, historic event that we watched with Hannah our daughter, her husband and their 9- and 5-year-olds. That was very special; our lives having been lived alongside that of His Royal Highness, we were able to explain the older royal family to the grandchildren, to enrich their experience of watching by adding what it meant to us. Conversely their wonder, interest, then feasting on scones and specially chosen foods enhanced our sense of occasion. In the afternoon, after the fly past, we played some of the parlour games of our childhood – what fun and laughter from blind man's buff!

We are the story-bearers for the grandchildren. Our son Martyn's daughters often ask us to recount the 'sillies' as they call them: the family stories of things that their dad and his brother and sister did. Our being their grandparents gives longer context to their lives; they understand that they are part of a continuum of tradition, not just random individuals cast loose alone on the sea of time. In turn we realise that our lives, now certainly in their later or maybe even last chapters, have a meaning within the ongoing context of their lives. They not only carry our genes, they carry our story, and it carries them. There is a responsibility here to pass on stories of the good things, as well as stories of the hurts and harms of things that happened to us. Moreover as followers of Jesus, we try to convey something of the living faith that we have found in him, conveying that not by fear or compulsion, but hopefully by living a joyful, abundant life that attracts them and is intriguing.

It has been traditional to say that one of the special things about being grandparents is that we can pass our knowledge to a new generation, so that all we have learnt over these many years isn't wasted. Occasionally that is true, as we share gardening, birdwatching or model-train operating with the grandchildren. But as this generation of grandparents, we have another new skill to learn. We have to accept that they are more at home in the current digital world than we are, and we need to learn how to humbly accept their help, even in being enabled to operate their smart TV set! But, simultaneously, as they face the fears and threats of climate change, a crisis that their generation is going to have to fix, we can retell the darkness of the nuclear threat under which we lived at their age and how the world tiptoed back from that.

We have lived long and very blessed lives, probably the most healthy and wealthy generation in history. We have so many good things to share with these grandchildren, and hopefully, the humility and emotional intelligence to listen to and value them too.

George and I, at one stage in our lives, helped lead a large church youth group. Within those years, young people would come to a firm faith in Christ, and they were sometimes the most unexpected ones. Our wise coleader, in whom they confided, noted how often there was a praying grandparent or god-parent in the background who held that young person before God. For those of us with a faith, that is another of the aspects that our special relationship can have.

What in this wonderful relationship should I guard against and what should I value? Tournier writes about the problem of those older people who refuse to hand over their prior parental position and are critical of everyone and everything. If direct inappropriate control is one danger, a linked one is the indirect form of control: 'There are grandparents who spoil their relationship with their children and grandchildren by giving too much advice on the upbringing of young people, especially be criticising their behaviour.'[7]

By contrast, in a packed page, he delights in several activities that are wonderful: a harmonious intimacy with grandchildren by taking an interest in them, going for a joint walk, observing nature with them, making things together (allowing them to lead in that) and giving a child a one-to-one personal welcome, akin to the good side of the experience of being an only child.

Here's a thought that gives a grandparent both encouragement and a challenge. As grandparents usually we aren't in the front line of having to bring discipline and seldom have to play 'bad cop'. Often we are there to witness participation, and sometimes triumphs, on the sports field or school play and to shower our praise on the performers. We can be playmates because we're not cooking the dinner. We are often the givers of small gifts and more important, though less predictably, the givers of undivided time. Charmingly, Fischer writes:

'The love of a grandparent is often one of the strongest experiences a child has of unconditional love.' Tournier adds: 'Grandparents can often understand their grandchildren better than the parents do and give them the acceptance they need in order to grow up.'[8]

I ask myself, 'Will that be how my grandchildren experience me?' I know they already remember me as the recalcitrant 'backwards camel' on whose back they used to ride and who, as he crawled across the carpet, always for fun did the opposite of what they commanded. I hope the love beneath the fun is getting through. I'm with Fischer once more: 'The most important spiritual role that grandparents play is simply *being there*.'[9]

In writing all this I am aware that it may be salt in the wound of single people or for those couples without children. Some in those situations have built relationships that act as the adoption of spiritual children. Others have found a vital role as extra adults in families. They may be amazing biological or adopted aunts and uncles. The commonality across all these examples is the joy of relationship and connection, in which the older people support but don't take over.

Fruits from the spring and summer of a working life

Along with many others, by the time I entered the autumn of life, the mortgage had been paid off and the house was ours. That's a sizeable fruit and a significant asset. Quite often in prayer I give thanks for the house we own and have lived in since 1997. For others, some of this owning process may have gone into reverse through equity release and the fruit is being used up, hopefully in a good cause. I hear mixed accounts of whether that route is a prudent way to go.

A related factor is that our house in Sheffield is very much home, but not just for us. It also acts as the magnet attracting in the wider family at Christmas or major anniversaries, and is large enough to swallow them all without much struggle. A home acts as a focus of memories, especially when it includes where the children grew up. Furthermore it acts as an indoor playground for the grandchildren, with particular toys and games, made more special because they only come occasionally. Nor is that fruit just for now. In one sense this home is like apples carefully stored away, and our children are aware that the house is a major asset to be passed on. In an age where the ratio of income to house prices is now a bigger figure than ever, it's a major factor in our and their long-term thinking. For all this fruit I am consciously thankful.

Staying with finance, receiving both the state and a work-related pension are also fruits of past labour. What we set aside in the past has now been added to, with the assurance that these sources will live as long as we do. And, like fruit which helps keep us alive, they contribute to our financial health. That can't be taken for granted, as we shall see later in the book, for many elderly people experience poverty and poor housing as part of institutional ageism.

It's only true for some people, but another fruit can be that one's career has topped out. That could be due to a variety of factors: achievements accomplished; responsibilities carried; people assisted; projects completed; good causes furthered; or influence exercised. I now wonder if my 60s were the happiest times of my life. I delighted in the team I led, our work was fascinating and esteemed, and I travelled the developed world a bit sharing what we had discovered. The adult children were all purposefully settled and grandchildren had begun to appear. I was in rude health, for we had walked the Cuthbert Way pilgrimage from Melrose to Lindisfarne, and I had completed a strenuous Sportive cycle ride in the Peak District in a gold standard time. I'm not alone in such thoughts; Carolyn Heilbrun, ex-Columbia University English professor, says: 'My sixties were my happiest time.'[10]

Yet I am both surprised and grateful that one way to see my life is as a late developer. Some years ago, perhaps foolishly, I unearthed my school reports and was reacquainted with discouraging familiar terms, like 'Lings could do better' and the faint praise of 'some work and progress'. I don't contest that assessment and admit that for years I considered myself as less able than my contemporaries and others I worked with. I thank God for the surprising callings on my life that eventually took me into stipendiary ministry and then, two decades later, into research. (I unpack the resulting shift in my self-understanding arising from this second transition more in chapter 5.) My point is that I see what I was enabled to discover and write about in the latter years of my working life as a kind of fruit. I hope that many readers can see their working lives in a similarly fruitful way.

I hope it also makes sense to see any mentoring or consultancy roles that can come along in retirement as another fruit harvested out of our working lives and arising from the experience we have gained through our work. In the next chapter I explore another fruit: the connected topic of the exercise of wisdom that is supposed to come with age.

Two nice peaches are the free bus or tram pass and the senior rail card. I may hang on long enough to get a senior's ski lift pass, but as people are living longer the age limit for one seems to creep upwards. When you are on that bus, tram or train, it's a mixed blessing to have a younger person give up their seat to you. It's very pleasant to take one's weight off the feet and be able to look out the window, yet somehow galling to realise that in their eyes I looked like I could really do with the seat.

Lifelong learning and being fruitful

Emilie Griffin in *Green Leaves for Later Years* refers to lifelong learning as one element that helps people find meaning in life and a way to live better with constant adaptation to its chances and changes. I can see how her title of *Green Leaves* links to this aspiration. To keep learning is to stay green. To stay green extends the time we can remain fruitful.

The so-called University of the Third Age (U3A) arrived in the UK in 1982 from France, where it began in 1973. This phenomenon acts as a public marker that expects and legitimates that learning should be lifelong and can continue through our older years. Presently in the UK there are about 400,000 takers. I drew on U3A to assist me in one aim of my retirement: to teach myself German and thereby honour my past and deepen my contacts with the German side of my wider family. I also picked up somewhere that learning a language is good for keeping the brain active and staving off its decay. Whether it's worked for my brain, I don't know, as I don't have a couch-potato double who stayed stuck on a sofa.

Trying to write a book is also a learning process. I find it involves acquiring and sifting written sources, paying closer attention to other people's experience and one's own, discerning how all these sources modify what I thought I already knew, seeking out an overall shape that does justice to this variety of old and new inputs, and then working it all through with a perceptive editor. I can see how doing that all fosters a future life in which ongoing learning is encouraged, and which exhibits staying fruitful. Any form of public speaking would involve some related dynamics, though taking much less time.

For me, another aspect of lifelong learning has been as a companion within the new monastic grouping called Northumbria Community. This belonging has fostered ongoing spiritual learning and shared discipleship in a more focused way than I found within congregational church life. But to whoever finds their church to be a source of lifelong learning I say, 'I'm glad; long may it be so.' There's no spirit of competition here, just a search for expressions of Christian community where the values and inner dynamics are such that its members continue to grow in Christ, and thus remain fruitful, as John 15 asserts can occur.

Recently I have had the benefit of one way that lifelong learning is sharpened, which I learnt from Neville, a Church Army friend. It's a process, not a programme, by which a small group of no more than six people – called a meet-up – agree together to work with material across a year. The meet-up could be online or on-site. I've done both. In this case the material happened to be my 2020 book, *Seven Sacred Spaces*,[11] but it could easily be some other source.

What is so life giving are a few factors. First, the pace is intentionally slow. Participants live with one chapter for a month. Second, the perpetual question during that month is not 'What didn't I know already?' but rather 'What is God saying to me through this text?' Third, each person prepares a four-minute, or 400-word, summary of the answer to that question and shares it at the monthly meet-up. Fourth, the other five listeners seek to discern what to feed back to the speaker about what has been said and how it came across. Each person occupies that hot seat in turn. One participant called it a group practice of spiritual direction. I have seen how transformative and life-changing this can be. It encourages lifelong learning and produces fruit.

There's a longer description of how a meet-up works in Appendix 2.

There are more fruits to harvest, and many are related to aspects of freedoms that occur in autumn, as I consider in the next chapter.

Application questions

🌿 When the annual season of autumn comes round, how do you tend to react?

🌿 Make some notes about what you think has been the harvest of your life.

🌿 Which would you say have been the best fruits?

🌿 If you've been a grandparent or great-aunt or great-uncle, what do you value about that relationship?

2

The fruits of living in freedom

Sacred Space is an annual publication from the Irish Jesuits containing a year's readings from the gospels with a brief commentary for each day. Across the years the series has placed significant emphasis on God-given freedom as part of setting the context in which a week's structured daily prayer occurs. Take 3–9 April 2022 as one example: 'By God's grace I was born to live in freedom. Free to enjoy the pleasures he created for me. Dear Lord, grant that I may live as you intended, with complete confidence in your loving care.'[1]

I have noticed that many of my interviewees were very positive about the years of their retirement. Freedom was a word that came up often. This freedom was composed of many elements.

'Free to…' factors

A key aspect was *freedom to choose*: what to do; what not do; what to take up; and what to put down. At times their descriptions of this freedom came across with lightness of spirit. There was real freedom to say no to invitations that in the past would have made sense or might have been taken dutifully, and also the freedom to yes. With a freer diary, one woman noticed she was responding to other people's innovative suggestions with 'Yes, why not?'

An associated and linked freedom was *freedom to spend time*. This would include time both for existing friends, in some cases deliberately building those relationships into stronger friendships, and time to make new friends. A few, including myself, have found some of those friendships cross international boundaries. These links, in particular, take blocks of time in order to travel to meet and when there, to stay for longer periods of time. In my case this wider set of relationships includes reinvigorating existing friendships with others from college days, via email and Zoom. The retirement gift of more time was also directed to doing those things that my interviewees enjoyed, whether indulging in a variety of cultural activities, watching or participating in sport, or developing hobbies.

Linked to the gift of spending time is the *freedom to notice*. One illustration of this is that my time spent birdwatching has increased during retirement. I have even bought a telescope. Telescopes are a bit unwieldy to use, but the magnification provides entrancing detail. I think that binoculars aid bird spotters, but a telescope turns you into a birdwatcher. More widely, one of my interviewees saw her retirement as the opportunity to notice 'the now' more. She related it to the R.S. Thomas poem 'The Bright Field', in which he reflects on the sun illuminating a small field and likens it to Moses being drawn to the burning bush.

Freed-up time was also linked by many interviewees with being *free to have time with the family*. I notice that the notion of family is more elastic than I realised. The closer end is the obvious, should I say familiar, relationships we have with children and grandchildren. This then can be stretched to include revived connections with extended family members, long-lost cousins and hitherto obscure members of the family tree. Martin, one of my two brothers, has been doing extensive research on the English and German sides of our family. Pursuing one's ancestry is much advertised today. Beyond this, some couples without children have evolved family-like surrogate relationships with younger or similar age Christians which is a mutual delight and support, but which takes time to nurture and foster. I also know of single people who have been informally adopted by a nuclear family and the time they spend together is highly valued. It's all time directed to relationships, and retirement is a chance to open those doors wider.

But this feature of more free time is neither an unalloyed benefit nor an easily defendable space. My most recently retired interviewee described its onset, and its time, as a liminal space, a time of leaving certitude and entering uncertain transition, and to what? I too recall the feeling that the early weeks and months felt more like a sabbatical from work than total release from it. I chose to mark that start in September 2017 with a trip round Europe, including memorable train journeys in the Alps. The suggestion of sabbatical carried the implication that a return to work was coming. Of course it wasn't, the sabbatical illusion was a form of denial, and it was only coming back home to apparent idleness which drove that home to me. 'Now what?' became a real question.

As for defending freed-up time, one classic observation of retirees is that they have never been so busy. They thought: 'When I retire, I'll have plenty of time to do whatever I want.' Yeah, right! It seems not only does work expand to fill the time available, but also that life abhors a vacuum. One interviewee described this stage as not just busy but giddy. She had been retired ten years and foresaw with some accuracy that her retirement would begin with an active phase and only much later a more passive one. In the gradual, or maybe sharp, transition that has begun to come for her now, the time issue will rear its head again.

Some interviewees spoke of finding more *time to pray*, which is true for me too. No less than five out of 14 people mentioned this, one way or another, and they were all clergy – people paid to pray, but only finding enough space for that now. I didn't push this issue with any of them at the time, as until I read all the transcripts I hadn't seen this pattern. Some expressed it as exploring Ignatian spirituality, others as going deeper or becoming more reflective, or moving towards the contemplative. Two women found they were drawn into intercession for the mess in the world, one with frequent tears over news items. She sees prayer for transformation as a calling for retired people.

All these routes require uncontested space, a background that preserves silence, and time. They have in common the questions 'How is God at work in my life?' and 'How does God wish to be at work?' These are good questions at any time of life, but great ones in the autumn of life when we have less ahead of us than behind us. I even wonder whether the other freedoms I have noted in this chapter would be so liberating without some of those steps forward in prayer. If our autumns are to be fruitful, they need to be purposeful; to find purpose and direction we need a spiritual compass. That is part of the benefit of a life of prayer.

The interviewees' responses, and the fact that these changes had only come at this stage in their lives, made me reflect on my years of service in local churches and my decades of research. I admit that I seldom found the freedom or length of uncluttered time which I now can and do give to prayer and spiritual reading. What follows is only what I have found works for me. It may be that broad elements of it are transferable to others, for they are elements of classic liturgical worship: praise, confession, engaging with scripture, prayer for others and a dismissal blessing.

I'm useless before breakfast, so prayer comes after it. I have a favourite chair in our study/dining room and a door that is firmly shut. The shape of this time is provided through the Morning Prayer liturgy from *Celtic Daily Prayer*. Within it, at points, I talk back to God from either a line from the liturgy that strikes me or what I notice in Bible readings. These are from *The Daily Bible*, a lectionary compiled by Michael Perry in 1980, and from *Sacred Space*, mentioned at the start of this chapter. Intercessions for family members, friends, contacts and issues are spread across the week on a sheet of paper, which means that I focus on nine to ten people per day. I also pray through the daily prayer diaries from BRF Ministries, Church Army and Northumbria Community.

That may make this time sound very organised and fixed. Yes, the shape is fixed but the human–divine conversation within it is not. The tail piece, dismissal or signing-off procedure, has become important to me, yet it remains fresh. I always finish with the two Christ-centred collects from *Celtic Daily Prayer*: 'Christ as a light illumine and guide me,' and, 'May the peace of the Lord Christ go with you.' I am still surprised that when I get up, often an hour has gone by. And often I notice that I am both stilled and more prepared for the day. Retirement has given me freedom to have time.

Don't think that this experience of more time to pray is an even one. As one interviewee, David, a spiritual director, put it: 'God has become more real... at times. He's naughty; he does have coffee breaks... sometimes quite long ones.' I asked him why that is so. He continued: 'Firstly, that is life. If you were going to live on cloud nine all the time, it would become cloud zero and you would be always looking for something greater.' He then added that to have life spun out, rather than all in one lump, is much more treasurable. It's similar with food. Most meals are just totally ordinary but occasionally you go out or plan to stay in, and you have a feast that you will remember. So it is in my life of prayer – much of it is ordinary fare and a daily discipline, but occasionally I enter a mountaintop moment of enlightenment.

Till now I've explored what interviewees highlighted as freedom to. There is also freedom from.

'Free from...' factors

A common theme among interviewees was *freedom from responsibility*. An associated word they often used was relief. They found themselves freed from having to be responsible for projects or parishes, freed from having to manage employees, lead volunteers or direct others' working lives. The freedom from having to exercise discipline over others, which is seldom a pleasure, was named as a special relief.

Some responsibilities came with role expectation, not formal line managing. A classic case would be features expected from a vicar's wife. This could range from providing the mythical cucumber sandwich, with crusts cut off, my dear, to being the insidious back door to power or the person deemed right by others to fix whatever the vicar had failed to attend to. It was so nice, interviewees said, to put those ones down. *Freedom from stress* was a related way to talk about this change that retirement offers.

Another common feature was *freedom from the tyranny of the diary*; that is, the diary as controlled by work and formal expectations from others. The old feeling of constraint, of having to do what was required by the job or by superiors was replaced by a sense of being back in control of one's own life and what was entered into the diary. No one stopped used a diary; indeed, some of us now had two – a paper and a digital one. No one complained they had an empty diary, although I notice that mine oscillates unpredictably between many close-coupled entries and blank spaces. While writing this book, I was glad of those diary spaces. In my paid working life, I'd have had to artificially create them.

Others mentioned *freedom from comparing ourselves with others*. A self-deprecating joke, enjoyed by my wife Helen, picks up this dynamic of comparison with others and how that changes in one's older years: 'When you were 20, you really worried what others thought of you. By your 40s, you noticed that you worried less. In your 60s, you realise that others weren't thinking of you in the first place.'

There is wider data that overlaps with this, provided by the insurer SunLife. According to interviews with more than 50,000 people who were aged 50 and over, 75% are less bothered about what people think of them than when they were younger, 61% enjoy life more than when they were younger, 59% live for today instead of tomorrow and 42% say their life is more exciting.[2] The joke puts emphasis on the decreased visibility that is felt by older people but the research says we care less about that comparison. This fits with the fun poem 'Warning' by Jenny Joseph that has her deliberately wearing bold, clashing colours.

In chapter 1, I mentioned Professor Price's international photography competition in 2016 called 'Ageing: The bigger picture'. She noted a second joy of ageing that bears out the Joseph poem:

The second major theme was that with ageing can come a care-free enjoyment of life, an abandoning, when people can be themselves and forget the cares of life. Dancing was indeed a recurring motif for photographers as a metaphor for the joys of ageing. So also was the recurring idea that you could play like a kid, let go, sometimes with the kids, but not necessarily.

This emphasis on 'freedom to' and 'freedom from' links to research which found that 65–79 is the happiest age group for adults, according to the Office for National Statistics. The survey of 300,000 people across the UK found life satisfaction, happiness and feeling life was worthwhile all peaked in that age bracket, but then declined in the over-80s.[3]

Another angle on this 'freedom from' that I found perceptive and had not thought of was from Sue, a lay interviewee who commented that in retirement she felt more equal to other people. This occurred because she didn't have an academic or professional background and had previously been surrounded in church life by those who did, so she felt not as good as other people. In retirement, she didn't know what others did and as other people didn't make much of their prior employed life, this brought a sense of equality. Perhaps retirement can be a more equal playing field with a common status – of being retired people – who have put the identity of a working life behind them.

But as our prior steadfast grip on life loosens and the thought that 'there's not so much time left' begins, another internal comparison question gets sharper; that is, what have I done that is significant or matters? For most people, it is the case that they have not been famous and don't expect an obituary in the newspapers, and they thus can feel desperately ordinary. 'Who am I compared to others?' some may say.

I was reminded of this nagging question by Iris Moore-Sparkes' booklet *A Grain of Sand*, with its cameos of her life story, which she wrote as a reaction to frequently wondering what the purpose of her life was. At one point, when she was feeling low, she was on a beach watching children making a sand castle. It was as though God said to her, 'I need millions of grains of sand to build my kingdom.'[4] In her own late autumn of her 80s, now with not so much time left, her booklet looks back on how often God had guided her way. She was one of those grains of sand that was needed. She sensed that she mattered, and this brought her comfort and reassurance.

Freedom includes 'Shut the door'

If our autumns are to be enriched by freedom, I think they need to include a freedom to live in the now and, in that now, to be neither dogged by the past nor intrinsically nervous of the future. I am not alone in naming such weighty dynamics. I have gratefully devoured Emilie Griffin's 2012 book *Green Leaves for Later Years*. She, in turn, in a chapter entitled 'Grief, loss, anger', commends the wisdom within P.D. James' diary from her late 70s that became her 2000 book *Time to Be in Earnest*. Griffin approves of James' humility and good sense: 'In old age we realize how little we can be sure of, how little we have learnt, how little – perhaps – we have changed.' Yet Griffin is glad that elsewhere, during an uneasy day, James adds: 'There is no point in regretting any part of the past. The past can't now be altered, the future has yet to be lived.' Griffin knows that memory is a gift but it 'can lead us into this sort of painful review of mistakes and sorrows.' She goes on to urge that though the past cannot be unwritten, our attitude to it can be changed. Fischer comments that memory 'is a reservoir of both joy and anguish'. She advises that the negative memories need a new lens which includes both compassion for oneself and forgiveness for oneself and others.[5]

I connect all this to a singular experience in my own life. In my book *Seven Sacred Spaces*, I wrote that I had latched on to the spiritual perception that though we have thoughts, we are not our thoughts.[6] Indeed, we can even observe ourselves having them. There are three in the room: me, the thought that has come into my head, and myself watching the other two. It is this third actor who helps me spot this triangle, for if I cannot even notice my thoughts, how may I discern their source, refuse those I should reject and bring in a contrasting good thought? In the past it has been too easy for me to look back over my life and identify many regrets. One day to my surprise when burdened by this affliction, I simply heard the clearly enunciated but whispered words, 'Shut the door.' What I take to have been the voice of God was, in tone, both kindly but insistent. The command was simple and not wrapped up in jargon. I know that came as a gift and include the story for any who find they are dogged by their past. I cannot promise that you will yourself hear those words as I did, but they are nonetheless good and enduring advice when facing regret or self-recrimination.

Shut the door. But be realistic, as I have had to be; habits take time to eradicate. There are still times when I have to choose once again to shut the door to the past, as it creaks open once more. As I quite consciously 'shut the door', so I choose to spot and refuse the thoughts of regret, failure and guilt which, if uncontained and uncontested, sap my energy and head to depression, when the black dog barks loudly. As a person with a significant early childhood bereavement, it's one of the negative cards I am likely to have to hold.[7]

But shutting the door is not simply a mind game, a psychological conjuring trick to dress up denial over regret in acceptable clothes. For the Christian, it is the active faith response to Christ's provision of real, complete and unambiguous forgiveness. It is applying the trust we have in God's promises about our past and his dealing with it through the work of Christ. As the apostle Paul said many years ago in Turkey: 'Therefore, my friends, I want you to know that through Jesus the forgiveness of sins is proclaimed to you' (Acts 13:38). It makes sense to shut the door to regret over past sins and any rancour over being sinned against.

I've told you part of my story about learning to deal with the past, a preoccupation of those of us who are getting older and have more past to recall than future to enjoy. I want to balance that with another account where the focus was the present and the future.

Freedom to accept the invitation to adventure

One morning in March 2021, I was praying the *Celtic Daily Prayer* morning office as usual. I came to its penultimate prayer, attributed to Patrick, which begins: 'Christ as a light illumine and guide me.' The prayer includes the words 'Christ under me, Christ over me, Christ beside me'. As I do not find this spatial language of 'over' and 'under' very meaningful, I instead say, 'Christ before me, Christ behind me, Christ beside me.' That speaks to a timeline of my future, past and present. Unexpectedly, and uniquely in my experience, I saw before me, in my mind's eye, the seated figure of Christ. His left arm was stretched out towards me in welcome and inclusion; his right wrist and hand were moving back and forth beckoning me. I heard this Jesus figure warmly saying, 'I'm waiting for you to catch up.' He spoke not as an impatient parent on a hike – 'Come on, do catch up' – but as a fitter, more experienced guide on an upward journey, one who knew the way better than I did. It felt like companionship for the present and an invitation into the future. I suspect and accept that catching up with where Jesus is will take time, and closing that gap may need to be repeated, but I'm grateful for this invitation and glad that he's patiently waiting.

I realise that to have told you those two seminal stories creates two problems. First, how usual are such experiences? That's not too difficult to respond to. I know they are rare and also that I must not chase after their repetition. Tournier had to respond to a similar question and wrote: 'To hope for constant illumination on God's will… is quite utopian.' At times we have 'to let ourselves be led by God blindly'.[8] He went on to underline that times of explicit guidance are rare. Perplexity and only implicit guidance are far more common. For my part, both times had something of the nature of a calling. They marked the need for a change of behaviour, of attitude, of mental direction.

In the Bible, hearing the voice of God is often linked to callings: think of Abraham, Moses, Joshua, Samuel, the prophets; or in the New

Testament, Mary, Jesus at his baptism, Peter in Joppa, Paul outside Damascus. All these figures are far more significant players than I am or ever will be, but it's the pattern of calling that intrigues me. That links to the rarity of this experience. When God announces a calling, gives a new direction, his voice is more explicit, but it is not repeated. In C.S. Lewis' *The Silver Chair*, something similar occurs for Eustace and Jill to send them out to rescue a disappeared prince. The voice and initial calling of Aslan are clear; from then on it's down to them to keep remembering the signs.

Second, can I even be sure these experiences were not mere wish fulfilment? No, I can't. However, a few things encourage me. Once more an insight from Tournier is realistic but supportive. As a fallen human being aware that we only 'know in part' (1 Corinthians 13:12), he advises: 'We must be careful – we are never safe from error.'[9] Then as a doctor he notes paradoxically that it is the mentally ill who are the most sure of the voice of God, and it is healthy people who are hesitant, humble and prudent about it occurring. I hope it is the latter spirit in which I have shared such confidences. I need to add that the experiences for me manifested the telling combination of the messages being both so apposite and yet so surprising. They fitted and yet were unexpected. How often that is a mark of genuine guidance, and this can come in much more subtle ways than believing that we heard a voice.

More widely in terms of perceiving guidance coming to us, one autumn-of-life fruit is the judicious use of memory. I find I can, and I hope you can too, look back and with hindsight sense being mysteriously led. Tournier notes a variety of ways this happens: meeting a person who said something crucial; picking up and reading a book (that's happened to me several times and changed the direction of my life); having a dream or a strange hesitation. In this wide list he also includes being seriously ill, which was Ignatius Loyola's story, and through a notable failure or a conspicuous success. Dallas Willard, in his book *The Divine Conspiracy*, not least in the first two chapters, sets out his belief that we are surrounded by the kingdom of heaven, or the reality of a spiritual life, far more than we commonly realise. We live in a 'God bathed and

God permeated world'. We can have confidence that God wants to guide. It's the hearing that is often less clear. Looking back and noticing God's presence, influence or intervention can help. Fischer commends this noticing as part of claiming our past.[10] It was a key Old Testament practice too; they recalled the exodus, at least annually at Passover, and also in times of crisis.

Having now lived with the gift of those two spiritual experiences for a couple of years, I realise that reflection upon their occurrence, and my own longer story, has helped me see life as an adventure, not just a challenge or a set of problems to solve. Seeing life as an adventure is another expression of living in freedom. Adventures don't have fixed boundaries; they have an element of surprise and unpredictability. What a gift to those of us in the autumn of our lives, when it would not be difficult to see more endings than beginnings. So in my case there is a calling to a relational, spiritual and moral adventure for me to catch up to where Jesus is and it will be a further adventure into which Jesus takes me. That takes me to the next section. It draws on the attitudes, and so the comments, of my interviewees and also the distilled wisdom of Tournier, who saw the whole of living as an adventure, though I will limit this adventuring to what can occur in the autumn of life.

Our years of retirement as adventure

The author Rob Merchant wondered how many people saw growing old as an adventure, and whether even fewer churches would see their older members as adventurers.[11] Nevertheless his book about the third age does include the word 'pioneering' in its title. That word has something of the adventure flavour.

I too wondered whether my interviewees would either use the word 'adventure' or use images that have something of that feel. Question 4 was deliberately open: 'How have you found life since stopping paid work?' Question 8 was more focused: 'What adventures have opened up or come along?' When asked question 4, David, now well into his

80s, paused, considered and said: 'Unexpectedly enjoyable, immensely creative, new opportunities opening up, and very refreshing and invigorating.' I'd call those the words of an adventurous spirit. Indeed, later to question 8 he replied: 'I do treat life as an adventure, just as I treat the end of life as an adventure. You know it will happen but have no clue how it will happen – that's what makes it an adventure.'

Question 2 asked what phrases, and question 3 what images, linked to life in retirement resonated for them. Four explicitly cited the word 'adventure', and four further people talked of retirement as an opportunity. Others used a variety of images that have tinges of adventure: climbing a mountain or a precarious ladder entering the second half of life, with four referring to a journey into the unknown. Another four used the language of entering a foreign land with its elements of discovery and challenge. One unusual image, used by Jonathan, a cricket-lover, was to liken early retirement to the third day of a test match, when there is everything to play for and the result is still open. Six found my own image of autumn worked for them, while three preferred not to use it, although they saw what it was getting at.

Nearly all interviewees were able to name the particular adventures that had come along. Only one said she wasn't adventurous, but then later she went on to be a leading figure in starting a drop-in centre at her local church. Many of the adventures cited had, to my mind, something of the flavour of a second career, which I will come to in the next section. Other adventures included: more far-flung holidays and travel, moving house and area, doing a marathon-length walk and joining a new monastic community. Three were about attitude more than practice: consciously letting God open whatever the next door was, wanting God to bring an adventure and not get bored, and choosing the directly spiritual journey from life as doing to being.

I have had to do my own learning about adventure. My teachers have been those I interviewed and Tournier. I have long been troubled by Revelation 2:4: 'You have forsaken the love you had at first.' The joy I knew as a 16-year-old newly committed Christian just wasn't there anymore by my 20s. The discoveries later on of life in the Spirit and charismatic renewal have become over time everyday and normal. Something similar is true in that I have been a companion of Northumbria Community for 20 years. Curiously the same has been true of my adventure with skiing. What used to be a passion, eagerly anticipated and excitedly prepared for, lived among the magic of the mountains, is now a routine conducted amid familiar sights. The modelling hobby too has dulled down from creation to operation. At times it feels like 'Been there, done that.' So I have wondered what is wrong with me, that this tale is so far from life as adventure. But I do see something similar has occurred in pioneering movements that I have known and been part of.

Tournier explains this problem. All movements, he says, get silted up. He calls it 'this law of the progressive extinction of all adventures'.[12] He even names their five-phase shape. Phase 1 exhibits dynamic growth and little external resistance to it. Phase 2 marks its peak, and resistance to it takes shape. Phase 3 requires the adventure to organise itself and defend its gains. The adventure becomes debate and its face changes. The prophetic has become reasoned argument for and against it. Formulas and dogmas begin to define the adventure. In Phase 4 historians start to measure and classify it within a wider picture. In Phase 5, even later students read and write about it. I name these phases with some sense of a heavy heart for I see parallels with wider church initiatives, such as the charismatic movement of the 1960s, cell church in the 1990s and fresh expressions of church from 2004. Others have seen this as a four-stage process: man, moment, machine, monument – an inexorable process of institutionalisation. Whether the earlier phases of these ecclesial adventures should have been sustained for longer, I don't know.

This book is more about personal journeys, and I began by noting my cycle of internal journeys. Tournier engages with that, too, writing of a person roused by the Spirit, seeking to sustain that fervour through spiritual disciplines and yet finding this lacks the initial ardour, for which he reproaches himself:

This man is mistaking a psychological problem for a religious one. He refuses to recognize the law of adventure which is that it dies as it achieves its object… The spiritual life consists only in a series of new births.[13]

That makes sense to me and modifies my view of the autumn of life as an adventure. It is not one long adventure; it is a time in which to live through a succession of them, accepting each one as it comes, realising that it too will reach its summit and begin to subside. The rise will be rapid, and the decline will be slower – not unlike the rush of a wave up a beach and its slower return to the sea.

He argues also that adventures are distinct from one another. I concur, having lived through the change from parochial to research work and with my diversity of hobbies: sailing, skiing, cycling and model-making. I agree with him that starting out on a new adventure is risky, for by definition it contains the unknown and amateurs in that field have to 'put their trust in a hunch'.[14] I was intrigued that for Tournier, like me, starting the adventure of writing meant nervously taking the plunge. It was a matter of committing himself and, having done that, now no longer being free to stop. As with me, the gestation before writing was long but the birth process more rapid. I haven't written many books, but all few were many years in gestation and only then could I commit to paper. I also have to admit that trying to write this book is one current adventure, and I already wonder what I will do when it is finished.

If anyone is intrigued to know more, I commend Tournier's seemingly timeless book and chapters 8 and 9 for exploring further characteristics of adventure. One adventure is launching into a second career.

Freedom for a second career

The newly retired still have gifts and energy. Tournier recommends that they embark on what he calls 'a second career', and he devotes chapter 4 of *Learning to Grow Old* to this. My questionnaire did not contain a specific one about whether people embarked on a further career. Instead, I put two wider questions: 'How have you found life since stopping employed work?' and 'How does the reality of your retirement compare with what you expected?' Of the 16 interviewees, 14 had taken on or been given roles that were not just a hobby or interest but were forms of work, drawing on their track record, gifts, skills and experience.

The range of roles was wide and many were out in the world: being a stopgap head teacher; a non-executive director; handling the closure of a college; becoming a fiction writer and pilgrimage leader; taking up spiritual direction; being a vocations advisor; working for Marriage Encounter; doing supply teaching; leading guided walks for the National Trust; and taking on a PhD. Others were part of local church life and its mission: becoming the treasurer; being PA to a vicar; acting as project manager; starting out as a cathedral chaplain; and becoming chaplain to a walking football club.

Writing this I was reminded of Stan, my father-in-law, who retired from a bank at 52 and then gave many years of invaluable service as full-time administrator to his local Baptist church, and of Mike, the voluntary full-time administrator at St George's Deal when I was vicar and without whom I doubt I would have survived. In addition, one person became a part-time violin maker. A quartet has played his violins, viola and cello. Another became a wood-turner.

These examples expose that the border between truly undertaking a second career and having a serious time-consuming interest or hobby may be porous and not easy to plot. Sometimes we use the term 'occupation' as a synonym for profession or career, as in the question, 'What is your occupation?' Equally we can speak of 'being occupied' to describe time working in the garden, looking after grandchildren or spent on a hobby. We talk of 'having a pursuit' for a serious hobby, which is quite a driven word. I have chosen to live with this uncharted, untidy boundary between career, occupation and pursuit.

These 14 examples, and indeed in a lesser way my own hobby of making a model railway, remind me that, as Tournier says: 'A creative work is always something personal; always an adventure… to restore work to its truly human status.' Perhaps, in the autumn of life, unearthing some sense of adventure is more important than knowing the precise difference between work and a hobby. 'The important thing is the preservation or rather reawakening in oneself of the spirit of adventure.'[15]

Tournier adds his awareness of the constant danger of work or relationships degenerating into routine. Maybe hobbies lovingly and seriously undertaken are among the best forms of work. That they are done with love is central to his thought, making it one of his five named characteristics of adventure and noting that 'amateur means lover'.[16] Listen once to a person talking about a hobby they are serious about and you realise they love it.

The duration of these so-called second careers, occupations or pursuits ranged from a couple years to a decade. Some were related to past employment patterns, others utterly different from them. Some roles still continue; some have ceased. One person said she expected her active stage of retirement to be followed by a passive one. Doubtless the art is knowing, which takes humility and discernment, when that transition should occur. Some signs may be obvious. The onset of a serious health issue can be a clear red light. Amber might be the sense of diminishing strength and the onset of failing memory.

More subtle is a sense of appropriateness and then a question begins to form. For example, in my case, when I reach 75 should I still be responsible for leading a Northumbria Community regional group? My wife asked herself a similar question about being 70 and leading a cathedral-based toddler group. In today's church, there are more laity with ability, but with less availability because of work pressures and life patterns. Even 25 years ago, in the parish I served, we began to see the volunteers who took up a variety of ministry roles in their 50s and 60s were reaching their 70s and 80s but without replacements in sight. That made the decision of when to stop and retire from the active stages of retiring more complex.

Freedom to use wisdom and the gift of listening

The contribution of older people is not limited to the fruit of what they can offer through the activity of their second careers or pursuits. There is a more passive, and sometimes reactive, role in the fruit of offering wisdom and the gift of listening to others. Ten of my 16 interviewees said listening was one of the gifts they had been given and three were using it in 'recognised' ministries.

There is an established view that older people can bring wisdom. Rob Merchant mines the Old Testament, which broadly saw older people as an honourable source of wisdom, in particular citing Job 12:12: 'Is not wisdom found among the aged. Does not long life bring understanding?' Tournier makes it a 'criterion of civilisation: the place we are prepared to give to those who, in the autumn of their lives are reaching the summer of wisdom.' Ian Knox spends many pages on what older people give to the church community: their participation in worship and ministry; their voluntary commitment to its organisations; finance; prayer; and time. He devotes three pages to wisdom and understanding, expanding that poignantly to include the telling of life stories, showing old age is good, demonstrating old age is a fulfilment and helping a good approach to death.[17]

But all this comes with a few caveats. Tournier is clear that the old need to wait to be asked before giving advice and warns that we avoid those older people who are too ready to dispense wisdom with largesse. In his words:

We ask advice of those older people who do not insist on giving it. The old have something better to do – to become confidants. We will open our hearts to those who listen in order to understand us, and not in order to judge or direct us… To claim the right to give advice, is to try still to exercise a certain power over others. The key to success in old age seems to me to be in the abandonment of the will to power.[18]

His words are congruent with another image for the autumn of life. We shift from being at the centre of life to its edge or, as in question 3 in my questionnaire, from the front seat to the back seat of life. No less than six interviewees responded to that, three recognising its rightness and three others disliking that it was what was happening. When you are in the back seat, sometimes wisdom lies in knowing what not to say and when to keep quiet! The same can be true even with the vantage point of the edge. Often in my experience, at those times when others have kindly told me that my comment was wise, all it felt like was sharing common sense or merely summing up what was already in the room. Conversely, at those very times I was tempted to think I had been wise, that pearl offered up went unnoticed.

One illustration of this shift from front seat to back seat is that on longer countryside walks, which we continue to do with our adult children and their children, I am no longer the principal wayfinder and navigator. My OS maps and compass have given way to the maps on their phones. This provision is usually more accurate, though vulnerable to a drop in signal. They have chosen which walk to do and take the lead in showing the way. These days we follow, and usually I don't even bother to take the map, even holding back a query about a strange turn taken.

Among the interviewees, Michael noticed his place in the wider family had shifted from the centre to the edge. We are no longer in the front seat in the minds of our adult children and that affects the matter of giving any supposed wisdom and highlights the need to keep listening. It's a 'two ears, one mouth' strategy.

Applying wisdom to ourselves

If those few paragraphs begin to value, as well as warn about, the use of wisdom and listening to others, what of the acquiring of wisdom in living with our ageing selves? Fischer explores this elusive and mysterious quality. She knows wisdom does not come automatically with age, but is needed for growing into more wisdom about living with oneself in our autumn season. She unpacks six features.

The first is *attention*. She commends attending to the present moment, from which gratitude comes. In so doing 'we learn the power of the ordinary to reveal the holy.'

From this grows the second practice, *awareness*. This she links to mindfulness, calling it 'a goal of Christian spirituality: living in the present and receiving gratefully its gifts'.

Associated with this is the third aspect, *centring* – a form of prayer – waiting in stillness for God's coming, of which the goal 'is to make God the centre of our lives'.

Out of that comes *imagination*, which for her embraces the contributions of beauty, creativity, the artistic and a journey into knowing God through many images, but having to face down unduly stern images from our past.

Only then does the fifth dimension, *action*, appear. In this case she names action for justice and care of the oppressed, even though it may only see progress little by little.

Lastly comes *darkness*. She sees it as a likely path during the autumn of life, and I have known times of it too. She knows there are many different kinds of darkness: of the soul, of depression or of grief. 'For some this darkness comes and goes; for others, it is the persistent path.' For what worked in our earlier years with God now doesn't. We find we are at an impasse, in which we are invited to surrender control. All these steps are a path to greater self-knowledge and we are forced to learn to trust and rest more in God. 'These then are some of the paths that open us to the gift of wisdom.'[19]

Griffin is more succinct, though a few themes overlaps with Fischer:

> What wisdom do I bring to the later years? Nothing more than the wisdom of dwelling in the present moment. No more than the courage of God's promises. Nothing more than the perseverance to walk through sorrow. No more than the unlimited future of God's love.[20]

I am grateful to the wisdom of others in books and interviews who persuade me to notice life more closely and intently. They advise me to wait before offering my supposed wisdom, guarding my tongue while perched on the back seat. They encourage me to learn how to live with my ageing self, on this autumn adventure in which some of the strategies of middle age no longer work.

Midday prayer, within *Celtic Daily Prayer*, draws upon Psalm 90:12: 'Teach us, dear Lord, to number our days that we may apply our hearts unto wisdom.' When in youth and into middle age the number of our days seems to stretch to an infinite horizon, we can be tempted to ignore the passage of time. Days come and go as an apparently infinite and renewable supply – not unlike the past attitude to the supply of fossil fuels. In autumn, when we realise that we have fewer days in front of us than behind us and we see that the horizon has got closer, numbering our days takes on a whole new meaning. Precisely because they are limited, we notice them more. This living more attentively is one aspect of wisdom for later years.

A related image came to Helen my wife, some years ago. She put it this way.

> I retired in 2013 pretty reluctantly, through redundancy from teaching, aged 61. Once I was used to it, I made sure that each

day had a volunteering focus: joining two orchestras, helping at an RSPB centre, running a Sheffield Cathedral toddler group and presenting Godly Play. I also threw myself with zest into engaging with our first two grandchildren, born around the same time. This was all alongside the ordinary chores of life, which before, as a busy teacher, I had had to do as efficiently and quickly as possible. Now there was time to be thorough and more creative, in cooking, gardening and writing cards and texts to friends.

One day in my morning prayer time, a picture floated into my mind. It was of a traditional sweet jar made of glass, and it was full to the top. I remember being given such a thing as a child, and helping myself to handfuls to begin with. As I watched the jar, in prayer on that day, it quickly got down to below half way. Oh help, I thought, this is my life and the days are running out. Then another childhood memory came, of being in that same situation and carefully only taking out one sweet, and making it last as long as possible, enjoying its flavour and the sweet sensations as long as possible. I felt God say to me: 'This is your life now; yes, there are fewer days left, so take each one and live it to the full; each day can be lived in committed discipleship, enjoying the world and its people. Every day is a more precious gift now, not to be squandered or unvalued.' The meditation for Day 18 in the Northumbria Community's *Celtic Daily Prayer: Book Two* is a poem expanding the title of a book by Dawna Markova called *I Will Not Die an Unlived Life*.[21] It expresses what I learnt.

The fruit of character

The list of the fruits of the Spirit in Galatians 5 is one of the better known New Testament passages. In my experience, it is usually expounded as a set of virtues for listeners to aim for now, whatever age you are. Of course there is sense in that, but now I have my autumn specs on I am more sharply aware of viewing those nine-fold list of qualities with several sharp questions attached. Are these virtues the harvest of my life? Is this what my autumn looks like to others?

By the end of autumn, the leaves are off the trees and you see the true shape of a tree's trunk and its limbs. Its individuality is more pronounced, not just an oak looking different from a beech or an ash, but each oak being its unique shape from its history. We might even say the tree has disrobed and become naked. We see it as it is.

One interviewee was eloquent about the naked tree, naming the starkness of its structure exposed, the tree being both vulnerable and strong. As autumn progresses, we see where the trunk is sound and true, where ivy has grown or where it was torn off, leaving scars. We notice where the limbs are healthy and proportionate. We also can see where branches have broken or fallen, where the tree may be damaged by a storm or punctured by a woodpecker making a hole that in time may be hollowed out by a squirrel or become the entry port to insects boring deeper inside to the living wood, which eventually will kill the tree. The tree leaves falling is about disclosure of the tree's heart, but it also heralds the opening of vistas.

The connection to this sort of stripping back to essentials is that, in human terms, as people age, what and how they are tends to become more pronounced. Inhibitions may diminish and character will out. Tournier concurs and mentions this at least three times in *Learning to Grow Old*: 'Old age reveals what a man really is, though he may not wish to see it'; 'A person's characteristics tend to become more accentuated as his life goes on'; 'The fact is that in old age we remain in general what we were before, but the traits of character become more marked.'[22]

The geriatrician Lucy Pollock is less definite: 'Many people hold a theory that character traits become more accentuated as we age… but that's not always true.' She adds: 'Dementia can change a personality utterly for good or bad.'[23]

The exposure of character will tend to reveal our virtues and our vices, our good habits and our bad ones. Both have been accumulated through life. My present understanding is that the autumnal stage of life, with its break from being an employed person and opportunity to explore what some call the second half of life, is a real chance to focus on the growth of character – to face down the bad and foster the good.

The passage to such virtues is no easy journey. The Genesis account of another kind of fall includes Adam and Eve realising they were naked and taking steps to cover that up (Genesis 3:9). To see oneself morally and spiritually naked is both disturbing and helpful. But only by living in the truth can repentance, change, renewal and transformation follow. Perhaps that search for honesty behind the externals of religion and the structures of belief is what prompted Brian McLaren to write *Naked Spirituality*, a book that also deals with learning across four stages of belief and life.[24]

Tournier also argues it is no accident that this facing up to who, and what, we truly are, is likely to occur in retirement. Then the loss of authority, power, wealth and position can bring a change in human values. 'From then on a man's value is judged not be what he does, but by what he is.' Tournier goes on to name some traits: personal maturity, their breadth of mind, a person's inner life and their quality of love. He concludes these are the value a person brings to the world.[25]

Freedom for hobbies and play time

Here's one warning. 'People who have no hobbies in their 60s become old people', said Harold, one of Knox's interviewees.[26] There is, in theory, freedom in retirement for taking our hobbies more seriously, but various constraints can hinder us. Tournier, writing in the 1970s, noted that our society values work more than leisure, and hobbies are usually classified by others as leisure. In addition, our being so used to routine, through our years of work, could be a trap in retirement by which our hobbies are dulled down to be just worked at. Moreover we can be afraid of what others think of our hobbies, and they can become but little fads we are ashamed of. At least one of my hobbies could be called 'nerdy', and I have often been reticent to go public about it.

There's another transition too. Pre-retirement, our hobbies acted as a distraction and relaxation. Now they become an occupation to help fill our time, an opportunity for contact with others who share our interest, and a chance to develop our skills and not regress. In short, they shift from accessory to a possible status of prime importance. But we should not imagine a binary view in which work is seen as routine and leisure as creative. Beneath both is life and, as Tournier notes, 'Life is a mixture of creation and repetition, of innovation and routine.'[27]

I wanted to show how these forces cash out across both work and leisure, so I put them in a diagram.

	Work	Leisure
Creation and innovation		
Repetition and routine		

My instinct is that we need to be able to live well with, and in, each of these quadrants, recognising the need for and the validity of each quadrant. I think it is false to believe that the size of each quadrant should be the same, or that what we place in each quadrant occurs with the same frequency.

I find in both work and leisure that the incidence of creation and innovation is less common and the repetition and routine occur more frequently. I note that the first pair are the greater bringers of life and vitality, the invitation to adventure once again. I hope that the latter pair will serve the former well, but I never imagined the second were unnecessary or inherently wrong in themselves. Even writing a book involves a lot of routine and repetition: sometimes daily re-opening the manuscript, ironing out bits of poor grammar, making sense of the nonsense you wrote last time and checking the references.

Danger: there's a hobby coming down the line

Is a hobby play time or not? I'm not sure. But I just about dare now to unpack one of my hobbies before you, which is making a model railway. The hobby includes going to see other people's models, because there is always more to learn. Re-reading Tournier has given me permission to re-classify this hobby as also a bit of an adventure. Part of the reason is the ongoing learning that is required; the other part is that something is created under your hands. So many varied skills are needed. Let me give you a guided tour. (Skip to chapter 3 now, if you are yawning already.)

One essential foundation is the perceptive observation of the real thing, as without it what you make won't really work. There are various early questions. Are you confident enough to build a layout based on your own ideas or do you need to copy somewhere on the real railway network? I did the latter, choosing Matlock Station in Derbyshire in 1938–39, aware of my slim knowledge. Then comes the issue of what scale to work in and what budget is acceptable.[28] One has to plan for both realism and operating interest, for one of the worst outcomes is to have spent hours building something that is boring to operate. The planning stage also involves finding the space available, which nearly always turns out to be too small for your first idea. Next comes making accurate drawings of the chosen plan that will fit in the space you do have. That stage needs to be conducted with a modesty that knows plans are only approximate, so when you finally do come to the actual construction, some jiggling will be needed. All this planning, in my case, took at least six months in 1999.

Only when all this thinking is done comes the first turning of ideas into action, by the erecting of an overall wooden structure that will carry the running lines, sidings, climbs and descents, cuttings and embank-ments, and enough space for convincing scenery to pass through. At last, some actual track-laying begins. This mechanical occupation I have always found particularly satisfying, though I am unaware of having navvies in my family history. Next, planned beforehand but now activated, is the darker art of electrical wiring and installation of controllers and switches to those railway tracks. There will also need to be electrical or mechanical ways to operate points and signals. Done right, trains will not derail at wrongly set points or run into one another. The layout design must also have the capacity to hide trains, to maintain the illusion that they are running through the layout not merely running in circles, chasing their tails like demented puppies.

Now we are talking about what will run on the railway. In practice some people just choose to run the engines they like. Others, like me, want to follow what would be seen at the real place. This leads to choosing and acquiring only the correct locomotives, coaches and wagons. These days the standard of ready-to-run items is high and the choice is wide. It's just a matter of cash. So in this comes the discipline of resisting modeller's curse. That is, to only have half of what you want, but twice as much as you actually need.

By 2001, there were lines and sidings, some items to run on them, but they traversed a bald, bleak, bare set of boards. Though I knew I was modelling Matlock Station in 1938–39, only an expert might have recognised the overall track shape; no one else would have a clue where or what it was. The next bit of the adventure presented itself.

There were no kits to make or models to buy of the buildings that were there. I had to make them from scratch. Mercifully, I found a book that contained simple architectural drawings of all the surrounding Matlock station buildings that I needed. After making a drawn copy, I used pic-ture frame card for the structure, covered with sheets of paper-based stone work and sheets of see-through plastic for windows. These all had to be slowly measured (twice), cut, glued, papered and painted. A small building like a waiting room could be 10 hours' work, a large goods shed taking at least 30 hours. Looking back at my records I only finished the majority of these buildings by 2014, making one or two a year.

So now there were buildings – and internal lighting to bring them alive, but no landscape. Once again, another adventure was on and needing new skills. A quarry face was fashioned from layers of sawn-up expanded-polystyrene blocks. Fine copper wire fed through a multitude of cut down kebab sticks fenced its top. I also had to make a hill, add grass and scrub bushes, make and stick stone walls and finally populate the slope with sheep. Being a genuine artist was a bridge too far, so friends with artistic ability came for the weekend, in which they and my wife painted the backscene of Matlock town and surrounding hills. I also incorporated my version of Monsal Dale viaduct into the overall layout, but that's its own story.

A further adventure was making trees, which are often plentiful by railways. Bought ones are expensive and often unconvincing, so learning how to make trees – using lengths of fine twisted wire, bulking the trunk and major limbs out with masking tape, all of which are painted, before adding the artificial foliage – all this beckoned. A forest tree can take another 30 hours to make, and there needed to be several. It is also drove me back to take in the real thing – to notice how the shape and character of an oak differs from an elm or a copper beech. I chose to make one of each, by the model of a real farm that lies below Monsal Dale viaduct.

The adventure of the search for realism is endless. In case you are getting bored, I only give you the headlines. Model railway stock comes out of its box as though it was fresh out of the real railway paint shops. In the steam era, they never ran like that; they were dirty from use. So there's a painting skill, called airbrushed weathering, by which the locomotives and what they pull are 'dirtied up'. Creating scenery is another endless art, including learning to use what's called 'static grass', which magically stands up like the real thing. And the overall result would look dead unless it was populated with people, animals and vegetation. Each new skill required was another adventure into the unknown. Maybe last of all comes seeing if the model can be run to a real timetable from that period. I'm still working that one out.

I'd be kidding myself and you if I said it was all adventure. It included much repetition and routine maintenance. The longer the list of tasks and the time taken to build the model in practice, the further time taken to repair what has already been created. The spreadsheet recording the time and money spent on my model of Matlock station shows it has taken 20 years and over 2,000 hours to make, including 300 hours to repair faults occurring or damage done.

There were also six years when I was not only fully occupied with full-time work but also tackling a part-time PhD. Creative railway model work stopped. There have also been years when I thought I had got as far as I could take it and all sense of adventure and challenge had gone. A concerning question was whether I enjoyed making it more than running it? Having nearly finished, should I now dismantle it and find another location to copy?

Railway modelling is a versatile exercise in both creativity and patience. I also see it as one manifestation of fruitfulness. Perhaps the fruitful harvest is those hours of purposeful creativity, and one sweet fruit is watching the faces of those friends, children and grandchildren who enjoy seeing it, as well as being allowed to drive a steam train out of a hidden siding. I like to show visitors a train running along, then stop it in full view. I then start it up again with the sound function turned on, by which the locomotive puffs, whistles and then stops applying squeaky brakes. People always smile and usually laugh. A whole new level of delight in its realism has emerged.

The guided tour of this hobby has now pulled into the final station. Thanks for coming, I hope you enjoyed the trip.

The autumn of life is not all fruit and harvest

Chapters 1 and 2 have explored the manifold fruits of the autumn of life. They are to be savoured with gratitude as they occur. And, like the harvest in the agrarian world, they are to be stored again for the winter that will eventually follow. So we maintain the health of relationships given and gained, retain storehouses of memories, photos and curios, and practise the lessons learnt along the autumnal way.

Yet to be balanced and honest, I must acknowledge that autumn isn't all fruitfulness. There are grey days, too, and our days have begun to shorten since the zenith of the sun of high summer. Some songs of autumn may be more like laments. That's a topic within the chapter on scripture and living out our autumns. There is much to give thanks over, for the diversity of autumn fruits, but it's now time to pay attention to the falling leaves.

Application questions

- What freedoms have come your way in your own autumn of life?

- Do you notice more 'freedom to' or 'freedom from' factors? Why might that be?

- Tournier invites us to see life as an adventure. How does that strike you? Is that thought inviting or intimidating?

- Willard wrote that we live in a 'God bathed and God permeated world.' You may or may not agree. If you thought that way too, how different would it make living your autumn of life?

- What further new adventures could exist for you?

3

Autumn: those falling leaves

During the autumn of life our capacities diminish. As we age, there are mental and physical losses. Our physical health and mental sharpness take some steps downward and our horizons begin to narrow, even if we have a bucket list. We may struggle to keep up in a fast-changing world. If we live on, decluttering beckons and downsizing may be needed, as well as handling anxiety as we head towards dependency. Let's unpack all those.

Loosening or losing one's grip

Nearly all older people begin to find that certain words won't come, names elude us and 'what's her face' doesn't take you very far. Several of my interviewees named this very loss, irrespective of their age, which ranged from mid-60s to late-80s. What is worse is that people start to finish our sentences for us, as we struggle to release that word or phrase that we can feel lurks disguised in some dark undisclosed alley in our brain. This elusive bit of data has lost the way down the winding tunnel to our mouths. Sometimes it doesn't really matter. A mildly tiresome example of suffering from elusive names was that although I had organised my retirement library at home alphabetically by author, this cunning plan, worthy of Baldrick, was flawed: though I might remember a title which I needed to pull out, could I remember who wrote it? The prospect of painstakingly reading the spine of several hundred volumes did not appeal. Nor could I bear the thought of reorganising the whole system of my books by title, or creating and maintaining a database that offered both. I shall have to continue to hunt and nurture the bitter-sweet fruit of patience.

I noticed too that, as I entered my 70s and this word block began to happen to me, both I and other older people whom I interviewed sometimes laughed nervously to cover a hesitant break in speaking, or apologised to companions and listeners that they couldn't find that name, word or thought that was needed. This sense of losing our grip can come with a vague sense of shame. (I'll comment on that word 'shame' later.) Our competence has diminished; we are no longer so sharp, or as penetrating. Half of those interviewed used those particular words in noticing this change. We might have some wisdom still, but the fluency to express it has begun to elude us. Early leaves are falling.

Only recently, I dutifully locked the house back door after completing some useful piece of gardening work under Helen's direction and went back to book writing. It never occurred to me that I had thereby locked her in the garden. An hour later, the front doorbell rang and a gracious, but justifiably irate, wife explained how she had resorted to using ladders and a spare trellis frame from the garage, to scale the wall to our neighbour's house and scramble to freedom. Oops, another leaf had fallen.

Slowing down

Those of us in the autumn of life find that we have to go slower. Even David Attenborough no longer travels out on safari with the camera crews, but instead does the voice-overs at a later stage in a studio. Intriguingly, at the closing scenes of his 2022 series *Frozen Planet II*, Attenborough got out of his chair, which was placed in front of the big screen, where he had sat as the wise man, famed commentator and representative observer, chronicling the disastrous effects of global warming, then walked slowly towards the camera, not looking at it, and went off into darkness. Was there some sense that he had now given everything he had to give – magnificent and hopefully significant though that has been? There is a time to slow down. Some of us are realising that, though we still go out for walks, we tread more carefully than in the past.

An irony is that we are all slowing down today for many reasons. It's not just a feature for the active elderly because of their decreased mobility, diminished muscle power or disobedient brain. Of course, it is that, and in my case my recorded performance times on the bike and the rowing machine show me getting slower and weaker. But it is also the fact that finding one's way through modern life seems to be getting slower.

Consider the time it takes on the phone, an app or some form of computer to get a doctor's appointment. I accept that the entire NHS is under enormous strain, and I applaud all they have been able to do, not least during the Covid pandemic. I willingly clapped them in our street alongside our neighbours. Yet the process is certainly both slower and more uncertain than it was decades ago. My doctor's practice has been good to me, but there have been times of trying to phone, every five minutes from 8.00 am, and finding the line is perennially engaged. Finally I would get through and be told the list was closed for the day.

Every app boasts that it is quick and easy, and indeed some are, but I find many that aren't. Then having done the task, made the booking, ordered the item, another slowdown is being asked online to fill in a review of your experience of that site or service. Doing so much of life online too often feels like being stuck in a traffic jam with no alternative route to choose.

That raises another example. In an actual traffic jam, sat there with the engine turned off and peering round the vehicle in front, you wonder if there has been an accident, is it roadworks or are the traffic lights broken. Behind that lurks the question of whether I will now get to my destination on time. These days I leave longer to arrive somewhere than

I did before. Motorway driving, especially in rush hour, is no longer fun. Smart motorway signage can be useful, but we all experience them becoming slower motorways, even though the hard shoulder has now become an extra lane. Have you noticed, too, that whoever programmed the illuminated lights to show slow-down speeds approaching some hazard only calibrated for 60, 50 and 40 miles per hour, whereas when you approach a halt, lights showing 30 and 20 would be far more realistic. I am amused by the irony that, though modern cars are designed to go faster than ever, often we are actually going slower, not least in towns where a bicycle may be considerably faster, as well as healthier and more ecologically responsible.

But back to the autumn of life metaphor and its attendant slowing down. We older people find ourselves going slower, both physically and mentally. My interviewees found this slowing was also linked to getting tired more easily, and this needs managing by building in recovery time. My sons even notice that I drive more slowly these days. The positive about slower motoring is the ability to notice my surroundings better and experience less stress in the slow and middle lanes – and I tell myself I'm saving money and diminishing my carbon footprint. With slowing there sometimes comes the added anxiety that, knowing we are eventually going to die, have all the various necessary things been done before time runs out? When will slowing become stopping?

Living in sickness and in health

That the autumnal leaf-dropping stage of life is happening to us is clearly marked by the medical aspect of our lives. Somehow it is clearer than chronological ageing, which can be quite confusing. Though daily I do increase in age, there is some meaning in the sentiment 'I am as old as I feel.' By contrast, the degrading of our health is unpredictable. It may either gradually creep up on us, or it may come more as a violent sudden blast, if you have a stroke, heart attack, major operation or unsuspected diagnosis of cancer. In early autumnal weather, a few leaves begin to drift off the trees, but many are blown down by a storm.

According to the National Council on Aging, about 92% of seniors have at least one chronic disease and 77% have at least two. Heart disease, stroke, cancer and diabetes are among the most common storms. Of my 16 interviewees, three had needed hip replacements, another three a major heart operation and a further two cancer surgery. Whether slowly or rapidly, what is true is that the leaves are falling.

My own story thus far is much less serious. Some changes are both gradual and so far eminently fixable. Take the example of needing glasses or contact lenses. In my 30s, I needed glasses for the first time, but only for reading and computer use. Out of vanity I never wore them otherwise, even for preaching. Then the day came when I struggled to read my notes, and out they had to come and perch on my public nose. In my 50s I began to think they were prudent for driving. Nowadays, except for horseplay with the grandchildren or turning over to go to sleep after bedtime reading, I realise I am wearing them all the time. My feather-light varifocals are so familiar that I don't even realise I am wearing them. I have been known to go and look for them round the house, complain that I can't find them and then discover I was wearing them all the time. None of my interviewees mentioned glasses; it's as though they have become accepted extensions of ourselves. We see life through them and become unaware of them.

The loss of a tooth is slightly different. I had my wisdom teeth out in my early 20s and this was easy for me to deem as progress, as there wasn't room for them. There dental matters rested until a year or so ago. Then pain at biting or when drinking hot or cold things meant an upper left molar was in trouble. That grew to a semi-permanent ache that I didn't want to live with. An hour's levering and tugging at the dentist and it's gone. There's now a gap that won't be replaced easily. If you get a denture it's quite a process and how will the adopted 'gnasher' cope when a crunchy apple comes along? A few people may have enough money – and sufficient vanity – to afford an implant. Whether you take no action or accept being given a substitute, you know that a part of you has gone forever. It's not much to fuss about, or is it? That smile I hope you liked is now flawed and part of what my body grew and gave me has now failed. Lose a prominent frontal tooth and all this is dialled up further.

Another technical replacement for a loss or diminution of a faculty is the hearing aid. Hearing loss had occurred for nearly half of my interviewees, and this mattered especially because of their continuing roles of listening to people. It was rare that I noticed that they were wearing such a device. Somehow, to be seen wearing a hearing aid remains an admission of failure or incompetence. Older people are quite expected to have to bleat, 'What did you say?', but I've never heard someone ask, 'What didn't I see?' Curiously and illogically there seems to be no loss of status in wearing glasses. The response from hearing-aid makers has been to make them as unobtrusive as possible. Preserving one's undying image and credibility, as remaining truly human, is an understandable response to this illogical specific expression of ageist prejudice over deafness.

I spotted a few other entertaining and sober responses. The two with engineering backgrounds took the view that they wouldn't worry about their health until something obviously went wrong, much as they wouldn't stress about a serviced car engine that ran well. I discovered that all the respondents who mentioned their being less strong were male. And it was the two railway modellers (not me, in this case) who feared losing their sight.

As to other fears, I noticed that it was the single women who named the vulnerabilities of tight finances and of dying alone. It all underlined to me that our health does not exist as a totally separate factor. Rather, how we view our health is significantly affected by our circumstances and our outlook. Some of this is beyond our control. In a forest there may be both sycamores and oaks. The sycamores drop their leaves early, the oaks far later. Neither chose to be what they were. So it is with us.

Our health issues tend to reveal our advancing age

We are privileged to live in a spacious semi in Sheffield. The house was built in 1904 and owned for many years by a member of the Thornton family – he of the boxes of chocolates. Mercifully, it was never modernised in the 1960s and thus retains many original features that give us much pleasure and enable us to be hospitable. The point is this – it's now 120 years old and starting to show its age. The original, lead-lined, wooden lavatory cistern started to leak, and we had to find a specialist plumber to fix it. There is a slight leak in the roof and the requisite small bucket is in place. Winter storm rain once came through an exposed corner of the stone walling into the parlour. It had been repaired years ago with the wrong cement mortar rather than correct lime mortar. The rendering below the sitting room bay window began to crack and fail, causing the large stones around it to wobble a bit. Our roofer has elegantly sorted those last two out by packing the gaps with pieces of slate and beautifully finished lime mortar. We see ourselves as custodians of a lovely building, but it is showing its age. I tell you this because the same is becoming true of me.

Recently, ill health has been niggling me. Previously my general health had been very good, and I sensed little change from the vitality I enjoyed in my 50s, 60s and early 70s. I expected this to continue unabated, but a few years ago that changed. Since then there has been an ongoing yet unpredictable stream of conditions. One dimension was worrying chest pains, accompanied by shooting pains in my left arm for which, one day, I did call 111. The delightful ambulance crew who came out ran tests and diagnosed it as heartburn from an existing hiatus hernia and from a trapped nerve in my neck. The latter was cured by remedial exercises from a physiotherapist actually called Tom Back!

Twice in recent years I was given an appointment for a 24-hour ECG monitor to see if the periodic fluttering sensation in the heart area and a sense of lightheadedness was anything to be concerned about. I appear to have an occasional ectopic beat, but Google says that's usually nothing to worry about. There matters have rested with occasional mild symptoms persisting and an ongoing unease that not all is well. I am currently being treated for low blood pressure, a low heart rate and possible angina. The resolution of this story is not yet clear.

Another trouble was my guts played up. Now Mrs Prune and Mr Fig are among my best friends. However, the appendicitis I feared has not materialised! In addition, planning a long car journey now involves checking beforehand where the service stations are and taking those pit stops. Countryside walks will probably need to include a wild wee, as my PSA (prostate-specific antigen) number has started to rise. Yet I am grateful that I still sleep through the night without having to get up. My low blood pressure contributes to my often feeling light-headed, and over the years this has led to my passing out on at least three occasions. Thus after any extended cycle ride or any vigorous exercise I am careful to rehydrate and take on salts. I notice too that hill climbs I used to cycle up at 13–14 mph are now being taken at 8–9 mph, but it feels like as much effort even to do that. Fallen leaves indeed.

A further factor is that my asthma has risen. Only twice in many years has that been truly alarming and life-threatening. However, quite often, and unpredictably, a throat tickle becomes a persistent but ineffective cough and out comes the blue puffer. Indeed, that small canister sits in my right trouser pocket on nearly all occasions. The result is a low level of semi-permanent vulnerability, which sometimes seems obsessional, but at other times justified.

I do worry that you now feel that you are reading the ramblings of a paranoid hypochondriac, and I admit that the number of times I have self-diagnosed a terminal complaint is ridiculous. I almost never Google these conditions because that would add to my morbid suspicions. To my credit, I deny ever having had man flu. However, I cannot deny being slowly eroded by the length and variety of these signs of decay, dis-ease and decline. It has been lowering, even depressing, such that I seriously considered pulling out of a booked skiing holiday in 2022 because I felt I couldn't face its physical demands and the Covid-induced travel regulations and uncertainties that accompanied it. I went and lived to tell the tale. But being reduced to tears over that episode had never been my way before.

In all these ways the turning from 72 to 75 years old has been quite a sharp downturn. Like our 1904 house, this 1949 body is beginning to creak. I still do not know whether all this represents a blip, or if it is the herald of my future to which I still have to learn to adjust. Fischer nails this nagging reality: 'Bodily decline is frequently one of the most difficult aspects of growing older. There comes a time when what we most fear is not ageing, but disability.' She wrote that about women, but I own it too. As Mitton admits: 'There is an autumn season in the human journey that is brought about by a loss of health that finds no immediate cure.'[1]

The body used to be my obedient servant, doing what I wanted it to. Gradually a set of shifts has occurred, with occasional rebellions, and my body is becoming more like a task master or tyrant, with me being only able to do what it will allow these days. Of course, there have always been limits, of speed, strength, endurance and understanding, but my body and I had adjusted to those compromises between ideal and reality. Now the nasty thought occurs that my body begins to be more like a traitor. It was my faithful companion and willing friend in games, sports and excursions. It carried me to and through work. Now there are mild protests at getting up from a chair and heavier breathing when climbing the stairs in our house. It is 43 steps from the cellars to the top floor.

I'm not entirely alone in these disturbing thoughts. One interviewee, Sue, gave this fascinating reflection on her health at this stage of life:

> I am aware of a strange thing happening: I am detaching from my body. It won't always do what I want. I am aware that there is a kind of dis-integration happening between 'me' and 'my body'.

It was Ann, a female friend in America, who made me aware of an additional pressure on women in the autumn of life. She writes:

> We women are so very aware that, whether it should be this way or not, society places a declared value on attractiveness in women, and we live with that awareness all of our lives. And when that attractiveness begins to wane, in our or the world's eyes, we struggle and are saddened at yet this one more aspect of the early latter years of our lives.

Concessions have been made to these falling leaves. I have stopped playing cricket, dinghy sailing and running, but I am still cycling, go for fairly long walks and from time to time use the static bike and the rowing machine. Others my age go to the gym. It's good that we attend to our bodies. As Fischer says: 'When we listen to our bodies we can become good caretakers of our own health.'[2] To my relief I still manage an annual skiing holiday, and here I'm grateful for the mystery of muscle memory. I took two years out from skiing because of the pandemic, but when I once more clipped into my skis in 2022, I did the first turn without thinking. Well done, my body, thanks for remembering how all that worked. Skiing can be quite kind to experienced older people, because as your technique improves, it takes less effort because the skis are working for you more efficiently. They are expressly designed to turn. All the body movements do is trigger what the ski will do for you: glide, turn or stop. So in that activity I am still very fortunate, but the lurking question is: for how long? My sense from our week's outing in 2023 is that the skill level is still there, for which I am grateful, but the stamina is waning.

February 2024 may have marked hanging up our ski-boots at the end of 55 skiing weeks. I have had to admit that the old sense of adventure has faded. I noticed that I fell twice, and while I was not injured, it could have been worse. I am thinking it's wise to quit while you are ahead. And curiously, just as I sat down in my coach seat for the return journey, a large leaf fluttered down just by my window. Hmmm.

How should I view all this? If leaves are a loss, are there parallels to the five classic stages of grieving: denial, anger, bargaining, depression and acceptance? I think so. In chapter 2, I mentioned Emilie Griffin's book, with its chapter entitled 'Grief, loss, anger'.[3] I was surprised that, being such a perceptive writer, she didn't start further back with denial. Related writing comes from Tournier in section five of his *Learning to Grow Old*, which is simply called 'Acceptance'.

I am not sure whether I should I regard all these things I've named as thorns in the flesh? Whether Paul's own 'thorn in the flesh' (2 Corinthians 12:7–10) was physical or spiritual, I'm not sure. His list of weaknesses, insults, hardships, persecutions and difficulties sounds very wide. What is clearer is Christ's response: 'My grace is sufficient for you, for my power is made perfect in weakness' (v. 9). I am sure that living the autumn of life means living with falling leaves – with some kinds of decline and some encounter with weakness. I will unpack hints of how to live Christ's response and other biblical material in chapters 7 and 8. I hope to be forgiven for all the above autobiography. I've wanted to be candid about living with these falling leaves.

Loss of leaves in a partner

I can only imagine the additional pressures borne by people, living in their own autumn, whose life partner is at the end of that autumn or even already in winter. I recall such friends expressing that a number of joys hoped for, or fruits of retirement, had been stolen away from them. At least two testing scenarios exist. Perhaps the easier one is when the decline is only physical and recovery may be possible. Some activities, hobbies and types of holiday have to be abandoned, but not conversation and relationships.

When the falling leaves are serious mental decay, other additional strains occur. A kind of pre-bereavement begins: the partner loved and known begins to fade away, and the spouse can do little or nothing to bring them back. Sometimes, what is worse is that underlying unresolved character traits appear in the afflicted partner and quite often these will be disagreeable. They can include irrational fears, buried cynicism, disinterest in life, serious anger or old antipathies. What is worse, the ability to banish or put right these 'demons' is all but lost. Time for amendment of life has run out.

The partner still in autumn can feel this is a case of 'winter but never Christmas', as was said of Narnia in the chilling days of the White Witch in C.S. Lewis' *The Lion, the Witch and the Wardrobe*, and they have no idea how long this burden will have to be carried. At the least, they need friends with whom they can talk honestly. Here they can unload something of their sorrow, regrets, conflicting reactions (like caring yet sometimes wishing the person would die), as well as recalling the positive memories, gratitude for what has been and fleeting moments of hope.

What a shame

Something else occurs alongside the loss of our own previously robust health. We can feel we are becoming a burden to our family, costing them time, effort and money. Some readers may have watched the BBC Two programme *Head On: Rugby, dementia and me*, about Steve Thompson, the English rugby hooker with repeated head injuries that have led to early onset dementia in his 40s. Such an onset is a fearsome autumn storm; at times he can almost feel the leaves falling, as he finds he even forgets his own daughter's name. Yes, there were fading fruits, like showing his children his England caps, but they were overshadowed by his sense of shame at becoming dependent, being no longer a provider and self-sufficient. In the programme, although he won a World Cup medal in 2003 and an MBE, he was recorded as reflecting: 'If I hadn't done it, I might not be such a burden on the family.' That's a dramatic and harrowing story which should lead to a change in the rugby culture to minimise head injuries. Yet the gradual or sudden loss during autumn of our abilities, mental or physical, can prompt a similar reaction.

A number of my interviewees were insistent that they didn't want to become a burden on their adult children, and they feared it might occur. My generation are the first to have four generations to relate to: caring for yet older dependent relatives in their own winter or fourth age; coping with our own third-age lives; dealing with our adult children's requests for, say, a loan from the Bank of Mum and Dad or for that nice free child-minding service; and also fulfilling roles as grandparents. All these relationships contain delights, but they also add to the pressure. We are reluctant to pass that pressure on to the next generation. Becoming aware of the onset of our own dependency may carry a level of guilt or shame that it is now happening to us, and we know that the consequences will fall on those we love. I link this prospect of burden and shame to what I noticed from my interviewees. Eight said they feared some form of dementia compared with only four who mentioned cancer. I'd link this to the reality that many cancers are operable, whereas as yet there is no reversal of dementia. Moreover, people went on to express fear of what hidden character flaws might rear their heads and what dreadful language they might use and things they might say.

Time in the autumn of life

There are periods when days pass without a milestone in sight; the future seems but a continuation of the present. All is familiar and you believe that you know how everything works. Several of my interviewees were in that happy state, and yet some were aware of niggling factors. David asked himself: 'How long can I go on at this pace?' Michael has realised that 'the future will be managing decline, and how I develop a spirituality for it'. Christine spotted a challenge: 'I am increasingly aware that health is not just something to be taken for granted.' An image that came into my mind hearing these comments is that our lives until now have been like an attractive, well-crafted sandcastle built on a sandy beach and we have just noticed that the tide has started coming in.

Beyond that stage and picture, there are times when you sense the wheel has already turned and the context and landscape are less familiar. Somehow you have travelled out of the familiar into new territory. This might be caused by one of those 'big birthdays' – you reach 21, you hit 50 or you encounter 70. Other milestones include: the first day of a job; getting married; the birth of a child; when someone calls you 'middle-aged' for the first time; the day you retire; the death of a spouse; or any of those birthdays that usher in a new decade of your life. Autumn marks the end of the summer season. The transition through autumn is a further journey, and there may be a winter coming quicker than you think.

Even the very word 'milestone' is congruent with living through time; there is the sense of movement, a journey is happening, we are not where we were. The catch with time is that you can't turn round and go backwards. There is no reset button to play the game called 'My Life' again. Yes, there are memories but that is calling bits of the past into the present, not the other way round. Memory can trawl the brain, but it cannot bring up live fish.

Circle or line?

Today not everyone accepts this essentially linear view of time. Katherine May in her delightful book of stories and reflections, *Wintering*, approves of Gaelic mythology, which she says recovers for us a cyclic metaphor for life that has been forgotten in modern society. She deprecates 'imagining our lives to be linear; a long march from birth to death in which we mass our powers, only to surrender them again, all the while losing our youthful beauty'. I guess many with pagan beliefs would concur. Fischer asserts that 'women's time is cyclical'.[4] However, I don't think the choice is binary, either linear or cyclic. I see both in action; the agricultural seasons are cyclic, but the chronological years are linear.

Some readers may be wondering why I haven't chosen to name and explore the metaphor of a journey. These paragraphs bear upon that deliberate omission. Journeys can be taken whether you adopt the cyclic or the linear view of time. Both have to be lived out. I accept that. But precisely because journey doesn't settle that difference of view, it doesn't work for me. The autumn of life is not cyclic. It has an end, and its name is winter. I also chose to omit much reference to journey because I think it is overused. Autumn is less explored, and I find it both more evocative and more demanding.

May's book lovingly explores the metaphor of wintering for those periods in our lives which emotionally and personally can be cold and dark, stark, isolating, painful and lonely. They may arise through various kinds of suffering and loss: illness, hospitalisation, injustice, fear, unemployment, divorce, bereavement, even the Covid-19 pandemic. She rightly observes that such 'winter periods' will happen to all of us. Then the cyclic view gives her hope that winter will pass. Winter can be redeemed through what she calls rest and retreat. We need to learn to take care of ourselves. She believes winter brings insights and those who winter well will gain wisdom. And, despite winter's gifts and virtues, spring will come.

I accept there are these cycles. I have done my own winters from a young age, when my father died suddenly and entirely unexpectedly. I felt its icy cold. Yet beneath and beyond the cyclic, I'd put the case that the Christian view of time is fundamentally linear. It runs from what we call creation to the return of Christ, the full coming of the kingdom, and the arrival of the new heaven and earth. Its principal milestone along that linear trajectory is the coming of Jesus. Until recently, history dates were either BC or AD. That, I would argue, is a Christian view of time.

Yet along that line there are also loops. By loops, I of course don't mean that during them time goes backwards before going ahead again. I suppose it is a way of talking about what feels like a repeating pattern. Some of these loops are mid-sized repeating ones, like the four seasons of the year, or the less predictable 28 different 'times' cited in Ecclesiastes 3. There are the tiny ones that may depend which side of the bed we got out of that morning. There are the much longer ones, such as in the Old Testament the spring time of the exodus, the summer time of David and Solomon, the autumn of their failing successors and the winter of the exile. There are story loops, like the start of enforced perpetual winter in Narnia, ended by the advent of Aslan's spring. In church history it may depend where you view things from. Is the Reformation a Protestant spring, a Catholic winter, or both? So, yes, I see both lines and loops.

Living the new unfolding line with its loops

There are loops and lines, but this book is written because I am getting older – and that's not a cycle, it's a line. The book is about that line, sensing that I haven't lived the autumn of life before and I have to learn how. As I adjust and change, emotional cycles will have their roles to play. The line may well contain big wiggles and loops. Like Katherine May, I too have hope, but not just that autumn can do what it should and that winters pass. My hope is in the God who works with and within time, who in Jesus intervened publicly within time and by the Spirit brings life into what I foolishly call 'my time'. I hope also in the God who has the authority and right to blow the final whistle and call 'time' on all existence, including mine. Whatever depth of winter precedes the blowing of that final trumpet, there then will follow a springtime far surpassing anything we've ever seen before.

But let's come back down to earth. I recall a saying related to time and particularly the season that I'm calling the autumn of life: 'I've never been this old before, and I'll never be this young again.' The original comes from Eleanor Roosevelt: 'Today is the oldest you've ever been and the youngest you'll ever be again.' Search online for either quote, and you'll find you can buy wall plaques and coffee mugs with her words, and more interestingly a number of websites that offer counsel and agony aunt responses to stressed young people who woke up one morning and found, to their alarm, that they are now 30! 'Don't panic,' I say to them, 'I'm writing this book in my 70s.'

Perhaps arrogantly, I prefer my version to Roosevelt's. It directly owns that this reflection is my problem, not yours. It tacitly admits that I don't quite know how to live at this age – it's a foreign land. How I negotiated life in my 50s or 60s doesn't feel that it has all the answers. On the other hand, today is the youngest I'll ever be, so maybe I have more resources now than I may have in the future, to live out the autumn of life, to wander through the foreign land of my 70s. Thankfully, most bits of my body appear to hang together, and at the last count the total of my retained marbles wasn't too bad. That's if you don't take the escape of people's names too seriously; it's just that the retrieval system has got a bit rusty. That name will come to me at a wonderfully inconvenient moment.

So yes, my life now is a foreign land. No, I can't reverse back into the land that was familiar, but I maybe do have the shoes and staff for the onward expedition of up and down loops and the periods of an even line. But mentioning a staff – oh dear, that's not so far away from having to have a walking stick and all that implies.

So far I've commented on the autumnal leaf loss involved in losing one's grip, slowing down and having health issues, including caring for a dependent partner. I have also touched on how this stage of life marches on in a linear time process, including loops, that is distinctively Christian. I now need to branch out and make more use of the metaphor of living in a foreign land, which our autumn time has taken us to. I think this set of losses hits those living the autumn of life harder, because we are living through a digital revolution, which for many older people is its own foreign land. I found that this way of speaking resonated for people I interviewed about their own life in retirement, even when they didn't identify with my metaphor of autumn.

An immigrant in Digitalopolis

If being older is a kind of foreign land, my second, newish, scarily changeable foreign land is the digital one. Among classic BBC comedies was the series *One Foot in the Grave*, starring Richard Wilson as Victor Meldrew. (Already some of you are saying under your breath, 'I don't believe it.') Apart from the humour, get in touch with his disbelief, anger, frustration, bewilderment and disenfranchisement. What's the link to today's foreign land for those of us living the autumn of life? Let me tell you how it has been for me and you decide what sort of status you would give yourself.

It is now commonplace for those teaching digital education to distinguish between digital residents and visitors or between digital natives and immigrants. 'Visitor' is the more transitory term. The visitor can behave like a tourist: they choose to do the sights, take the photos, get a suntan and go back home, maybe intrigued, maybe pleased, maybe shocked at what they saw. The 'immigrant' has had to engage more deeply; they have left a homeland and entered a foreign culture and are being forced to work out how to live there. Such is the prevalence and universality of the digital revolution that I think of this aspect of my autumn as entering a foreign land. Thus I find the word 'immigrant' is more honest and demanding for how I experience the digital world, than my simply being a come-and-go visitor, which might just be fun.

In the digital world, I seem to get by much of the time. But here's another contrast. It's not my identity, it's about my capability. I'm not digitally fluent; it's as though I have to use a second language that I've never been properly taught. I am coming in from the outside. Like a digital parrot, I know some of the vocabulary, but I stumble and can't always find the word I want or express what I need to say. I'm not fluent; it's not my mother tongue or my natural environment. Worse still, the analogue world I was born into has suffered from 'digital warming'. Its ice shelves have shrunk and parts of its coastline has disappeared. Goodbye encyclopedia, OHP, SLR camera, service-it-myself car, spare parts shop, wind-up goods or toys, repairable goods, petrol pump attendants, local bobby, even many department stores. Yet, in some places, to my surprise, the milkman has walked back out of the sea and wasn't extinct after all.

Three cheers for digital

Though I could be called a digital visitor rather than a resident, and though I consider myself an immigrant not a native, I have to say there are many benefits. I am grateful for word processing; it truly helps me compose. Without it I would be lost, and I doubt I would have written anything for publication at all. I only discover what I really need to say because my first go on the screen clearly doesn't hack it and I can easily edit it. I also needed the database Access and the spreadsheet Excel to hold and shape the data generated in my research life. Excel continues to be how I store data for my finances, motor car histories, holiday arrangements, and even the log of work done and costs incurred on the model railway. It panders to my preference for detail. I enjoy using PowerPoint to communicate something more than putting on a screen the very words that I was also saying and giving people images that do other work and start further thoughts.

I love the way our family keeps in touch so frequently and instantly on WhatsApp, with quips and pictures. I truly appreciate how, during the Covid pandemic, Helen and I, via Zoom and email, kept in meaningful touch with many groups: local and international friends; members of our regional Northumbria Community group; and the European-wide members of our extended family. I value all those gains, and I would struggle to live well without them.

I haven't yet added praise of access to the sheer volume and range of useful information because of the digital world. Like many people, I have a collection of apps and programmes which, for example, tell me how much energy our solar panels on the roof are making; show me where I am on an Ordnance Survey map; keep me in touch with sports news; help me learn German; inform me what the weather is likely to be doing; and provide a digital concordance. Not to mention the wider world of podcasts and YouTube, where I can find plenty of material related to my hobbies and interests.

Yet in all this, I sense that I am a receiver of digital benefits rather than a creator of them. I have learnt to respond adequately to what comes into my email inbox or through various apps, but I am not confident to explore those worlds and venture out further into them. I stand at the back of the digital squash court and send back a few shots but rarely, if ever, hit a winner.

Is there anyone out there like me?

There are even times when venturing into the digital world that I surge with impotent anger. 'Oh, it's so easy to do online,' a website, an official or even a young friend may say. But does anyone else share my frustration at now needing to use at least 30 different sites that all need their own password, and that your favourite one has been deemed not strong enough, or you don't remember whether the one you are chasing had a capital letter in it? Have you ever gone on a website and found that it's like looking at a map of an unknown place? Sometimes I'm not even sure that the map is the right way up. Can I find the one link I need? I wish. Anger and frustration bubble away. Then you ask a younger member of the human race for assistance, and they sit down and crack it quickly. What have you learnt? Only that they know how to do it and you don't. Who said all the dinosaurs were extinct when there's one sitting in this very room?

Or what about discovering that there's a phone number on the website? 'Ho, ho,' you think, 'there might be a person to talk to.' You dial and several minutes later a nice-sounding pre-recorded voice gives you five options to select – and you don't know which one really would be best. You hit key 4 in hope; it was the least clearly wrong. You are now in a queue, bombarded by inane music on a short loop. Eventually there's a pick up, and who's there? Either it's another computer trying to fit you into AI-generated categories or you have been re-routed to another team with another assistant who isn't actually much help! Whatever happened to real customer service?

Yes, I confess to being a reincarnation of Victor Meldrew. But I seriously fear that we have created a digital world in which the ability to create and send information exceeds the average human ability to access or process it. Ever felt you get too many emails? Ever wondered where that lost email went? Ever wished that those unwanted adverts would stop popping up? Ever wished your phone wasn't on during a meal or that you shouldn't have picked up that call during a meal? Ever cursed the spate of nuisance phone calls? Ever read through the day's offerings in the TV guide and been glad that at least you have some DVDs? Ever found yourself considering having a fast from the phone, tablet or computer? Ever worried about the advent of AI? Too many 'evers' there I know, but is anyone nodding out there?

Do not pass go and nearly lose £200

My worst digital nightmare began in January 2022. I needed a new passport to go skiing. The website said it was easier, quicker and cheaper to apply online. Stupidly I believed it. I input the relevant data, but then needed a digital photo. The website tests that photo, and immediately tells you whether it passes. After five attempts, I got one accepted. Relief and job done.

Two weeks later an email arrived, saying, 'Your photo doesn't meet our standards.' My worry level clicked up. I just had time to nip down to the station, get a passport photo, do a traditional, counter-signed application and send it with my existing passport to Peterborough. A week later came another message: 'There is a delay in processing all paper applications.' The new one wouldn't come in time. Anxiety notched up higher. So I completed an urgent-in-person application for Peterborough, costing £147. I quickly got an appointment.

The official there asked, 'The form is fine, but where's your old passport?' I said it was in his office, with my paper application. He looked worried and went to consult. He returned. 'Sorry,' he said, 'we can't get that passport because of GDPR.' I was furious. 'You mean I can't give you permission to go and get *my* own passport? How ridiculous!' I now hit mega-anxiety level: all options exhausted, no holiday, total waste of money, stupid bureaucracy, etc.

I don't know how it happened. Maybe he saw that I was about to cry. Maybe his compassion surged. Maybe I missed the hovering angel. 'I shouldn't do this,' he whispered, 'but go down to the secluded booth. I'll take your picture.' He took it first time and assured me it would be fine. He also advised me to contact the complaints team and tell my story. I would have hugged him, but I guessed he was in enough potential trouble already.

I am not alone in having a passport renewal horror story. But I tell it to illustrate a digital mirage, that everything digital works. This exhausting, painful process took me to the edge, and showed me that digital sometimes promises more than it can deliver. Little wonder that I think I'm an immigrant in a foreign land.

Immigrant or exile?

Perhaps I should have expected that my autumn of life would in some way have aspects of being in a foreign land. And it's not just that I haven't been this old before and this stage of life in retirement is different in important ways. As a long-time companion of Northumbria Community, that identity has asked me to live with the following exilic question, sourced from Psalm 137:4: 'How shall we sing the Lord's song in a foreign land?' And, as I've just illustrated, that's exactly what I call the digital world – a foreign land.

That question ratchets up the understanding of who I find myself to be in relation to the digital world. You have read already that I see myself as more immigrant than visitor, as working in a second language and never becoming fluent. But the exilic metaphor goes further. There is a sense in which I am an unwilling captive in a foreign land. I didn't choose to be here. I have to write, keep accounts, pay taxes, maintain contacts and store photos digitally. I cannot avoid a lot of buying online, and I wish I could be free of nuisance calls. The digital world has invaded my privacy and my prior antediluvian country – complete with typewriters, people who answered phones and wrote letters – and I have no choice but to work with it, to be appreciative of what it has opened up and to learn what I need to survive and even thrive in it.

There is another aspect to a contemporary sense of exile, and it reaches far wider than the retired. We are aware that we no longer live in a world whose future we can take for granted. The term 'existential threat' or 'crisis' is more often used. Sarah Pillar of Northumbria Community wrote in its newsletter of November 2022:

> Today we ask questions in the face of existential crises: conse-quences of war, degradation of habitats and climate life-cycles, mass movement of people fleeing for their lives… In a time of great lament, how shall we sing the Lord's song in a strange land?

We, in the developed world, are returning to living with a perpetual sense of frailty. Pillar named some major sources above, but the years 2022–24 have added political turmoil, a clearer loss of the centre ground in politics, unending industrial strikes, strained and creaking health and transport systems, all to a background of a widening gap between rich and poor. For Christians in Europe, perhaps the whole developed world, there are overlaps between autumn and an exile of the church which is its own topic and explored in chapter 6.

Decluttering of both house and life

Before entering the onset of the dependency of winter, an autumn task is decluttering and in part an early preparation towards death. It is another helpful, even necessary but seemingly endless, expression of what I call learning to let go, the topic of the next chapter. Maybe decluttering is also an adventure in exploring living more simply. Fischer concurs; the ageing that is autumn 'calls for the simplifying of our lives'.[5]

When we simplify, we find out what it is that we treasure, and treasure is linked to where our important memories are parked. Especially for those who find they have a poor memory, treasures could be in books, diaries, pictures, clothes, furniture or houses. Even those blessed with a retentive memory invest in such things. Whatever is hard to let go of is probably a treasure. Dallas Willard comments: 'Treasures are things we try to keep because of a value we place upon them.' He works with the sayings of Jesus about treasures, that culminate with: 'Where your treasure is, there your heart will be also' (Matthew 6:21). He points out that we all have them, adding that 'this is an essential part of what it is to be human'.[6] It's not wrong to have what is important to us; what matters is whether what we have chosen is treasure on earth or treasure in heaven.

If I understand Willard correctly, by 'heaven' he is not primarily thinking of the afterlife, but of the quality of kingdom-based eternal life now that begins as we walk with Christ. I can believe that our beneficial memories can be among those heavenly treasures. So letting go of objects that carry such memories is not straightforward. Those I interviewed often expressed ambivalence in dealing with decluttering. Words like dreadful, hard and disturbing lived alongside liberating, releasing and freeing. To throw away is to reject the tyranny of things, but also to risk the loss of a memory and to cast away something that might have been useful to others. I also noticed the number of people who told me that their attitudes were formed by what they saw their mother do.

Some elements to decluttering are big and mark the end of an era. For two years I had been trying to sell the flame red MG Midget we had owned since 1975. It came with the amusing number plate EGO 420J, which at one stage was worth more than the car. It had been a faithful friend and a pleasure to drive for short distances. Tootling along city or village streets, people on the pavement would turn their heads, smile and even wave. But latterly it was just not being used, because we have two other capable cars. Disuse is not good for a car. I could still get in and out of EGO, but I knew that saying goodbye marked the end of an era, when I enjoyed tinkering and upgrading it, when cars were simple enough to service oneself and when my body didn't mind lying on a concrete garage floor to do repairs or servicing.

This story then ended on 31 May 2023, when EGO was sold to a nearby classic cars firm who would sell it on. As I write I sense a bereavement, remembering it being towed away on a trailer, noticing the empty space in the garage and doing the post-death clearing out – cancelling the insurance and throwing out past editions of MG magazines. I have only just had the happier resurrection-like thought that the car's restoration is about to begin as the buyer will undoubtedly beautify the bits of bodywork that are showing their 53 years and make it look like new.

Some parts of decluttering have an element of humour, if not farce. In September 2022 my own decluttering took another step towards facing down my hoarding and sentimentality about some possessions. Helen and I cleared out an outbuilding, among which we found a white crash helmet bought in 1966, when I began a few years of motorcycling. It had not been worn since 1972. Why did it take me only 50 years to part with it? I suspect an untidy mixture of treasured memories, a sentimental hoarding disposition and inertia.

Davina, a friend at a similar stage in life, was describing her progressive decluttering to me and acknowledging the burden of her being a life-time hoarder. Pushed by trying an antidote to this trait she parted with some books, only to wish later that she had kept some of them and said, 'I felt I had betrayed some old friends.' What a fascinating and insightful comment. There are objects with which we feel we have relationships. One pleasure of retirement is picking up a treasured book you have not read for some time and getting reacquainted with it, laughing at the same places as before, marvelling once more at its verbal artistry, only half remembering the plot and even wishing that the character you are intrigued by or admire really did exist. More goes on between a person and a thing than we sometimes admit. I spotted that among those I interviewed who had occupied teaching roles, within and beyond church life, the parting with books was a notable milestone. One even said, 'I can't bear to part with books.' While others at retirement took the bold stroke of giving away 90% of their working books, such as commentaries and theological tomes. At that point they also ditched their university notes. Helen and I did the same on both counts. Some now have a Kindle to compensate for those losses.

Davina also likened decluttering to peeling an onion. It can be tricky work to get that tough and now useless outer skin off, but having done so, all you find you have achieved is to expose the next layer. 'Peeling an onion' is a metaphor for an ongoing task that you mistakenly think you have finished. Helen and I did clear that outhouse, and that was therapeutic. But three lofts and two garages await, let alone over a thousand books, 200 video tapes and a similar number of DVDs. And that doesn't account for a large cellar with a serious model railway that represents 20 years loving labour, and another smaller one built, I insist, for the grandchildren. Here comes the further point. All layers of the onion are part of the onion, so we need not be surprised that much decluttering is both painful and liberating. In doing it we are stripping back part of ourselves with the layers of activity, and even identity, that we have constructed over years.

Curiously and disturbingly, at the same time we know that many of those treasured possessions are seen as junk by our children or grand-children. Mahogany furniture, beautifully crafted, perhaps inherited, eagerly acquired and once admired, is now seen as clunky, dark and forbidding. In 1985 I inherited a single pillar mahogany table, which seats six with ease and has served ten. It goes back at least four gen-erations on my father's side, and I hope in future some family member will love it. Holding something in trust admits that it has come to you and will depart from you. A number of those I talked with also cited items of historic furniture that were treasures. I can only trust someone else in future will care about this one. I wonder, will all such family heirlooms just become firewood? Might they make it to a charity shop? Other examples of decluttering historic items have been much easier. We decided to sell some family heirlooms that have skulked in a cupboard and that no children will want. I cite an ornate silver Victorian tea service, fit for use in *Downton Abbey*, in which the sugar bowl was as large as the teapot, and also three gold sovereigns from the Victorian and late Georgian period. I don't even know where they originated from and how they came my way.

But we have only scratched the surface of decluttering. Lofts are the classic corner of sentimental clutter. Those who have cleared them tell me that it took years to do so. We have vintage clothes we loved, pieces of old luggage, redundant fishing gear, a massive Scalextric set that does come out annually and more duvets than make sense, not to mention the Christmas decorations. The adult children are also complicit in this. The lofts and some cupboards contain childhood toys and games and their university notes, as they don't have space to store them nor much time to inspect them. We shall have to turn up the dial on that last one. As one person said to their children: 'We are no longer your depository.' But when we've gone will the next generation have time to put what we have left behind on eBay, Gumtree and so on? Which things will they decide to keep and why? I wonder, do many people manage to declutter to their entire satisfaction voluntarily; that is, without a radical enforced change in circumstances such as bereavement or a house move? That takes me to downsizing.

Downsizing

I've not done downsizing, so I wanted to learn from my interviewees. Seven hadn't faced this yet, but the other nine had. Of those, three had moved to a bungalow or flat, with the long-term advantage of no stairs to climb but a higher price in relation to land area. More had only moved into a smaller house. For all these people the issues and lessons raised by decluttering became necessary, acute and time-bounded.

There is one more major aspect around downsizing, which is the question of whether this will be the last home we choose and own. There's a tension between two sets of factors. First, we are grateful for our existing spacious house, which is in a quiet area of Sheffield yet very convenient for getting into town, easily accommodates visits by the wider family, and has garage space for cars and cellar space to house a workshop and model railways. But second is the growing weight of maintaining a garden and veg patch, keeping the paintwork up to scratch, climbing steep stairs and the rising costs, not least to heat it in winter. It's a nice problem to have, I know, and presently the balance is to stay.

A year ago, a smaller house down our road, which we has always liked the look of, came up for sale. We duly went round it, pondered whether to put in a bid, talked to our children, and concluded it wasn't the right time. Yet it was the first concrete alternative that met the awareness that the home and garden we love will become more than we can maintain. Our daughter Hannah's response was we should get someone in to tackle the overgrown trees we can no longer prune from the top rung of an ancient ladder and another person to do the technical painting jobs. That all sounds like we stay, and we recall that our house's first owner lived here, girl and woman, from 1904 to 1987 and was carried out by the undertakers. Not a bad way to go for one of us, but quite a burden on whichever spouse is left and taking on the roles previously carried by the deceased, and with income halved. No wonder many do downsize.

Having a bucket list

This term is related to an earlier colloquial term for dying, 'kicking the bucket', and was popularised in the 2007 film *The Bucket List* (dir. Rob Reiner). Exploring a bucket list gives you permission to think and do the things you always wanted to, but it is also admission that time is running out. None of those I interviewed had a written list, and it tended to be true that the older they were the less they saw any point in having one – either potential items were already ticked off or the ability demanded by activities such as foreign travel was now out of reach. Many of those younger in the autumn of life did have unwritten aspirations. Some were distinctly active: foreign travel, whale watching and a walking pilgrimage. Other aspirations were more reflective: time to read, choosing to observe life more closely and maintaining a sense of purpose.

Whether you have a list or just vague thoughts, one tricky question is: what if you complete it? For example, among the interviewees are friends who sailed round Britain, which was a notable lifetime achievement, but within a year they decided it was time to sell the boat. I don't have any sort of written bucket list, but I had always secretly hankered for the opportunity to drive a full-size steam locomotive. In June 2019 the family bought me that opportunity, and I was instructed on a 060T tank engine and was entranced to learn how to drive it up and down the preserved steam line between Rowsley and Matlock in Derbyshire. That choice was especially apt as the model railway in our cellar is of Matlock Station and that very line. Having yearnings for some privately long-held dream is then affected by the next topic.

Creeping dependency

By dependency I mean needing others' help with tasks in life that we used to manage on our own – from spouse or children, if we have them, or from friends or wider family. I chose the word 'creeping' from my own experience that in my 70s this feels like a very gradual change. Other interviewees chose similar terminology: 'a subtle change'; 'one watches a slow movement'; 'a gradual change of dynamic'.

I've begun the slow slither on the slippery slope. I earlier mentioned how trying to remember the names of people and things is becoming more difficult; I mention it again here because it is allied to a slowly rising tide of dependency. Helen and I have tried to make a game of this. It goes like this: 'Give me a clue, what's the first letter of her name/that flower or bird/where we went on holiday three years ago.' Often I just need the trigger pulled and the memory is fired back up and has the data.

There's also the lack of competence in a changed world, such as when we ask our children or younger friends, 'How do you do X on the mobile phone?' It's not that we've forgotten; we simply don't know. We are out of our depth. Then our children or younger friends become our tour guides to parts of the digital world. At best, we learn a lot, try to remember it and sometimes pretend that we really get it. At worst, in watching them show us a new move or function, all we actually learn is that *they* know how to make the darn thing work, but that particular IT mystery has not been cracked. The reverse happens when we explain some nugget of wisdom about life or work to our adult children or even grandchildren and get the 'Yes, I know, Grandad' response or that raised eyebrow and amused smile that conveys much the same.

But more is going on than a less keen memory and digital dinosaur syndrome. I learned, from how people responded to my question 17, how our relationships are changing with our children. A couple of interviewees explicitly commented that the balance of power and energy are shifting in the children's direction. One person saw it as simply natural and the other as the conscious making of space for the coming generation. Some saw that change of power and position as being well summed up by the spatial image that we, the autumn people, have shifted from the centre to the edge of the family. Others talked of it as a generational or gravitational shift, marked initially when our children begin to assert adult independence and not even want our help, and clearly when they begin to have children of their own, who naturally become their first priority.

A further stage comes as children also start to become our occasional carers or take charge for medical reasons. Several interviewees named the Covid pandemic as marking them out as vulnerable to their adult children, who then felt responsible for them. Two others found it happened as they lived through a major health issue. Another two said they were beginning to be parented by their adult children. Bill had comments like: 'Dad, you shouldn't do that anymore,' and 'Can we come and help you with XYZ?' Another noted the same but underlined the kindness and gratitude motivating such concern; that is, 'You've done so much for us and now it's our turn.' A number knew that adult children still occasionally came for wisdom, inevitably faced serious problems in life and could turn to their parents and the Bank of Mum and Dad was mentioned. So, where the relationships are open and good, it isn't one-way traffic.

Most interviewees rightly said they were not yet dependent and did not qualify for being in what I would call winter. Yet a number added that dependency will creep up on them. It is inexorable.

A rise of anxiety

Feeling one is losing one's grip, perhaps with an attendant feeling of shame; having had to let go of our status and role in society; our past achievements being forgotten; knowing we are slowing down; experiencing an increase of health issues; wondering how dependent on others we are becoming; and the advancing prospect of death – all of these can easily be sources of anxiety. Because this wide range of concerns is relatively recent in our lives of retirement, and we didn't ask for these intruders of the mind to come knocking at our door, it can feel like being at the wrong end of a mutiny. The crew of which we used to be master is making a bid to take over the ship.

Emilie Griffin poses a multitude of sources of anxiety. I am amused that she calls them 'a short list', but then takes two pages to list them. I have selected most and sought to summarise these:

- Will we be provided for – will we have enough to live on throughout life?
- Do we have good relationships with our grown children?
- What should happen to family heirlooms?

- Will our house continue to stand up against decay, storm and drought?
- What about our health and those terrible diseases that eat both people and finance?
- Have we lived to our potential and met others' expectations?
- What do others think of us, are we liked or respected?
- What do others say of us when we are not there?
- Have we achieved enough in life?
- Do we really have friends, people we are genuinely close to?
- Is our wife or husband a friend?
- What about the culture we live in – is it really going down the drain?
- What about all the negative trends and disasters the media delight to portray to us?
- Have we played our part as a positive contribution?

She admits that many of these are legitimate concerns, but counsels: 'Anxieties may start small but they can escalate readily. A habit of anxiety can take charge and begin to dominate our lives.' Mitton knows the ubiquity of the problem: 'We all know the power of fear. Anxiety is a close relative of fear and regularly stalks the human heart.' Tournier teases out the serious far-reaching consequences of living with anxiety: 'Anxiety engenders fear, fear paralyses, breaks the spirit, takes away joy, deadens life and engenders self-centredness, absorbing the mind and turning it away from adventure.'[7]

An image discloses how this response drifts to become a habit. Being anxious about something is like taking a path. Then when something happens in life of a similar character that provoked the first worry, it is so much easier to take the same familiar path again. A related image is that anxiety becomes the rut in our road of life that is easiest to follow and progressively difficult to escape from. Griffin doesn't develop another image she mentions in passing, but it adds something more. She likens anxiety to weeds in the garden; they sprout no matter how often we've pulled them out. It isn't just that we can acquire a bad habit, but somehow the anxiety itself continues to lurk within us and generates its own continued responses. All these images are ways of saying that anxiety easily becomes a habit, and we become addicted to it. This is especially likely when what we face is long term, like living with a disease or a failed relationship.

Anxiety is the doorway to fear. It is alleged that the phrase 'Do not be afraid' occurs 365 times in Bible. Why is it there so often unless it is a real temptation? I'm intrigued by Romans 8:15: 'The Spirit you received does not make you slaves, so that you live in fear again.' Despite this encouragement, even Christians can be prey to fears that can enslave. Moreover, some measure of fear is sometimes the right reaction, such as being near an angry poisonous snake. But living with too much fear is enslaving. Having a fearful anxious disposition casts a shadow or cloud over all aspects of a person's life.

It is not difficult to become a modern-day Martha, to whom Jesus said: 'Martha, you are anxious and troubled about many things' (Luke 10:41, RSV). So what to do? It is simple to read the advice of the apostle Peter: 'Cast all your anxiety on him because he cares for you' (1 Peter 5:7). The easier part is the casting; it's then leaving them there that is more tricky. I almost see myself as carrying a heavy suitcase full of anxieties, opening it before Jesus and either taking the items out one by one or, on a bad day, tipping them all out at once. The temptation, having exhibited the anxieties, is either openly or surreptitiously putting them back in the case and sidling off with them. Leaving, not casting, is the real act of trust, which is what Griffin recommends. I'll keep coming back to trust in the next few chapters.

I air such fears, hoping that it helps my own generation be more emotionally honest, but also to help the next generation prepare better for their own ageing and in response to my generation now. If Tournier is right that how we have lived our past is highly significant for how well we live our present, then I want to explore an aspect of that perception in the next chapter, because I am convinced that what I call 'learning to let go' is a vital attitude, the need for which crops up across a lifetime.

Application questions

🍂 How are you coping with those words that won't come?

🍂 Is your body still your obedient servant? What signs of physical decline are you noticing and what adjustments, spiritual and physical, are you making?

🍂 Digital visitor, immigrant, second-language user, exile – how many of those terms resonate for you, and what stories do you have to tell about them?

🍂 How do you find living with anxiety these days?

🍂 Which leaves have you found are the hardest to lose?

4

Learning to let go is a necessary positive response

Chapters 1 and 2 explored the obvious positives of all kinds of fruitfulness which characterise an autumn of life. There is yet a more subtle positive to identify. It is linked to the falling leaves, but it also occurs well before they start to fall. Learning this art early will help us live our autumns. As Mitton puts it: 'Autumn has that feeling of life being let go.'[1]

For many years I have seen life as a process of learning to let go. Some stages that are common to most of us are not that difficult to name, though we may not be conscious any longer of having lived through them. I suggest all of them are congruent with Jesus' enigmatic words in Matthew 16:25: 'Whoever wants to save their life will lose it, but whoever loses their life for me will find it.'

This letting go is necessary; but these times of change can be fairly insistent in their demands, as Tournier says: 'All through the course of our lives, even amidst all the creative adventures, acts of renunciation will be forced upon us.' Some give us no choice, while others are big choices we make. One reason this happens at all is the sheer fact that we age. Fischer notes: 'Ageing is a mosaic of transitions or passages.'[2] Because these transitions will come, how we handle all of them matters.

What does 'renunciation' mean? Neither Tournier nor I mean a dull, defeated attitude that can be common in later life. A willing letting go is acceptance, and acceptance is not 'fatalism, passivity, resignation'. Tournier continues:

> True, active, personal surrender to necessity is the great task of life… To accept is to say yes to life in its entirety… Neurosis is always linked with an inability to evolve… The adult who cannot accept growing old… is in the same difficulty.[3]

So come with me as I tell the lifelong tale of learning acceptance, learning that life is about letting go.

The times to let go

Earliest years

Some argue that letting go begins from the moment of birth, as we leave the security of the womb and enter a new world, with the additional symbolic factor of the cutting of the umbilical cord. Never again will that physical link be present, though a glance at our belly buttons reminds us it was a past source of life.

Then before too long, the young child experiences being weaned and another level of intimate and sustaining source of physical and emotional attachment to a mother ceases. Yet this transition can be transcended. As Psalm 131:2 has it: 'But I have calmed and quietened myself, I am like a weaned child with its mother; like a weaned child I am content.'

At interview, a friend, Alec, showed me his poem about that process and a comment on that verse of scripture and the challenge it presents.

Denied…
Luscious founts of
daily sustenance
Unfailing cornucopia
of suckling consolation
… withdrawn

Aggrieved…
tempests of self-assertiveness erupt
howling gales of tyrannical tantrums
an Atlantic of self-pitying tears
… ignored?

Pacified…
pitiful sobbings cease
stillness slowly falls
as silence spreads her wings o'er
… the weaned.

Here I let the poem dig down into this painful and resolving process.

Going to school

A few years go by. Then comes the first day at school; never again will living at home be the sole centre of life. At the age of eight I changed schools. My mother had to take my three-year-old brother to his first nursery. My new school was a bus ride away across south-west London. We did a practice run, but on the day it was down to me. I had to let go of what would have been a reassuring hand in catching the bus, getting off at the right stop and entering the school premises. The last was my undoing. The school was a repurposed enormous private house. So assuming the front door was the way in, I mounted the front steps and tried the door. A vexed school secretary popped up and told me in no uncertain terms that the pupils' way in was via the cellar entrance to the side. Not an auspicious beginning. Letting go has some risks.

Next comes the transition from junior to senior school. That might be at 11 or 13 depending on which part of the education system you inhabit. But it is another letting go – leaving behind being one of the oldest in the school to starting again at the bottom of the ladder. I can remember how in 1962, as a 13-year-old, the 18-year-old prefects had an almost godlike aspect. That attitude to authority was let go of during the turbulent 1960s, and by 1967 being a prefect was almost despised.

Overlapping with such changes come the teenage years. What is left behind is the relative simplicity of childhood and then famously, sometimes fiercely, comes the ending of parents being the unquestionable authority. In teenage years, the poor things are shown up to be manifestly ignorant, though as a number of wits have remarked, it is surprising how much they have learnt by the time one is 21.

So the first 20 years mark a progression of several stages, the first a step away from utter dependence, including a step into independence. But then, if all goes well, comes learning the more complex steps towards interdependence which characterises adult maturity. In two decades a cascade of processes of letting go have already happened for the young person.

Leaving home

The letting go doesn't cease there. Classically the time comes – possibly for university, maybe for a job or perhaps to travel the world – when the young adult leaves the parental home. I recall the gradual shift by which during my first year away, 'home' was Barnes in London, where I grew up. Yet by the fourth year, 'home' was Nottingham and St John's, its theological college. When the flip precisely occurred I don't know. The clearest demarcation point was 29 December 1973, when I married Helen, one of the other students, and we set up another 'home' in a rented cottage down the lane from St John's.

Of course, not all young adults marry, but for those who do, there is both a letting go and a life-changing welcoming. The letting go is of no longer being single, letting go of having options – by forsaking all others – and becoming married, which is a lifelong change of status, however the marriage works out. The divorced and the widowed were still married once; that cannot be utterly undone even though the relationship may have died or ended.

Becoming a parent

There's another letting go, this time of comparative relational simplicity, as well as joyous arrival, when the first child is born. Life and identity have changed forever. I found I was no longer just a married man, but also a father, in my case with only a few childhood memories of what that role meant in practice. I remember bringing Helen and one-week-old Hannah home from hospital, closing the front door and thinking, 'What do I do now?' And fatherhood and motherhood express being a parent for life. Our three children are all now taller, probably smarter, in some cases richer, but I am still Dad – that eternal source of quips that make them purse their lips. But that stage of having them at home is not forever, though there can be times it feels like it!

Henri Nouwen puts it neatly: 'Children are their parent's guests.'[4] Yes, they enter our space for a transitional time, and then by stages leave to create their own space. This further life they embody is fashioned only in part by what they learnt while with us. I've noticed several stages in this sequence of letting go of our children. Early ones are when the first child, and then when the last child, start going to school and having them at home all the time stops. Perhaps those particular changes are felt more keenly by stay-at-home parents. Another emotional and symbolic step for me was walking my daughter Hannah down the aisle in 2004. That process took a more final step for us in 2023 when our youngest son Julian got married. We love his wife Hortense, and they are great together, but the process of handing over beloved children to a partner, to someone else, who now is their prime concern and prime source of support, has the pain and the pleasure of release. In *Autumn Gospel* Fischer relates a level of pain: 'A mother describes the experience of having the last of her three sons leave home. "I don't know if I will ever get over it. I may always feel this mourning."'[5]

Empty nesting

Watching them go and seeing them do life differently is part of a mutual letting go. They too let go – of our perpetual presence, our patterns, our priorities – and peccadilloes – and must fashion their life together. Tournier writes: 'One cannot make a success of marriage without detaching oneself from one's parents.'[6] So the empty nest at home, with its own letting go once again, is not all that's going on. Paradoxically, the only way to stay well connected with our adult children is letting them go. Leaving and cleaving is a creation pattern (see Genesis 2:24), which is both an ending and a beginning. Similarly, a bird that I hold in my open hands I will never crush, and it is free to take flight. And then, like with love, curiously the more you give away the more you find you have.

As I was writing this account of my own times of letting go, which I hoped cited much of what is common to humanity, Fischer's *Autumn Gospel* woke me up with a jolt to realise that I had omitted some key female transitions. (I hope it is not then mere tokenism that I have included citations that struck me and begin to address that lack.) One of these is menopause: 'At menopause... our bodies signal the end of our reproductive phase and we begin to learn a new way of thinking and feeling... that is no longer tied to the possibility of creating children.'[7] My wife and female friends tell me this transition can be complex, bringing both a sense of loss but also a freedom to focus on and pursue a career without the background question, 'What if I have another child?'

Big birthdays and job changes

Chugging along in the background while all these familial steps occur is the inexorable passage of time. Too much can be made of it, and they aren't all significant to an individual, but we do talk about 'big birthdays'. A decade has not just passed, it is gone, and youth is turning to middle age, probably denied at first and let go of reluctantly, before the comments of others on our advancing age and our looks become irrefutable. Making this personal, I recall, over 40 years ago, how at 31 to my surprise, for the first time, some of my leg muscles were stiff the next day after playing football at a teenager's party. The enforced letting go of the illusion of endless youth was going on. Today the decade markers are mitigated by comments like '60 is the new 50'.

Other stages may be less about specific years and more about work and opportunities. I recall the endings of various local church ministries, including letting go of certain responsibilities and particular friendships, moving on and starting again. In my case at 48, I let go of serving in parochial church ministry, with its given status, its special belonging to particular community and familiar patterns. I started out, with not much in my knapsack, on the new, unknown path of a research life with Church Army. I realise now that it was a striking example of Tournier's observation that our adventures get more personal as we get older. I stopped doing what is shared by thousands of clergy and set out on my own adventure of watching other people start fresh expressions of church.

Finding me and losing the old me

It also changed how I thought of myself. A vicar must at least pretend to be a generalist, competent in many fields: leadership, pastoral, liturgical, homiletical (preaching), apologist, social graces, and not least change management. I was ruefully entertained by a piece I ran across many years ago that I think came from the magazine *Parson and Parish*:

When churches see a new incumbent, they expect the strength of an eagle, the grace of a swan, the gentleness of a dove, the friendliness of a sparrow and the night hours of an owl. Then when they catch the bird, they expect him to live on the food of a canary.

Trying to be that bird had left me exhausted, and it was only a few years into the research role that I realised why it suited who I was. I do better investing lots of time in a few things rather than giving little bits of time to many things. In short, I am a specialist, not a generalist. The specialism is that I am a watcher not a doer. I love watching what others do, trying to work out what it all means and putting that in a way that others can understand. So the risk of this change was to me an example of the fact 'that letting go is a kind of finding: new beginnings, coming home'.[8]

But the first steps were not easy. Fischer observes: 'Making a transition is like entering another country' and she calls this standing between a receding landscape and unexplored territory.[9] I was very aware of that uncharted region. I had no formal training in research methods, in writing or statistics. I had never lectured at higher education level. I only had a sense of call that watching new ventures and making them known was what I enjoyed and that this field was a crucial step forward for a church in a century of decline.

So I pottered ignorantly into this research field, where I tried to detect the finger prints of God within the adventures of various people who were evolving fresh expressions of church (fxC). By incremental linked steps, these fxC were connecting relationally with those who had either given up on church or who wouldn't have been seen dead in it in the first place. These fxC communities were both necessarily unlike the ways of being church rejected by many, yet at root they had the same essentials, so as to deserve being called young churches.

Other people will have their own stories of where their jobs took them and what was set down, in order to pick up the fresh challenge. But common to all working lives, significant or menial, retirement begins to beckon. Its inevitable advent crossed the horizon of my perception after becoming 60, an age which, at the time even then, seemed impossibly old.

Retiring

Retirement is not the end of life… it is a period of transition from the vocations that filled middle age to the callings of this third age.[10]

I stopped work for Church Army at 68, and, while again people's stories will vary, for me it was definitely a letting go. It was a parting from colleagues I was deeply fond of and from a working community that I had helped to build. It was also a putting down of a field of enquiry that I thought was important for the future of the church. People were extraordinarily kind about what they thought I had achieved. I was astonished to be awarded a Canterbury Cross by Archbishop Justin Welby for 'an unparalleled contribution to the Church of England and its future health'. Yet it was time to stop, to face that I had less energy than before, that my view of the past was sharper than my vision of the future. I have long learnt, as a leader, that if you can't see the future at all, it is very unlikely that you are supposed to be an integral part of it. I had to let go once more and to enter the uncertainty of retirement. The very first page of Tournier's *Learning to Grow Old* includes the following:

Retirement and old age must, of course, be accepted. *We have to give up all sorts of things*, and accept with serenity the prospect of death while remaining as active, as sociable and friendly as we can, despite an unavoidable measure of loneliness.[11]

In retiring, the spring and the summer of my life had now gone, autumn was upon me. Only in truly letting go once again, sometimes easily, sometimes with a struggle, would I be ready to begin to live out this autumnal season with its joys, opportunities, perspectives, obstacles and losses. These seeming opposites of loss and opportunity are related. Mitton, writing about autumn, advises: 'The willingness to let go and grieve creates space for new possibilities.'[12]

This undulating terrain will be the path to the end of my life, and this book may be its sketch map for the autumnal phase. This sort of language conveys a scent of risk. Taking risks takes courage, and as Fischer says: 'Courage is what enables us to let go, to live in the darkness, to begin again. It gives us strength to risk.'[13] Such letting go is not easy. I appreciated the realism and candour of a newly retired skilled and highly sociable relative by marriage who said to me: 'The hardest thing is that I am no longer needed, and it is taking me months to get over that.' Letting go can be hard. We can be tempted by a desire to assert control, as it feels control is taken from us.

Shrinking horizons

Another ending and letting go has been to call time on summer holidays in France, taken about every other year since 1989, staying at a friend's farm. These many visits have provided a host of treasured memories. There were a number of subtle hints that the wheel was turning, such as the closure of some of the local bakeries and cafés which we had enjoyed. Were they a door closing for us too? Equally symbolically, a road bridge we would cross almost daily had been closed for repairs. This closure also scuppered a favourite bike route.

Life out there was moving on without us. At the farm itself, an attractive vista from the house to the fields beyond was becoming eclipsed by the growth of mature trees. It felt like a window closing. A more obvious factor was our diminishing endurance when facing the three days it takes to motor there from the north of England, with two overnight stops. Maybe deeper than all these, we woke up to realise that we knew the area so well that there were no more surprises and the sense of adventure had leaked away. What had been a welcoming familiarity was now less sustaining and reassuring. Time to let go.

Leaving autumn

I have no idea when or what my winter will be, what independence will have to be let go and what elements of impotence will need to be faced. I have already told Hannah, my sensible warm-hearted daughter, that she has my permission to tell me when I should stop driving, and I have promised to obey. At present it feels as though that element will be a hard release, for I enjoy the two vehicles we own and the linked freedom to travel. There is much I don't, and can't, yet know of life's winter, though as an inveterate watcher I have been observing the lived experience of older friends.

But it is certain that one day the last letting go – of life itself – will be asked of me. I hope that my learning to let go, throughout my life, will make that seem more normal. I am fortified by the reminder in Jesus' teaching that in letting go, what he called losing life, will be how we find life (Matthew 10:39; 16:25). Fischer put it this way: 'Faith tells us that this circle of loss and gain is a crucible of transformation. It is the paradox of the gospel.'[14] Indeed, this letting go will be the prelude to another receiving. I am glad that at present it is not difficult for me to trust that this last ending will turn out to be the best beginning of all. However, though I don't know when it will be, it is prudent and kind to family members who will have to cope with this change, to do various practical things.

Paul, as an older man, drew to younger Timothy's attention the universal truth that 'we brought nothing into the world, and we can take nothing out of it' (1 Timothy 6:7). So it makes sense to let go of what you can't keep, but to do it with the least aggravation for the next generation. We've made and signed a legally validated will and filed it under 'W' in the filing cabinet. We are arranging power of attorney against the time either or both of us shed too many marbles and access to funds by others is needed.

Realising that it is likely that one of us will go first, we have begun providing instructions to operate the roles each of us had when there was a spouse. I still don't know how to operate the washing machine and online banking is a bit of a mystery, though I am a consummate dishwasher stacker and learnt ironing as a teenager. My scrambled eggs are pretty good, and my Shrove Tuesday pancakes are widely praised. Other interviewed couples were on similar learning paths.

My funeral outline has some content and requests. What about the tribute? Some people, not liking the white-washed eulogies delivered by tearful relatives, who didn't really need to tell us that their grandma fell out of bed when she was two and won the form maths prize when she was twelve, have drafted a concise account of their loved one's life headlines and pleasing character traits. This is then printed out as the centrepiece of the funeral service leaflet for people to read when they arrive. When I first met it, I thought it a good idea.

Letting go is both acceptance and adventure

My re-reading of Tournier has connected two strands to take forward in my own life thinking, and I offer them to you. One is my own long-cherished view that life is a succession of learning to let go – a chosen acceptance of major changes in life. I've taken you through the stages I see. He has added a second – that every stage of life is to be seen as an adventure: whether that be birth or death, youth or old age. This connects with the meaning of life. 'In this light the successive abdications demanded by old age are seen quite differently: no longer as an impoverishment but as an enrichment in a new adventure.'[15] We both believe that holding on to past adventures is a mistake, even a prison. That is why learning to let go and living each adventure for its own life cycle are intrinsically bound together.

It's time to look wider than the letting go and the falling leaves.

Application questions

🌿 What have been your own most significant 'letting go' stories?

🌿 Which ones are you glad that you managed to do well? What do you think helped you?

🌿 If you are aware that another 'letting go' is coming, name it before God and pray for his intervention to assist you release it.

🌿 When in your life did you find that Jesus was wise and correct that a 'losing of life' can turn out to be a 'finding it'?

5

The active elderly, society and church

Please note several disclaimers. This book is only my jottings, the reflections of one man who counts himself among the active elderly, or third age, and has not yet reached the fourth, dependent elderly, age. I've also interviewed 16 people about their autumn of life. Don't look here for any definitive view of the current treatment of all older people today, who range from the newly retired to those in their last days.

But it has been intriguing to have access to a few sources that come from different periods in the recent past and to see how they compare. Tournier wrote 50 years ago from a European perspective, Knox 20 years ago from a British one, and then there are my own snippets gathered during writing.

The most recent viewpoint was assisted by my former research colleague, Michael Collyer, who headed up a group of Church Army employees focusing on ministry to older people in the years 1995–2003. He then pursued that speciality full-time within Church Army's Research Unit until he retired in 2009. He has kept that focus ever since.

Tournier's perception of the treatment of old people in 1972

Part two of *Learning to Grow Old* is called 'Towards a more humane society'. It is striking that it begins with unpacking 'contempt for the old'. He argues that this attitude exposes the faults of wider society. It is particularly felt by older people because at that stage of our lives, like when we were children, we 'find ourselves powerless once again'. The contempt shows, in that the retired and aged are not looked upon as of equal value. He finds the origins for such attitudes lie both in there being more older people, who now are living longer, which is supposed to bring a *burden* (note that derogatory word) on the rest of society, and also that the rate of change has speeded up, with which many older people are not coping that well. Deeper than this, he argues that 'we have built up a civilisation based on things rather than on persons. Old people are discounted because they are purely and simply persons.' We are no longer 'producers' in a world that values that function very highly. The backdrop to that distortion is a skewed view of humanity fed by a messianic view of the value of economics and from attitudes shared by an affluent society. These discriminate in an inhumane way in favour of those who work. These pressures on retired people can make them 'feel themselves to be a dead branch of society'.[1]

By way of riposte, Tournier urges that 'the old have a real job to do – the restoration to our impersonal society of human warmth, the soul that it lacks'. Again by contrast, he welcomes those who see 'how vital it is to a person to be accepted by others, to be valued, to be welcomed, to be taken seriously, to be listened to with attention, respect and kindness'. Back then, he noted that these humane attitudes were becoming truer of relationships with the mentally ill. He pleads that this progress should apply to the elderly too. He also draws another parallel of welcome progress with the legitimate and necessary rise of feminism, seeing women as equal partners in attitudes and life. Similarly, he shows that attitudes to children had improved, moving from seeing them as empty vessels to fill to taking them and their cast of mind seriously: 'The discovery has been made that a child is not miniature adult… In the same way the aged person is not a shrunken, amputated, wrinkled dried up adult.' He goes on to note that neither the child nor the older person is a producer. He recognises that social care of the elderly has improved, but thinks this is no substitute for family-based personal contact and personal love. All this teaches us that we need to love a person, of whatever age, for who they are, not what they do.[2]

To my surprise Tournier dismisses as legend the view that respect for the elderly, and them being held in honour, was true in the past. 'Contempt for the old does not date from modern times.' He references studies that reveal past centuries of cruelty and brutality towards the elderly who, until the 19th century, except for the rich and powerful, 'were rejected, despised and despoiled'. He then returns to other changes that need applying to the old. During his lifetime he witnessed what he calls a revolution by which adolescents moved from being in the shadows of adulthood to being 'a recognized age-group' – teenagers, complete with their own society or culture and its gathering places. His book calls for something similar for older people, one group among many deserving and demanding to be seen as persons. He pleads for personal contact between all people groups, including the elderly, in a time where our cities are notably crowded, matched only by 'the solitude of our spirits'.[3] The chapter acts as his call to reintegrate the old into society and recognise the part they have to play in it, not least, as many have better health and longer life to contribute to society at large.

However, Tournier does not hold that the view held by society of the elderly is the only factor to consider. The whole of the first section of *Learning to Grow Old* unpacks that how we older people have lived out our lives up till now is highly significant. This is congruent with what I've explored in chapters 1 and 2, above, celebrating the fruitfulness of autumn, together with chapter 3 urging the necessity of recognising the leaves falling in that same season and then chapter 4 on how learning to let go is a lifelong discipline. As he puts it:

> Retirement and old age must, of course, be accepted... We must learn to use leisure profitably, take up new interests, interest ourselves in young people and new ideas. We must learn how to pray, how to meditate, how to acquire wisdom, how to be grateful.[4]

He then adds a further factor, which he calls the particular circumstances of an older person. Depending on what these turn out to be, 'their fate is radically different'.[5] The circumstances he has in mind and explores in turn are very wide: managing the transitions of retirement well; having meaningful hobbies though with less resources; facing solitude; growing old in a comfortable relationship with a partner; enjoying one's wider family; having deep conversations; staying fit and having good health and health care; continuing to learn and explore.

All of these factors contribute to our well-being, although only some are within our control. Our part is our response to their presence or absence. As such, though older people can be victims of attitudes and practices in society and vicissitudes in life, these are not the whole picture. We have responsibility for our responses. His long experience of dealing with diverse groups of people, as colleagues, patients, friends and neighbours, leads him to call out two well-defined categories of older people:

> There are wonderful old people, kind, sociable, radiant with peace... they are grateful, even astonished that things are done for them and that they are still loved. They read, improve their minds, go for walks, are interested in everything and are prepared to listen to anyone. And then there are awful old people, selfish, demanding, domineering, bitter. They are always grumbling and criticising everybody.[6]

He adds that old age is just a detector or magnifying glass which shows up what has been there all the time, and surfaces now more clearly in old age. Some readers may be thinking that his list of circumstances ignores whether the older person is still active or is dependent; are they in what I call autumn or winter? He does mention in passing the third age of life and has spotted the recent rise of the terminology of the fourth age. He wryly comments that he suspects that third age vocabulary has 'only recently been invented so that old age can be delicately referred to without the term actually being employed'.[7]

To my surprise there is a total absence of discussion of how older people were then viewed by the church and how it treats them. He is far more interested in the personal spiritual path of the individual's acceptance of learning to grow old, and beyond that how old age foreshadows death. But the latter is a winter topic, and this book is about living our autumns. Readers may want to ponder how today is similar to, or different from, what Tournier laid out. Between Tournier and Knox comes my own little story.

A young curate meets work with older people

It was 1975. I had emerged from theological college and ordination with a deluded, often disguised, hope to change the world. In practice, as one of two curates at St Peter's, Harold Wood, Essex, I was given responsibility for its work with senior citizens, rather attractively called Good Companions.

Started a year or so previously by the vicar, it was a weekly Wednesday lunch club in the adjacent church hall for about 25 older people, run by a dedicated team of St Peter's third-agers. It then seamlessly flowed into a seniors' afternoon for some 70 takers, providing tea, biscuits and cake, and much chat, around lots of tables of four to six people. Some weeks a visiting speaker came, addressing mainly secular or special interest topics, such as illustrated talks on holidays taken and diverse hobbies. A long-remembered case was the visit of George Cansdale, the retired superintendent of London Zoo and TV wildlife presenter, who brought live snakes for people to touch and handle. I stayed clear of that one. The afternoon included a brief 'thought for the day' by the curate, and I set myself the task of working through passages in John's gospel which focused on Jesus.

Good Companions drew older people from the wider community who were not church attenders, with a minibus that collected the less mobile. It provided an outing of interest in the week, gave people a chance to meet and talk, helped offset loneliness and seemed to offer a side door into church life. A highlight was a coach day trip to France. We took a bus load to Le Touquet, 45 miles south of Calais. The upside was a memorable day. Many of them had never been out of the country in their lives, but fortunately in those days they did not need to acquire passports for a one-day trip. It was so good that we could offer a stretching of the boundaries of their experience. The downside was that we had not done thorough enough research. The day we arrived was a public holiday, and municipal day off, and all the public conveniences were closed. We never asked how our coach members coped with that stretching of their boundaries.

As I reflect now, I see more clearly elements I then missed, despite coming from a radical-thinking college. I failed to see the need and value of visiting folk from Good Companions in their homes in order to build relationships and when appropriate to explore Christian understanding and faith. I never thought to find out whether Good Companion members had dropped out of church in the past or whether they were non-churched and had never had that link. Only later did I realise that these are in effect rather different mission fields and need different onward paths. I remained content with servicing what I hoped was an attractional event.

I also assumed that some of them would somehow shift beyond attending the Wednesday afternoon to wanting to come to the weekly Sunday morning family service. It proved a vain hope. Less than a handful did that, out of some 70 people. The faith and cultural gap between middle-class church and working-class people was still too wide for them to make such a leap. I remember a conversation with one attender, Bill, a retired trade union shop steward, who thought the Church of

England was 'for the toffs'. It might have been far better to discover who among them had spiritual curiosity and to ask them how that could be developed. Three years later, I moved on and any specific focus on spiritual care of older people went off my radar. It has only now returned because I have become one of them.

Let time now roll on 30 years from Tournier's epoch. I offer some headlines and contrasts from further sources.

Ian Knox's 2002 book *Older People and the Church*

This widely researched book, with 19 pages of bibliography and four pages of questionnaires, feels like a thesis turned into a book, including a masterly opening overview chapter. It contains a wealth of citations and a critique of his own research methods, as he investigated the elderly's experience both of today's world and also the church, as well as that church's attitude to an ageing population. He was not alone writing at this time; I've also included a few contributions from Rob Merchant's 2003 book *Pioneering The Third Age*.

Knox begins with a clear assertion: 'The question of old age is one for the whole of society', here citing but slightly modifying Tournier, who wrote that the treatment of the old exposes the *faults* of society. The two writers concur of course that growing old happens to all of us, but deeper than that, 'we would all like to know how to do it well and what we should make of our older lives'.[8] An incremental change since the 1970s is that Knox produces copious evidence that people are living longer. He notes that the biblical figure of 'three-score years and ten' (70) as a social norm was reached in 1982, and that by 1996 life expectancy for males was 74.4 and for females 79.7. Merchant concurs, but adds a wider perspective that during the 20th century the number of over-65s has more than tripled, and now older people are more numerous than children.[9]

Whereas Tournier focused on living out one's old age well, despite a society that looked down upon it, the majority of Knox's text deals with older people and the church. One of his early headlines is to cite Paul Beasley-Murray from 1995: 'Many feel the church has adopted a youth culture.' Merchant agrees with this critique. Knox points out the irony that this is despite 'the older age group being the only one to see a rise in church attenders in the last few years'. He explores what his interviews revealed, that 'some older people feel there is now no place for them in the church and that they are not needed.' Delving deeper through other interviews with local and national church leaders, he found what he generously called a paradox: 'Older people are spoken of in glowing terms… [yet] provisions for older people are often sadly (and badly) lacking.' He poses whether by this emphasis on the young and through 'new, unfamiliar forms of worship, the church is implicitly aiding and abetting this.' Merchant digs a bit deeper and spots an underlying church focus on activity and seeing older people as no longer active.[10]

All three writers are acutely aware of the disgrace of ageism. A difference I detect is this. Tournier in 1972 was at pains to show how out of step ageism was with other positive changes in social attitudes, such as towards mental illness, children and women. Knox, writing 30 years later, can say 'Only in very recent years has ageism been recognized as a social evil akin to racism and sexism.' That sounds as though the progress which Tournier called for has taken some steps forward. Yet Knox in his third chapter finds ageism rife in society. Merchant agrees, saying 'Ageism exists at all levels of our society', and later discussing how elder abuse can increase with age.[11]

Both Merchant and Knox record a derogatory vocabulary within ageism, so much so that it leads older people to believe these negative dismissals of them are true. Consider boo words and terms for older people that are reported across Knox's book: wrinklies; greybeards; decrepit; infirm; narrow-minded; past sell-by date; doddery; those who have lost their marbles. Merchant adds 'old duffers' and 'old dears' and points out that ageism combined with sexism discriminates yet more against older women: 'Men can grow old gracefully whereas women are merely faced with a life of steady decline.'[12]

Both writers explore the fact that defining 'being old' is tricky, not least because 'becoming' and 'being' old is so often denied. A manifestation is to ask a person how they would define 'old' and the classic answer is 'Someone ten years older than me.' That answer assumes that age is the determining feature. Both Tournier in 1972 and Knox in 2002 deny this and go wider and deeper. As we've seen, Tournier says growing old well means working with three factors: a lifelong inner attitude to change and ageing; living fully despite the values imposed by society; and working with the varied circumstances people find themselves in. Knox is working with an apparently simpler question – who is an older person? His chapter 2 unpicks what turns out to be a complicated knot, and he concludes from his reading and interviewees that what counts in realistic self-understanding and quality of life is not chronological age but matters of health, attitude and circumstances. Those three factors can vary without much correlation to chronological age, and he shows people at different life stages disagree with one another about what age actually counts as old. He concludes: 'Old age is almost impossible to define and it would be folly to put any date for its beginning.' I enjoyed his apposite witticism: 'Your birth day only tells you when you were born, not how old you are.'[13]

Having spent two chapters looking at what people mean by old age and the continuing problem of ageism, Knox then writes eight chapters exploring the two-way relationship between older people and the church, as befits the book title. He begins with what the church and its leaders are saying about its dealings with older people. He spotted its dilemma: with few young people in church, there is the need to go for youth, but thus no urgency to reach the rising percentage of older people. He also identified a breakdown between thinking and action, in that several denominations had produced worthy reports on addressing issues linked with ageing, but few had read them and no substantive work had been done since. He also found that, across the denominations, theological colleges did little to train students for work with older people. Yet fine words were said about older people as givers and volunteers, along with the worried observation: 'They are getting much older and we are not sure what to do when they are too old.'[14]

He unearthed a minority view that you can't build a future from older people, a group who are often unwilling to change. Similar dismissive language was also found by Merchant.[15] Moreover, some current provision was actually accounted for by the ageing of prior existing groups. I recall the average age of those in so-called young wives groups in parishes I have known, and grin at the illusion that these groups could just be rebranded as mid-wives, let alone old wives! Knox concludes that there are many older people in our churches but, with notable exceptions, few churches are doing much to help them, which is a contradiction. Merchant adds two telling points: first, that the church can wrongly assume that older people are more spiritual and will just naturally return to church, and they are therefore excluded from its mission priorities; second, that the particular spiritual needs of older people still in church are overlooked, such as tackling issues of growth in Christ, working at consistency of life, facing issues of meaning and handling doubt in later life.[16]

When it came to exploring what older people thought of the church, Knox immediately noticed that views markedly differed between attenders and non-attenders. Among attenders, those who were positive saw the inherent value of being part of the church; it was a community they both gave to of themselves and from which they received, not least having friendships. Furthermore it nurtured their faith in God. Other attenders, outweighed by those who were positive, specified negative factors: the failures of leaders, not least new vicars imposing change; a lack of welcome from other church people; and the modernisation of spoken and sung worship.[17]

Responses from non-attenders were, almost without exception, from those who were de-churched. I was initially surprised that the research had not differentiated between the 'de-churched', those who had attended at some stage in their lives, and the 'non-churched', those who had never attended except for something like a funeral. Then on reflection I recognised that this more accurate terminology only became widely known through the Church of England report *Mission-Shaped Church*, which came out two years after Knox's book. Moreover, researching among those aged at least 70 just before 2002 meant he was canvassing opinion from those born in the 1930s, if not earlier, when church and Sunday school attendance were much higher. So a predominance of de-churched was not surprising. Twenty years later and the retireds now include both the boomer generation and Gen X, and hearing the voice of the non-churched would thus need to be sought.

Returning to what Knox disclosed in 2002, he found that older people had stopped attending in reaction to past compulsory attendance, such as at school or in the Forces, or because of some offence by the minister. He also found that many in the past had been devoted attendees with still some residual sense of loyalty to the denomination. This lingering attachment was more common among folk who had been Catholic or Free Church. There remained some sense that at best the church stood for something valuable and still helped some people. Certain words stood out in response to being asked what older people thought was wrong with the church: inflexible, intolerant, not holy, hypocritical, boring, out-of-date. Knox also chose four major reasons for non-attendance: disbelief, the church as an institution, other priorities and family networks coming first.[18]

These sources do overlapping but not identical work. Tournier highlights the need for individuals to learn how to grow old, and he advocates change in society's attitudes. Knox deals less with the first of these, but goes further with the second, specifically what the church can do. In two long chapters he unpacks in detail, and with diverse practical suggestions, both what older people can do for the church and how the church can care for them. Merchant adds detailed examination of how ageing was viewed in Old and New Testaments, as well as in the first four centuries of the Christian church. The focus of this book is closer to what Tournier majored on. I can but commend study of the books from Merchant and Knox, both as waymarkers on the long road to combating ageism in society and the church and as sources of ideas for the church, giving due focus to work with and for older people. Towards the end of his book, Knox flags up for the church, despite its rhetoric about the value of older people, 'what I believe is the paramount question: is there a will for a way forward?' For this occurs against a backdrop explored in his chapter 3: 'It became clear ageism in our society is alive and kicking,' albeit 'usually passively within churches'.[19]

Older people and society in 2022

There are considerably more older people today than there were in 1972 or 2002, partly because of population growth and because people are living still longer. That trend, noted by Knox in 2002, has continued. From 2002 to 2022, average life expectancy in England had increased from 74.4 for males and 79.7 for women to 82.3 for men and 85.8 for females. In the years 2018–20, the modal (or most common) age of death for males was 86.7 and for females 89.3. Beyond that 'between 2012 and 2017 the number of people living to be 100 increased by 85%. By 2030 it's predicted that 1 in 5 people will be over 65.'[20]

The percentage of the elderly population has also increased due to the falling birth rate. Moreover, people are living longer during the fourth age, or winter, of their lives than they were decades ago. Staff shortages, poor wages and low investment in care homes have been frequently in the news. A quick visit to the internet informed me that in 2022 there were over 17,000 care homes but that number is falling. Four percent of those aged 65 and over were in one, and 15% of those aged 85 or more.

The marginalisation of the elderly continues to be a cause of concern. I cite two recent reactions. Dame Esther Rantzen, founder of the Silver Line helpline for lonely older people and who is now in her early

80s, was interviewed on BBC Radio 4's *Today* programme on 23 May 2022 and called for the appointment of a Minister For Older People. And Katherine May, writing in her 30s, comments: 'We are, after all, a society that has done all it can to erase death, to pursue youth to the bitter end, and to sideline the elderly and infirm.'[21]

Covid may have made ageism worse. I and a number of friends of a similar age concur that during the pandemic it became possible, as an older person, to feel that one was not only highly vulnerable, but also, as a particular subset of society, an intolerable burden on the NHS. From being 'active elderly' we became among those most at risk. What's also different is that I have joined this 'vulnerable group' and that makes a significant difference to me. I am no longer only the observer but now also the participant. That can be a dangerous position and make all I say be dismissed as subjective. So I am relieved to have the informed research from prior and present decades, the corroboration of my interviewees and at least one current specialist.

Michael Collyer and *The State of Ageing 2022*

I met with Michael Collyer, a Church Army specialist in ministry to older people, mentioned in this chapter's introduction, for a day in May 2023. He supplied me with this summary report by The Centre for Ageing Better, dated March 2022. Its headline is bleak: 'The state of ageing in England is getting worse.' Various elements led to that conclusion. Of the 11 million aged 65 or over, one in five were living in poverty. Life expectancy for the first time has dropped a little, as has the number of years we can expect to live without a disabling illness. Life expectancy varies with income levels and where we live. Older people living in private rented accommodation has nearly doubled in the last ten years, which is the kind of housing most likely to fail a government test of being decent. A larger number of older people are living alone. This is notably true of 1.3 million males, up 67% in 20 years. The UK state pension is now one of the lowest in Europe as a percentage of previous earnings. The last three factors mean a greater number of older people with less financial security.

Two conclusions were drawn. First, 'England is becoming a more challenging country to grow old in.' Second, there was the need to appoint an 'Older People's Commissioner for England with statutory powers to protect and champion older people.'[22] This last point chimes with that of Esther Ranzten in May 2022.

Collyer then added comments from his long experience. Older people are seen by many in society as dispensable and have a low priority compared with others. One illustration during Covid was older people being moved out of hospitals into care homes to free up beds for younger patients. Similarly, health service budget decisions, regarding the allocation of resources, are being set by QUALYs (quality-adjusted life years). By this method, it is clear that operations and treatments to save or improve the life of 30-year-olds, with a future before them, will outgun the claims of an 80-year-old. Economic benefit is still being used to set the value of different human beings.

Collyer noted an irony which creates a gap. Advances in medical science and resources for it have increased life expectancy over the last 50, and even 20, years. But resources to improve social policies for the subsequently rising number of yet older generations have not kept pace. The chance to live longer is outstripping the chances of living well, socially and personally. He read out a sentence he prepared earlier:

> The public regret the process of ageing as it is associated with retirement and less status, declining energy, illness and loneliness. These are ageist values, the root of which is the fear of dying and death. Society's ideologies highly value success and economic activity. Productivity and consumption are at odds with the ageing process.

Collyer was glad to give praise for some aspects of progress. Access to modes of public transport and to buildings has improved substantially.

I guess this is where the disability lobby and the anti-ageism lobby have made common cause. There is much more awareness of dementia and Alzheimer's, with improvement in diagnosis, concern and resources to respond. The value of third-agers in voluntary work is widely recognised, in contrast to 20 years earlier. Most older people now have access to, and sufficient competence in, social media and can keep in touch with friends and family and across geographically spread extended families. Third-agers are wooed by businesses, as they are broadly seen as a large and prosperous market. There are even instances of product designers making them key to the design process, though more often the design of fixings in goods and clothing, and the size of print chosen about them, are disadvantages to older people.

One positive story in the 1990s was the motor manufacturer Ford. Knowing from market research that older people were significant buyers, they wanted to make their future Focus car easier to drive. The designers worked with a body suit, goggles and so on that simulated an older person's more limited range of movement. This set a precedent in Ford's general ergonomic design principles and led to the sales success of the Focus. So working smartly with limits can have benefits to all. I read that Ford do not make this story very well known as the motor trade believes 'you can't even sell an old man's car to an old man'.[23] When did you last see a TV advertisement for a car where the driver was an older person?

The last point links to the powerful factor of image. 'Image' is highly thought of in society, such that female television news readers dare not show a grey hair, for being or becoming old is a poor image. A negative illustration of image is the slow down signs by road crossings showing a frail couple equipped with sticks. Few of us third-agers are in that condition and many fourth-agers aren't either.

At least some writers are urging those who study markets to see beyond one stereotypical take on what older people are like or even the twofold third-and-fourth-age taxonomy. David Metz and Michael Underwood explore four stages affected by five factors: health, mobility, family ties, finance and major life events. They borrow four descriptors from George Moschis, who worked with these kinds of variables.

The first he called 'healthy indulgers', who behave like younger consumers. Stereotypes of these prosperous time-rich third-agers are those jetting or yachting round the world or going out for meals and buying clothes. The next group are 'ailing outgoers', who have had significant health issues yet remain positive. Their needs for healthy foods and appropriate clothing are seen as a big market opportunity. Third come the 'healthy hermits', who have known tragedy; they stay fit themselves but are withdrawn socially. They don't buy much. I wonder how that category who reduce buying is being reframed today by those of us who have a keen sense of ecological responsibility. Fourth are the 'frail recluses', for whom support is needed at their home or in a home. Importantly these four stages are not predominantly determined by age. Though it may be that the second and third categories are transitional stages towards the fourth – unless one dies before then! I don't like these labels very much, as economic utility to the sellers seems to determine them, but at least I appreciate that variety of situation and variety of causes is being discussed, rather than simple dismissal of those in retirement as one stereotyped group.

Overall, Collyer thought technology tended to discriminate against older people. For example, this group are used to 'real money' and no one has taught them how to use the alternative. We both had seen at supermarket checkouts how the young flock to the unmanned card-only payment machines and to others reserved for those for who self-scanned as they bagged the items off the shelves. We oldies head for the personal touch – spot the nicest-looking checkout staff member who has the shortest queue, let them run-up the bill, chat about how life is and then offer them either cash or a card. He added that older people don't seem to be part of levelling up. They remain a source of untapped potential for wider society, and training for them to live more fully is lacking. They are still seen as unable to learn, resisters of change and unable to cope with technology. His first words in our two-hour conversation were: 'Institutional ageism persists.'

Ageism has not gone away

It sounds to me as though the problems linked to ageism have not disappeared, despite 50 years of advocacy that they should be addressed and solved. Perhaps the equally long-held frustrations felt by those trying to right the wrongs of racism and sexism should have warned me. It is one thing to have fine well-thought-out rhetoric calling for change. Collyer's comment here was: 'It's all words and no action.' It is indeed another step to see helpful precedents established, praised and then for those to be reproduced elsewhere. Sometimes the very creation of a precedent seems to engender an illusion that enough progress has been made and further progress stalls.

A further step is to have legislation passed that penalises abuse and exploitation and which establishes a right of equality. But, as theologians rightly point out, the passing of laws does not create grace. Laws may help prevent ills and punish those who transgress them, but of themselves do not change inner attitudes much. It is yet another and further step for an entire culture to change and decades of ageist attitudes to be undone. Listening over the last year to news items, coverage relating to the ills of racism, sexism and now gender identity is frequent. News items relating to ageism are rare, despite the very large number of people affected.

Older people and the church in 2022

My data comes from the 16 interviews and one-to-one conversations with other friends that savoured of a stroke of serendipity. 'How well do you think church provides for people at your stage of life?' was question 10 to my interviewees. No less than ten out of the 16 thought the church provided pretty well, though some used a typically English response – 'not badly'. No one said 'poorly', though a few noted that with tiny elderly congregations and fewer clergy, stretched across larger benefices, resourcing was a sharp issue. However, here follow some serious qualifications to that rosy picture.

New lamps for old?

In 2002, Knox raised the issue of how to provide for older people in the face of a rising focus on ministry to and with young people. This sensitivity is still around. Some interviewees acknowledged a genuine two-way pull. At one end is the care of the many older people, in church and society, many of whom who are still major financial contributors to today's church. At the other end is the desire to grow the church for tomorrow. A few then raised the dilemma of whether either to travel the idealistic road of genuinely all-age church (not just disguised provision for children) or to provide diversity. Only one person specifically mentioned the need for mission to, and with, older people.

Fourth-age provision won't cut it for most third-agers

Nine of the 16 people, all of whom I would call third-agers, made clear that by provision for the old they meant what the church does for those older than them, that is fourth-agers; that is, activities usually run by third-agers. I was struck by a concurring comment from another person that I happened to meet, not one of the 16 interviewees. Suzanne is the community evangelist in a deprived northern Sheffield estate. Her drift was if you ask churches about their ministry to older people, they will describe making provision through services, events and clubs as well as visits, for people becoming dependent in their 80s and 90s. She is not alone in seeing that emphasis.[24]

There is nothing wrong with those activities or concerns, and much that is right about meeting these needs. One fine example is Anna Chaplaincy. I am glad that it began under Debbie Thrower and now is spreading around the country. But its focus is not on people in an active and healthy autumn, but rather to love and serve those in the winter of their lives, having become dependent and having entered their fourth age. Part of Anna Chaplaincy, which draws on Messy Church's emphasis on creativity and celebration, is Messy Vintage, which brings a further communal dimension to Anna Chaplaincy. The Messy Vintage website has a downloadable support pack, which provides templates for many tabletop creative activities for older people. Who exactly is this for? The closing two sheets of the pack make it clear: they cover what is expected when operating in a care home and guidance for such a volunteer, and they use words like 'residents' and calling those who come 'guests'.

To cite an example at parish level, Connections has been running for at least twelve years at Holy Trinity Claygate, with the church laid out in café style on a Tuesday morning and drawing over 100 people. It is favourably described by Tina English in *A Great Place to Grow Old*. But from her account and my own knowledge, it is thoughtful, stimulating provision for those in the late third age and fourth age, or in my terms late autumn and early winter. English admits: 'Younger seniors are looking for something different, even though some are happy to come as helpers.'[25]

A classic sign of this segmentation is Connections' development of a further series they run, called 'Hymns we love' with the chance to sing and hear a linked talk. Wisely, they want to encourage older people to be committed on their faith journey. But this approach assumes they do know well-loved hymns. Among the boomer generation and the increasing proportion of older people who are non-churched, that is not going to work, except among the lapsed.

This and other positive provision for fourth-agers can make churches blind to the gifts, wants and needs of the active retired, or third-agers, or the 'young-old' (a term from Knox). The Methodist Church wrote a report called *Third Age Discipleship* in 2013, which agreed:

> Whilst there are responses to the ageing agenda in our churches, the focus has tended to be on the provision of pastoral care, reflecting an emphasis on the issues faced by those now deemed to be in their Fourth Age. Third Age issues have been given less attention.[26]

Third-agers also prefer not to be classed with fourth-agers. They can think that it's the fourth-agers who are truly old. Three interviewees said they didn't want to go to events such as a Mothers' Union meeting or a coffee morning, all of which were seen as for the 'really old'. A number of authors concur with this distinction. The Methodist report said:

> What is also evident is that each generation will have different norms and expectations... For example, later generations may be less driven by duty and display less commitment to community and interdependence than their predecessors, while there will increasingly be a lower proportion who have experienced Sunday School and worship and who have a memory of the Christian story.[27]

Or consider the view from Jo Cox, author of *Going on Growing*, a 2012 Church of England official paper: 'Recognition of differences between generational cohorts is key to interpreting much of the writing on ageing and to planning for future action.'[28]

Thus stereotypes that lump all those aged over 55 together won't help. For example, Merchant warns: 'If you think to be older means joining the five million who watch *Songs of Praise* then you are failing to understand generational change.'[29]

Third-agers are different

Let me try to summarise what Merchant and Cox see as those differences. Both agree they are rooted in the fact that third-agers experienced the massive societal shift of the 1960s. Merchant, writing ten years earlier than Cox, adds that those who, in 2003, were fourth-agers had dutifully lived and served in World War II. Having lived through the 1960s, baby boomers tend to be those who are suspicious of creeds and reject Christian tradition. It was the previous generation who could be called *back* to church and the Bible by evangelists like Billy Graham in the 1950s. Other factors for boomers, and how life has gone for them, include the rise of individualism, the liberation of ethics, expecting a long, fit life, enjoying all that the company Saga might offer them, and having a market tailored to their wants and needs. I've heard of us described as the generation who had it all. Collyer highlighted for Cox the following four differences:

> Compared to the older group, the 'saga' group is likely to be spiritual rather than religious, be more likely to think for themselves rather than expect to be told what to do, expect choice, and be less likely to expect institutional structures.[30]

Within all this is a complication caused by two sources of difference: our attitude of mind, formed through cultural or generational background; and our physical health. The first tends to be connected to age in years because of the era in which we grew up, but the second is far more variable and not determined by age. There are people in their 90s who are wonderfully fit, culturally aware, alert and active, and there are those in their 60s who are chronically sick and, in their attitude, shut away from society. So I think it doesn't fully work to define a so-called 'Saga group' as 55–75 and 'Seniors' as 75+, though I note both terms avoid the dreaded word 'old'. Reverting to my seasonal terms, I can see some meaning to using terms like 'late autumn' for active 80- and 90-year-olds and using 'early winter' for those struck down by a health storm in earlier years. Simple labels are tricky.

If those are real differences across cohorts in society, how does it work out in church life? The few years I've been interviewing, reading and writing for this book makes me think there is a problem. I begin with the headlines of a widespread story.

Being neither young enough nor old enough

English writes about her parents in their 70s who resist being called 'old' but can accept the term 'actively retired'. I was intrigued that what they wanted from their church was a chance to serve meaningfully, to be listened to, 'but they don't want to be ignored'.[31]

This triad of comments from Tina's parents rang resonating bells with me. In private conversations with other people from previous parishes I had served in, I met sadness and frustration because in prior decades these third-agers were movers and shakers in their local churches. Now they feel that they are almost cast aside. All they are told to do is to fit in with what is already provided. They feel neither listened to nor understood. It seems to me that they exist in a chasm between two different, legitimate and necessary priorities in church life.

Mind the gap

On the one side exists the programme, worship, music and groups for young families, their teenagers and children. On the other side live a yet more traditional group of people. The latter genuinely value the poetic prose of the 1611 Authorised Version of the Bible and the similarly elegant words of the 1662 *Book of Common Prayer*. To put it starkly it can feel to these third-agers as though they are being asked to either buy earplugs and lump it, perched among the young and trendy, or to leave their spiritual home and get themselves into the spiritual equivalent of a care home or retirement complex. Maybe it was ever thus for ageing trailblazers. As Tournier says: 'There is the eternal conflict between the heirs of yesterday's adventure and the adventurers of today who push them aside.'[32]

I cannot know how widespread this alienation is, but I hear enough anecdotal evidence to bother to write about it. And I take seriously that a number of friends in my generation no longer find that congregational forms of being church really work for them, nourish them or handle their questions.

Move over third-agers – don't block progress

Late in writing this book, Glen, a Baptist friend, alerted me to a quite different strand in this overall story. He hears from others of churches where laity in the autumn of their lives are hanging on to power and their chosen style of worship, preventing those in their 30s to 50s from taking on leadership and reimagining church for younger generations. I freely concede that the overall picture is complex. The commonality is exposing how difficult it is to be an all-age church when the context contains genuine generational cultural differences. Then opting for believing one congregation can meet all cultures is delusional.

I'm sorry, but...

Reading my notes and listening to the recordings of the interviews, I found I began to make a growing list of direct yet often apologetic comments that revealed that congregational church is failing to engage with people in the autumn of their lives. Four noted that congregational church only still nourished them to some extent, because they were still involved in providing public ministry. The practice of leading helped keep them going spiritually, yet one of them could at the same time say, 'It's not me at all.'

One complaint could be summarised as congregational church doesn't go deep enough. Consider the following anonymous statements from my interviewees.

> *Church services don't rise above the lowest common denominator.*
> *I've heard it all before.*
> *We're not stretched.*
> *Church just churns up the old stuff.*
> *I want more, but don't get it, so I have to do the job myself.*
> *I want some deeper theology.*
> *My local church is Radio 2 and I'm a Classic FM person – that's what connects me with God.*

The last comment opens a group of further comments that I can't eas-ily find one right label for. They are wistful and to some extent regret the confessions made.

> *It's not where I encounter God, though I hate saying that.*
> *Personally, I find church less energising these days.*
> *I don't want to be there in church; I don't feel welcome.*
> *There's a lack of community; people just walk out at the end.*
> *It doesn't provide for people like us.*
> *A bit of me got fed up with church; I'm sick of words, words, words.*

Two factors were identified as elements of ways forward. The first was the search for being part of a small group of equally committed and able people, who delved deep into the Bible, who genuinely wrestled with its application to life, while also being committed to one another. At least three people had known this kind of small group in the past and still valued it, although they were aware that the request for its return could sound elitist. I could easily add my own vote for this provision.

The second element was a shared perception about a change in them-selves and this stage of life. Words used now about themselves were: reflective, meditative, contemplative and living with uncertainty. Paradoxically, there was both the desire for more silence and for a quality of deeper conversation.

What is disturbing about all these comments arising from twelve out of the 16 interviewed is that this is not a new problem. In 2001 a Method-ist book called *Older People and the Church* reflected in part on earlier well-known work on those leaving church, meaning its congregational life: 'Francis and Richter found that 28% of their older respondents felt that the Church no longer helped them to grow and rather more that a questioning faith did not seem to be acceptable.'[33] Eleven years prior, an Anglican report simply called *Ageing* could write:

What is essential is a greater honesty about both the spiritual needs and the riches associated with growing older... For some growing older is accompanied by feelings of isolation and uncertainty about God, compounded by a sense that these uncertainties are shameful and cannot be admitted.[34]

At least here my respondents did not feel they had to hold back.

I sang it my way?

My questions 11 and 12 asked what kinds of music they found spiritually life-giving and how often their church provided it. What I did not expect was that all directly answering number 11 said they gained benefit from a wide variety of music: from early medieval to contemporary, classical to jazz, instrumental to sung, hymns to songs. It was therefore unsurprising that no local church could satisfy such wide tastes. On a narrower consideration of the balance between classic hymns and more modern songs, people's experiences were very different. A few enjoyed the variety and choice provided, but those seeing themselves as more reflective or contemplative didn't find the choices offered uplifting, one even calling the songs facile.

Part of the alienation felt was their being obliged to sing too much contemporary Christian music, an opinion with which I concur. Whatever happened to what I thought were valuable songs from the 1970s to the 1990s? A quarter of my interviewees raised this specifically. I leave aside whether such items should be classified as hymns or not. I cite twelve examples on the following page, put in date order, from my squirreled away copies of Spring Harvest songbooks. See for how many were used by your church last year.

Title or first line	Composer	Date	Spring Harvest songbook
How lovely on the mountains	Smith	1974	1987 No 28
Jesus is Lord, creations voice…	Mansell	1979	1987 No 38
Christ triumphant ever reigning	Saward	1981	1999 No 18
There is a Redeemer	Green	1982	1987 No 83
From heaven you came	Kendrick	1983	1987 No 18
Great is the Lord and most worthy	McEwan	1985	1990 No 29
Be still for the presence of the Lord	Evans	1986	1990 No 7
Meekness and majesty	Kendrick	1987	1990 No 75
Jesus shall take the highest honour	Bowater	1988	1990 No 56
Lord I come to you	Bullock	1992	1999 No 92
My Jesus, my Saviour	Zschech	1993	1999 No 103
King of Kings, Majesty	Cooper	1996	1999 No 86

I do not expect that the above selection do much spiritually for devotees of the *Book of Common Prayer*, who will prefer hymns from further back, and I expect most of those on this list are unknown to young families. There is a gap. It may matter, because one aspect of our personal and cultural identity, as part of the boomer generation, is the kind of music that we identified with, especially that which was significant in our spiritually formative years.

Let's sing it for the ninth time

Beyond the eclipse of a collection of music that still resonates for many baby-boomer Christians, my interviewees and wider contacts have expressed concern to me about contemporary worship groups. This phenomenon, as one interviewee said, has ironically reproduced all the worst dominating aspects, linked to the paid organist and robed choir, that they were glad to see replaced. It is another example that revolutions tend to produce the next dictatorship. Here the parallel ills include: occupying a prominent position in the front of the venue; having great power over what music is chosen and delivered; worshipping the music style more than God; and choosing music that is best performed rather than shared by a congregation. Half of my interviewees specifically criticised worship songs designed for, and delivered as, performance.

Beyond the above catalogue of concerns, there were other widespread criticisms and dislikes. In no particular order: weak or bad theology; songs lacking melody; trite crass matey vocabulary; a lack of poetry in authorship; interminable guitar-strummed introductions; unclear long intervals between verses; turning the word 'God' into 'Gaaaard'; enduring uncertain repetitions of a closing line or a verse; and the breakdown of communication between the worship leader and the person operating the overhead screen. Nor did action songs get many house points. Much of this left my friends cold. Worse, they wondered, 'Where do I fit anymore?' In fairness, there was praise for acknowledged items of gold among all this straw and appreciation of the lasting value of some material from recent decades, which now even appears in cathedral services, played on the organ of course.

Beginnings of ways forward

AfterWorkNet

I have begun to notice that there are others on a similar quest. Happily, Tina English alerted me to the existence and aims of AfterWorkNet, who also have spotted and worked with the important differences between third-agers and fourth-agers. One of its leaders, Peter Meadows, whom I remember well from Spring Harvest days, writes: 'If your church has a ministry to seniors, this is not going to meet the needs of those now retired and active.'[35] I entirely agree. If that is the closed door, what is the open gate? Certainly it is not done by putting on an event, service or group that contains the word 'old'. That would be the kiss of death.

AfterWorkNet suggest eight related actions church leaders can take. Here's my summary from English's longer account:[36]

1   spend an hour with each retiring person so they know they are valued and supported
2   treat this group as a distinct church segment
3   encourage their spending time with their peers and addressing the issues of change that they are facing
4   be realistic about their (limited) availability
5   don't use them; develop them to grow spiritually as well as in service
6   encourage them to be salt and light
7   help them reach their peers
8   think intergenerationally.

All these action points make sense to me. They flow from the second factor listed, that is, recognising those in their third age as having a cultural identity, not operating by the stereotype that all older people (i.e. everyone aged 55–110) are basically the same. I am glad not to be a lonely voice calling out for this approach. I only wish I knew more about how the last three factors in this list cash out in practice. It may be that their website, with its activities, and their Facebook group would enlighten me. Meadows is not alone and some of the other voices have been around for some time demonstrating how the 'young-old' are different from the prior generation.

Reaching the Saga generation

Earlier than Jo Cox in 2012 and the Methodist report in 2013, in 2008 Chris Harrington, Church Army evangelist, wrote about mission to third-agers. In *Reaching the Saga Generation*, he named what was culturally distinct about those growing up in the 1960s and how, now as a generally wealthy generation, they value their retirement freedoms and autonomy over any remaining work and their lifestyle. 'For them "old age" is being pushed far into the future... old age is now thought of as 80+.' At the time of writing, he knew of no 'Saga churches' but urged that they should be created, despite knowing the calls of others that church should always be all-age. To that end, he describes features of that generation's spiritual seekers and helpful instincts to work with, culled from American churches that have made advances with church for the baby-boomer generation.[37]

I have long been provoked by the question: 'If people like Paul McCartney, Twiggy, Joan Bakewell or Mick Jagger became Christians, I wonder what sort of church would nurture them and be intriguing to their friends?' Maybe that's a leap too far and too soon; halfway houses might be better. Harrington offers a few of these, which need to be resource-light yet culturally acute: a film-and-faith night; a walking group; going on a pilgrimage (TV programmes have filmed these); forming a book group; a body, mind and spirit group; acoustic café via the web linking around creativity; or a motorcycle group. Harrington suggests that they all embody earlier hints that these avenues are big on participation, offer experience and discussion, model equality and innovation. They minimise hierarchy, any formal membership and being institutional.[38]

I can see here some links to the inner dynamics of the University of the Third Age. These seem to me to include that all participation and learning is active, not passive. It is a 'model of self-help'.[39] There is freedom to engage with groups that cover a wide range of broadly cultural interests; contacts and friends are made, new avenues are explored. Groups are self-led, though a visiting expert or indigenous previous expertise can be one contribution. My mid-level German class included shared food and drink at some point. Maybe that exists in other groupings. Congregational passivity and institutional church are a painful contrast to such a list of self-help dynamics.

Cox raises yet one more question to ponder. It will be an error to think that third-agers and baby boomers are the same thing. It just happens to be so now. But we boomers will age, no matter how many anti-ageing treatments we take, and will become fourth-agers, if we live that long. Coming up pretty shortly, and maybe even with a foot in the door, are those in Gen X, which begins with those born in 1964. By 2024 those born that year will hit 60. That will mean yet more learning about cultural connection to successive generations and discerning in what ways Christian content and cultural context engage with one another in a two-way missional learning, formally called inculturation.

My own suggestion

I have come to the view that it could be wise for churches to start groups or even congregations for those living this autumn stage. We already think culturally, by age and stage, when we provide children's groups and when we differentiate between groups for younger and older teens. The focus on provision for young families is often taken for granted, and BRF Ministries' Parenting for Faith is only one example of a good resource to aid it. Anglican parishes have long provided for traditionalists at the Book of Common Prayer Holy Communion, usually at 8.00 am. Why discriminate against autumn-of-life people?

There will be at least three objections. One is practical. In today's church there is a shortage of money and people resources. My response is: don't *provide* for the third-agers; set them free to discover and do it themselves. That's what they are used to.

Second, some autumn people don't want to be linked up with others of the same generation and instead find life by being with younger people. My response is there should be no compulsion to join and plenty of opportunity to experience intergenerational church life elsewhere. I think this both–and response leads to a 'mixed ecology', in which old and new ways of being church value one another.

It seems to me, from direct experience and from the process of writing this book, that what can work for third-agers are two things. One is active participation in shared activities, such as serving others and exploring together, rather than receiving provision passively. The second, which I have enjoyed for some years, is being part of profound small groups whose interaction and agenda is about living out, as Christians, the practicalities of the autumn of life, with its fruit and the falling leaves. These are at least two avenues to explore the missing 'more' that many are looking for beyond congregational church life.

The honest examination of that journey will dovetail with questions like 'What is deeper discipleship?' and 'How can we grow in character as the naked autumn tree of our true character appears?' The style will be adult learning, alive with questions and exploration; people bringing together their own work and new material. It needs 'a safe space where there can be honesty and openness and thus a confidence about sharing difficulties and personal stories'.[40] I add that this sort of search for a 'more' to the Christian life is what contributes to the steady stream of those, like me, becoming involved in the communities and practices of new monasticism. I wrote something of this in my 2020 book *Seven Sacred Spaces*. Many, though not all, of those joining are in the autumn of life.

The third objection will be that churches should be aiming at all-age provision. My response is not just that we don't apply this for other groups; it is more that I believe in diversity within unity, for which the body of Christ image in 1 Corinthians, with its distinct yet interdependent parts, acts as adequate precedent. In practice, it seems easier and maybe more natural to begin with allowing the creation of diversity and then encouraging expressions of unity across that diversity to grow up naturally and relationally. Also don't assume that those expressions of unity must be through an act of worship. Using the vocabulary of the seven sacred spaces, expressions of unity are much easier through refectory than via chapel. Eat and meet together across diversity before you try to worship together.

Gone, but in what direction?

I need to name one more dynamic, which is a bridge to the next sub-section. It is undeniable that a vast number of people, including older ones, have given up on congregational forms of church. Broadly there have been two strands of research and approaches about this. One is typified by that of Philip Richter and Leslie Francis in their expert books with the word 'gone' in the title. The research was to explore why people left and how to get them back. The other strand is linked to Alan Jamieson and Steve Aisthorpe, writing separately. They too researched why people left, but their questions are 'How are some people being Christians beyond the church?' and 'How can we go and join those who have given up on congregational church, out where they are?'[41] I guess there are more third-agers in those spiritual addresses than those longing to be back in the old normal of congregational church.

There is some link with what we know about fresh expressions of church for older people.

Fresh expressions of church (fxC) for older people

Towards the end of my working life, from 2012 to 2016, Church Army's Research Unit researched all the known fxC within half of the dioceses (21) of the Church of England. Among 20 varying types of fxC, we found 63 out of the total of 1,109, or about five percent, were specifically for older people. That there were any at all may surprise readers who might assume existing church provision would do. We analysed them in various ways and compared them with other types of fxC.

Who came? These fxC were dominantly comprised of adults, though two percent of the attenders were children. These fxC were quite small, 25 being the average attendance size. When they reached that number they usually plateaued, though only a couple subsequently shrank or ceased.

What were the attenders' backgrounds? Almost half (46%) were existing Christians, compared with an overall fxC average of 39%. They drew the highest proportion (41%) of dechurched attenders, compared with the average of 28%; 13% of the attenders had no church background. These figures fit with the overall context in two ways: first, the number of church attenders declines with succeeding generations; second, many people have left the church during their lifetime, but when offered something new and different may be open to join.

How did these fxC develop their internal life? Fitting with this data of who came, they scored above average in holding Communion (71%) but naturally low (6%) for holding baptisms. It was encouraging to hear that many of them had started through leaders spotting a gap in the parish cover and seeing the elderly as an unreached people group. Of these fxC, 54% met monthly and 38% weekly. Meetings were dominantly on a weekday (75%), with half of the fxC using church premises and half of them meeting in public venues. Two thirds of these fxC were led by women. Over half (55%) were lay led, usually accompanied by a team of three to twelve people. They are found across all traditions of the Church of England.

There are several marks that separate them from the long-known provision of a service in an old people's home or a secular older people's social gathering: 78% are taking at least one step towards discipleship, of which one-third have small groups and well over half (57%) choose one-to-one meetings, which older people may appreciate very much; 43% advocated devotional reading of the Bible.

I wish we had asked whether those who came were clearly third age or fourth age, and if both, in what proportions. From digging further, I know from the venue name that nine examples were for fourth-agers in some form of residential home. Twenty-four examples had either 'songs of praise', or the word 'service', 'worship' or 'praise' in the name of the fxC. I doubt those appealed much to third-agers. By contrast 27 out of 63 venues chosen were secular. That and the number of fxC working at development of the spiritual life could be evidence of pursing community and active participation, so there would be some attraction to third-agers.

A tail piece

This data is still the last we have and only shows a valuable and vulnerable beginning to reconnect with older people, more on their terms than on ours. Is that worth noticing? My wife knows only too well that I have been writing, and from time to time she sends me snippets that might fit somewhere. Helen found herself wondering one day in prayer. She wrote in her journal:

> Jesus, your journey for us your church may be to be taken back to the church in tenements of the pre-Constantinian Roman Empire. These were little committed groups, whose lives reflected your glory in a different way – the Celtic vulnerable way rather than the Roman powerful empire-wielding way. We will no longer have a place in which church and state are equal in power and influence. We will be powerful only in our weakness, but it is hard to learn that. In this we have something to teach the children of spring and adults of summer.

Part of living the autumn of life is becoming more vulnerable. This chapter has demonstrated how enduring ageism is still with us in society, contributing to that vulnerability. Church connection with the elderly was described as arguably mainly for fourth-agers, which has been good to provide, but it doesn't appeal to third-agers. Thus third-agers often find themselves in a gap between provision for the young and yet not fitting with the yet older fourth-agers. Congregational forms of church life were shown to appeal less to them now than in the past, when they were part of setting its agenda. Now they often no longer have access to those songs that nurtured their faith in previous decades. Ways forward may exist in shared activities, creating autumn-of-life small groups and finding life through expressions of new monasticism. All these are elements which contribute to vulnerability; some are unintended and some chosen.

This enduring sense of vulnerability acts as the portal to the next chapter.

Application questions

🌿 What signs of ageism do you still see and which ones affect you?

🌿 As a third-ager, how well is a church you go to engaging with you and those like you?

🌿 Which suggestions for work with third-agers began to interest and motivate you?

6

How shall we sing the Lord's song in a strange land?

I'm a companion of Northumbria Community, and this chapter heading, taken from Psalm 137:4, is one of three foundational questions with which we are asked to live. The three questions are related. First comes: 'Who is it that you seek?' Seeking God is our primary calling. But that calling has consequences, which the second question makes explicit: 'How then shall we live?' Seeking God leads to living for God. Then the third question gives the context in which the first two questions are being lived out. That context is the backdrop behind my living out my particular autumn.

Post-Christendom is today's strange land

For those of us old enough to be in the autumn of life, I think it is clear that our context or backdrop has changed. We can just about remember the 1950s, when the church was still fairly central to society and was thought to have some say and even power over people's lives. Going to church was a normal thing to do. Clergy were respected members of society. Decency in public behaviour was expected and required. Christendom appeared to be alive and well.

Now in the 2020s, we are living in what is called 'post-Christendom'. Today's Christians have a history to draw upon, but also a heavy burden to carry, both of inherited structures and, worse, shameful elements to apologise for. By 'post-Christendom', I mean a cultural context in which the Christian church is no longer in power. 'Dom' suggests a power word, as in dominion or kingdom. Christendom stretched back many centuries. Many people are glad its power has ended, because it was more controlling than liberating. We, the church, now find ourselves rejected at the margins of society. Our previous power is despised and dismissed. There is also widespread complete ignorance about what Christianity is all about.

It is now delusional to think that the British population are 'our people'. Church attenders can be called that, but there are four times as many dechurched, those who 'used to be our people'. Among younger generations there are even more of the non-churched, those who were 'never our people'. They have never met a living church community. That is the backdrop behind which we are living out our autumns. This is something more than coping with ageism in society and church, that chapter 5 unpacked.

So older Christians can feel lost, aliens in a world that we thought we knew, belonged to and thought we would retire into. Today's western world can feel 'a strange land', and singing the Lord's song in it is very 'not you'.

How far has the tide of Christendom run out?

In England there is considerable variety of how talk of post-Christendom may feel and the extent of being in a strange land can vary. I sketch three quite different scenarios.

In some villages, where as much as 10% of the population still attend church and the lord of the manor has been the church warden for

generations, talk of post-Christendom may seem alarmist and unbelievable. But, I wonder, is this delusion? How lasting is this future? Anna
Norman-Walker was the missioner in Exeter diocese. In October 2014
she sent me an article anticipating the adoption of palliative care for
dying parts of the rural church, in which she said:

> In the Diocese of Exeter we have 607 churches… Over 200 of them
> attract less than 20 to Sunday services and 106 attract less than
> 10. The average age of our committed member is 65.[1]

A second contrasting context is the public profile and the inner state
of the church in poorer urban areas. In inner-city east Sheffield, where
I live, over 20 years ago I received a sobering document from three
local clergy called 'Change and decay in all around I see.' Feel its pain:

> Welcome to the church of St Anywhere in Urbanland. It is in
> decline. It has known better days when it felt itself part of a
> developing community. Not anymore. In ten years the parish
> has moved dramatically up the scale of urban deprivation. It is
> small. The joint congregation (there were two churches) of 40
> represents less than half of one percent of the total parish popu-
> lation. And most of those are over 60 and female. It is suffering
> from an identity crisis. The patterns of ministry which worked
> well in the past don't work as well anymore. As a consequence,
> the church has become inward looking and feels powerless to
> face all the changes happening around it. It is enough to survive.
> In playing the 'victim' it becomes reactive, defensive and insular.

Their paper lamented a lack of lay leaders, financial difficulties, being
in maintenance mode, disconnection with the local community, and
many leaders being overworked and drained. Here the church has
become almost invisible and post-Christendom is a reality. The church
has already gone into a strange land. It has lost its prior honoured place
in society. It is now bewildered and trying to come to terms with an
unfamiliar reality, for which it knows no precedent. It's a kind of exile,
as it didn't ask for this all to happen.

For a third scenario, consider a thriving existing suburban church, a new resource church or a fresh expression of church experiencing fruitfulness and growth. Here there is hope and delight in a vibrant church community. There is life-giving connection with the surrounding people. In this case, it is not that the church is using its old Christendom power and influence. No, in this strange land, these examples are living out countercultural values, just as did the early church. The epistle of 1 Peter urges this stance. The opening verse, in the NIV, is addressed to 'God's elect, exiles'. 1 Peter 2:11 continues the theme: 'Dear friends, I urge you, as foreigners and exiles...' Peter then urges them not to be contaminated by surrounding values but to live such good lives as to provoke questions in those who watch them. These church people may be strange, but their common life is attractive.

The diagnostic difference between then and now is this. In Peter's day the church existed within pre-Christendom. Christianity was brand new and *came from* the margins. It had no history to live down. In our day the church exists in post-Christendom. Christianity is seen as having been tried and found wanting. Its history is its problem. It is *consigned to* the margins. In that way the New Testament is only half helpful. We need other parts of scripture to know how we may respond.

What will help us all, especially the older ones who remember a different past, to sing the Lord's song in this foreign land, but with our history? I suggest we need to draw upon the Old Testament literature which deals with the exile. These narratives and prophetic writings bring me insight and perspective. They help me stay with hopes I entertain and to cope with fears I cannot banish. There are further reasons to turn to the exilic literature. I don't suggest that there is an explicit repetition of the Jewish history around the sixth century BC, but there are some uncanny echoes.

Similarities to the exile story

1   Consider the decline of influence

Just as the northern and southern kingdoms declined in political influence from the heyday of David and Solomon, so the church in the west has seen marked decline of its influence in society and the proportion of the population who are active attenders. The 1851 English Census revealed that less than 50% of the population attended church. In its day this was an enormous shock. In 2021, the proportion of the population who were attending Anglicans had declined to under one million. Patrick Whitworth, writing in 2008 about an exile for today, made it but 1.7% of the population.[2]

In the Old Testament history of descent towards exile, there were the bright periods of significant prophetic ministries and the benign rule of better kings, but, in the wider sweep of history, these represented a stay of execution rather than a reversal of history. In our own day, we may be glad of the influence of thriving churches and renewal movements, but these have not reversed overall declining numbers. In 1998, in the opening pages of *Threshold of the Future*, Michael Riddell wrote:

> The Christian Church is dying in the West. This painful fact is the cause of a great deal of avoidance by the Christian community. To use terminology drawn from pastoral care, the terminally sick patient is somewhere between denial and bargaining.[3]

Whether you agree with Riddell's diagnosis, it is not a matter of argument that the great days of our political influence and power are gone. We are no longer in power. We no longer control society by influence, money and in decision-making.

2 Note that decay is a long story

In the kingdom of Israel, the seeds of spiritual corruption were sown at the height of its power under Solomon. We too have such a history in the medieval church. This apparent strength was followed by the break-up of this power into divided kingdoms. In 1054, Christendom split into a Catholic west and an Orthodox east, and in the 1520s into European Catholicism and European Protestantism, which itself further split into several denominations. All these contribute to the ongoing scandal of a divided church.

Furthermore, just as the ancient northern and southern Jewish kingdoms fought against each other, we too have a history of conflict, culminating in the Thirty Years War (1618–48) in Europe. In it, both sides claimed God had given them definite understanding of him and his ways. This poisoned the trustworthiness of revelation from God as a reliable source of knowledge. If claims of revelation had failed, what was left was reliance on human reason. Moreover, this disgrace, which was a religious civil war, sowed the seeds of rationalism and secularism.

I gladly commend Whitworth's *Prepare for Exile* for any who want to dig deeper into what I headline here. Explaining why he uses the word 'exile' for today, he writes:

> There are four reasons… why the church in Britain may be facing a new kind of exile: the building of a secular and pluralist state; a change in culture and its underlying philosophical presuppositions; the erosion of Christendom with its church-state links being further dismantled; and the reduction in the number of people who regularly worship in church.[4]

3   Discern that distorting changes come to prominence

There are two points of similarity. First, note the change in Old Testament Jewish society from tabernacle to temple. This centralising change occurred at the height of political power under David and Solomon. God was locked into one place. The connection to church history may be seen in the profound changes brought about under Constantine, when some of the wildness of the church was tamed. For a recent protest against this and a call for a healthy wildness to return, read Steve Aisthorpe's *Rewilding the Church*.[5]

Second, as the Old Testament people headed towards the experience of exile, Jerusalem and its temple became viewed as an inalienable blessing. Jeremiah's criticism was: 'Do not trust in deceptive words and say, "This is the temple of the Lord, the temple of the Lord, the temple of the Lord!"' (Jeremiah 7:4). We too have a heavy emotional dependence on, and heavy financial burden of, our religious buildings and an emphasis on public worship. This exaggerates the importance of place in guaranteeing the church's future stake in society. What might today's Jeremiah say to us?

4   Beware of superficial change

The Jewish people are called stubborn and rebellious by Isaiah, Jeremiah, Ezekiel, Hosea and Zechariah. Prophetic calls for reform had some impact under King Josiah, but the overall response for centuries was dismissal of, and ignoring calls for, radical change. As a lifelong Anglican, I know something of the resistance of my own church to calls for deep change.

For example, consider of the fate of two Church of England reports, written in 1974 and 1975, by the clergyman David Wasdell. He was employed centrally to research church attendance. He showed from meticulous national work that the larger a population of a parish, the lower was the percentage of attenders from it. He showed also that the maximum number of congregational attenders a single cleric could support was around 170, irrespective of the parish size. So the larger the parish, the less effective it was in practice. He advocated multiplying more lay-led smaller churches within one parish as the way forward. As such, he concluded that the parish system was inadvertently designed to fail. His contract was terminated, and his work has disappeared from view.

In 2015 I repeated his method, as closely as I could, using the 2011 Census and the then Church of England figures. They showed the same features and proportions, with the exceptions that many smaller parishes (the most effective ones) had been merged and that the clergy numbers had halved. It was fair to conclude that the Church of England had learnt precious little from Wasdell. Incidentally, he went on to research how institutions defend themselves against change.

Two decades after Wasdell, in the 1990s large parts of the Church of England found it interesting to listen to speakers about the report *Building Missionary Congregations*,[6] and to hear others from the Springboard team urge mission and renewal. But looking back, it is sad to reflect that apart from changing some labels, little else seems to have happened. At the end of the 'decade of evangelism', I agreed with the cynics who observed that the language of everything had changed to mission, yet nearly everything has remained much the same.

When I was still working for Church Army's Research Unit, from time to time when speaking I would jest that the Church of England has an enviable track record of producing well-researched, thought-provoking, change-invoking reports, stretching back to 1944 and *Towards the Conversion of England*. However, the church then did little, or anything much, about them. This raised a rueful laugh but never rebuttal.

5   Surely there's no idolatry today?

Having aired some similarities, you may reasonably ask, am I suggesting there is some equivalent to the widespread blatant idolatry of the exilic period? No, I'm not. I think our situation is less obviously troublesome, and yet it is serious.

My concern is partly that for too long we have been satisfied with church attendance as an adequate measure of being Christian. I am glad that in my own lifetime I have seen the rise of calls in books for discipleship to be the measure to value, and I have advocated the same myself.[7] This call first came across powerfully to me in 1981, when David Watson wrote trenchantly on the topic; his introduction included:

> The vast majority of western Christians are church-members, pew-fillers, hymn-singers, sermon-tasters, Bible-readers, even born-again-believers or Spirit-filled charismatics – but not true disciples of Jesus.[8]

Forty years on, BRF Ministries rightly make much of Andrew Roberts' work *Holy Habits* – a practical way to turn the desire for deep discipleship into a rooted part of everyday life. The terms used by Watson also touch upon my second and deeper cause for concern.

Put bluntly, one form of idolatry today is 'consumerism', which is alive and well in church life. 'What I and my children get out of it' is many people's measure of church life and where to attend, irrespective of whether they live near that church. I accept that there can be genuine reasons to belong to a church other than a nearby one. They include enduring connections to a wider network of people, a past history of connection elsewhere and profound convictions about different church traditions.

That said, loyalty and commitment always count. Being a choosy church wanderer is never a promising attitude. We wait to see how things will work out, in term of lasting commitment, with the advent of digital church, where people log in across considerable distance, time zones and even nations. In all such cases, we need to find out how attendance can become discipleship, for true discipleship and consumerism don't mix.

These five factors bear out that our post-Christendom context has similarities with the exilic period. This affects all western Christians, not least those of us in the autumn of life, who can remember the earlier good times and feel the loss more. The Lord's song has got harder to sing.

Differences from the exile story

I see two points of divergence.

1 The rise of worldwide mission

The exilic period does contain a call for the people of God to see themselves as called to be a light to the nations (Isaiah 49:6). But the reality was that this call was seldom grasped beyond the inward facing response for proselytes to join the Jewish faith. However, the Christendom church in the west has a different history, in part. Starting with the Jesuit response of the 16th century and from the 1790s in Protestant denominations, it engaged in a worldwide missionary movement on a scale never seen before. Through this, despite some regrettable elements, a more vigorous worldwide church has been planted in the two-thirds world. There is no equivalent to that in the Old Testament exilic story.

2 There is no 'fall of Jerusalem' today

Some may think: 'Surely there is no obvious equivalent to the fall of Jerusalem and the exile of its people to Babylon in 587BC?' This is to misunderstand the nature of what has happened to us. The enemy of the church in the west is not physical persecution, and the issue is not political power. The issue is spiritual credibility and relevance in the equally real battle for the affections and minds of human beings. Faced with the onset of secularisation and the re-emergence of new age or pagan spirituality, the contest to be the leading spiritual force in the western nations is being lost.

In that sense, the judgement on us is falling already. Today's 'Jerusalem', understood as the church in the west, is neither 'the joy of the whole earth' (Psalm 48:2) nor the centre of society. It is not even the place where it is generally expected that God will be found. Rather, the western church is seen predominantly as an institution, a relic of a bygone age and a minority sport for those who like that sort of thing. Even among Christians, and not just those in the autumn of life, I detect an increasing tendency. Their yearning for God is in tension with a sense that this hunger can no longer be fed by attending congregational forms of denominational life. They are dropping out, into the so-called new churches, into forms of new monasticism or into private religion. The growing cry among some of my thoughtful friends is: 'We can't go on like this.' My sense is that, like the Davidic dynasty, today's church is at the end of an era, though as the exile would tell us, this is not the end of the story.

Autumn and exile: overlaps and differences

I have catalogued five plausible parallels and two differences, though you may have noticed that one of those differences is in fact a similarity, just less obvious than the previous five, between our day and the descent to the exile. This is the backdrop that those of us in the autumn of our lives are having to cope with. Our world has changed, as has the church's position in it. The autumn of life and exile do overlap emotionally, in that both include handling a response to decline and decay. But I am not saying that the autumn of life is itself some sort of exile from a fullness of life that spring promises and summer may deliver. What I am saying is that the shame, disorientation and challenge of today's post-Christendom exile make the autumn of life harder to live through.

Yet we third-agers should know about coping with the loss of the falling leaves. We are also learning this reality is held in tension with gratitude for autumn's fruits, trust in God's continuing presence, openness to what he can teach us in a new season and hope for a better future. So I turn from comparison of the exilic period with todays' church, to pick up the prophetic messages that apply to us all as part of the post-Christendom church in exile. Some are challenging and some encouraging. But that is how it is with this dark cultural backdrop to living the autumn of life.

Strands in the prophets have echoes for today

The exile produced a diversity of responses, from the deep pessimism of Jeremiah to the lyrical hope of the later chapters of Isaiah. We too need to hear voices across and from both ends of this spectrum. I begin with Daniel.

Daniel 9: repentance and the people of God

Bishop Jack came to Sheffield diocese in 1998. He brought these three priorities: rejoicing in God; compassion for the needy; and repentance for the church. I valued the variety in these three, but the last one is sadly rarely named as he did. That emphasis reminded me of Daniel 9:15–18:

Now, Lord our God, who brought your people out of Egypt with a mighty hand and who made for yourself a name that endures to this day, we have sinned, we have done wrong. Lord, in keeping with all your righteous acts, turn away your anger and your wrath from Jerusalem, your city, your holy hill. Our sins and the iniquities of our fathers have made Jerusalem and your people an object of scorn to all those around us... We do not make requests of you because we are righteous, but because of your great mercy.

Two links occur to me. The first is the awareness that all of us in the western church are also living under the judgement of God. It is easier to think God may be judging an increasingly frenetic and decadent society, but I cannot believe God has nothing to say to a church that has known great influence, fouled its own nest and been in decline since the start of the 20th century.

But any talk of judgement is always perilous, not least if it sounds judgemental. The second point is therefore essential, though it could be missed. Daniel may not even have been born in 587BC or, if he was involved, he was but a child. He was not personally the cause of the exile. Yet he prays 'we have sinned'. He takes up shared responsibility. Repentance for our own position and not blaming other bits of the church is a healthier stance to take. From this chapter I hope you pick up that I am saddened at what church life has descended to, but I freely admit I am part of this problem. As of the time of writing, I have been a church member for 75 years and ordained for 49 of them. I hang in there with hopes and fears, with sorrow and repentance.

I suggest that corporate repentance should become part of contemporary Christian spirituality and a proper response to the many voices of criticism, inside and outside the church. Some of those people will speak out of sorrow; some out of anger. I cannot simply dismiss them as pessimists who are to be rejected for both the content and style of what they say. Such dismissal is far too typical of exactly what was wrong with pre-exilic attitudes. I don't want to collude with those who want to be told *only* the good news. To me such denial is psychological testimony to an underlying malaise. Failure to compose and sing contemporary songs of repentant lament is an unhealthy sign.

Of course, I find the voices of those who wish the church well are the easiest to hear, but they are not the only ones I should attend to, if I want the truth. That truth leads me often into repentance for the church, at times with tears. I have no choice but to love her still, because Christ loves her, and I am a product and a part of her. This is not a comfortable place to be. I am not alone in this and have friends of my era, also in the autumn of their lives, who sense they are no longer at home in the denominational church of their earlier years. They feel as though their homeland has been lost and they are already in some sort of exile. Their tears are more painful than condemnatory. Part of our response is repentance for the church of which we are part.

Jeremiah 12: living in times of judgement

If we are in a period of judgement we shall find ourselves caught up in some disagreeable consequences. Take Jeremiah 12. Verses 1–4 contain the prophet's complaint about God's lack of apparent justice: the way that the wicked and powerful flourish; how the vulnerable are exploited; and also that the perpetrators have lost any sense of accountability to God for their conduct. How similar that is to strands of life today. God's response to Jeremiah was not comforting: 'If you have raced with men on foot and they have worn you out, how can you compete with horses?' (v. 5).

It is as though God's reply is to say, 'Yes, it is tough – and it could get worse.' I wonder if one application today is that we have found it difficult in the past to race with secularism and modernism and often found ourselves lagging behind them. How then shall we fare with changing and slippery customers like pluralism and postmodernism, in which everything is relative and there are no truths? Don't hear me say we shouldn't try; I simply say it may be less easy. I am amused though alarmed at the aphorism I recall: 'You should start with where people are, but this is more difficult when they keep changing their address!'

Pluralism and postmodernism are topics in themselves. Whitworth's book on exile offers us at least seven pages on them.[9] Forgive me for naming mistaken responses rather than airing solutions, but during my working life, too many presentations on evangelism to postmodern people have been very modernist in style. A condensed example is the approach of 'We can be sure that Jesus rose from the dead, so Christianity must be true', to which the easy, and often final, reply is: 'That's fine as your opinion, but it doesn't work for me.' It is therefore good that there is now more talk about postmodernism and evangelism but, worryingly, less on forming church for postmoderns. We must do both if the fruits of the evangelism are not to rot in the fields.

Jeremiah continues:

> Many shepherds will ruin my vineyard and trample down my field; they will turn my pleasant field into a desolate wasteland… They will sow wheat but reap thorns; they will wear themselves out but gain nothing. They will bear the shame of their harvest because of the Lord's fierce anger.
> JEREMIAH 12:10, 13

It is clearly not new for the people of God to be apparently bent on destroying themselves and bound up in hard-working futility. The present church has at times suffered both. Living under the judgement of God on society and on the church will never be a picnic.

There is a variable within this backdrop of the exile period. Some individual churches and whole denominations may find resonance with the impending doom of the immediate pre-exilic period. Others will identify with being in the very period of exile itself. And a third set may find themselves genuinely caught up with the hopes of a return from it. Yet for all three categories, enduring themes include the following: living with both the faithfulness and severity of God; the need to be honest about our church past; and the permission to acknowledge our present difficulties.

God's judgement places us in a vulnerable position. Sense the bewilderment within Psalm 137:4: 'How *can* we sing songs of the Lord while in a foreign land?' It is a lament. Yet that exact difficulty of being worshippers surrounded by a hostile and alien culture, both then and now, could be precisely the point. God's people do have an exilic call to be a light to the nations, which is easier to do when you are among them. It is not a calling to withdrawal and being comfortable by ourselves. A later writer, from the apocryphal period, got this point:

> We give thanks to you O Lord before the nations, for you have
>   scattered us among them.
> There we make your greatness known and exalt you in the
>   presence of all the living.
> TOBIT 13:2–3[10]

Curiously it could be that those of us who are getting used to living the autumn of our personal lives have something to teach others living through the post-Christendom exile. In autumn, the whole art is to accept where and what we are, in terms of challenges from our increasing age and diminishing capabilities. We are called to live through the mixture of fruits and freedoms alongside the losses of the leaves. In the living out of both aspects well we testify to our experiences of God which we have in that season.

Haggai 2: don't give in to fears

In any genuine experience of exile it is hard not to look back wistfully. As one wag put it: 'Nostalgia isn't what it used to be.' Here is a message to older Christians who can recall the former glories of life and to whom the present achievements can look insignificant by comparison: 'How does it look to you now? Does it not seem to you like nothing?' (Haggai 2:3).

That context was a temple-rebuilding programme that got stuck for 20 years. The incomplete foundations were in painful contrast to the temple of Solomon that had preceded it. In verses 4–5 Haggai calls them to be strong, but this is not the same as a call to power. The call is not to remain stuck or cave in, but to hold on and complete the task given. After all, God originally neither offered, required nor promised his people previous kingly power, and those returning from the exile were never called to rebuild the Davidic kingdom. I think the same about any calls to bring back forms of Christendom. By contrast, I see much in life and vitality of the apparently powerless pre-Constantinian church that looks a better way. My most instructive read on that topic is Alan Kreider's *The Patient Ferment of the Early Church*.[11]

The call is to not fear; it is a powerful temptation facing us in a changing and uncertain society. Years ago I found, I know not where, a prayer by Bishop George Appleton that was natural to make my own when surrounded by intimidating factors and my own weaknesses:

> O Holy Spirit, whose presence is liberty, grant me that freedom of the Spirit, which will not fear to tread in unknown ways nor be held back by fear of others or misgivings of ourselves.

Haggai 2 also contains hope for the future, that God will shake the existing order and fill his own chosen place with glory. There is even the audacious verse 9: 'The glory of this present house will be greater than the glory of the former house.' These days I interpret 'house' not to mean church buildings, but church people. And as for the temple as a house, it is clear to me that Jesus saw himself as the ultimate expression of the temple or, in other words, where God is reliably found.

I do not yet see how this 'greater glory' can happen in the 21st century, but the promise is there. If it does not appear in history, it will be delivered in eternity. For hope is a permanent mark of genuine Christian spirituality. It will be based in the presence and promise of God, not our ability, strength or wisdom. There is hope. It is Christian to think so. The hope is in the God of mercy and judgement, the one who does not break the bruised reed (Isaiah 42:3), who blesses the poor in spirit (Matthew 5:3) and is ever working to make all things new (Revelation 21:5). The hope is not in human wisdom, better apologetics, slicker marketing or sophisticated digital AV equipment; nor is it in the power of persuasion, particular courses or any of these preferred human strategies. 'Be strong. Do not fear. Hope in God,' says Haggai.

I can't think that doesn't speak to us, whether all of us in some form of today's exile of the church or those of us in the autumn of our lives, when our strength is diminishing. In those losses, fear can stalk our lives, and I named various anxieties in chapter 3 on falling leaves. Even the apostle Paul admitted to fear and being downcast (2 Corinthians 7:5–6). It is pertinent that in Romans 8:15 Paul says: 'The Spirit you received does not make you slaves, so that you live in fear again.' The operative word here is *slave*. Fear can be a controlling taskmaster; it can deny us freedom to choose and command us to submit. I find it a fight to live out what Paul says that I have received, 'adoption to sonship'. That identity conveys my being an heir, and in that there is a basis for hope. Sonship, not slavery, underpins hope, which itself is a staple diet item in living the autumn of life.

Zechariah 4: don't despise the day of small things

Zechariah and Haggai were contemporaries (Ezra 5:1). Both prophets dealt with small beginnings, involving discouraged and distracted people. My cursory reading of introductions to Zechariah tells me there is much in its 14 chapters that is hard to understand. I am only paddling in their shallow end and making links that help me negotiate a post-Christendom exile as the backdrop to living the autumn of life.

I begin with Zechariah 4:10: 'Who despises the day of small things? Men will rejoice when they see the plumb-line in the hand of Zerub-babel.'[12] It makes sense to me to think that the plumb-line refers to the intention to see something built straight and true. Back then it was a reference to picking up the abandoned temple construction work that Haggai also called for.

In today's post-Christendom exile context, the last 20 years of my working life were spent watching people exploring how, with a new start, they have the chance to build church again. They aimed to build straight and true, reimagining what church is, when freer from those parts of the inheritance that ossified, compromised and distorted what she should be. Equally, building straight and true must mean faithfully following the essence of what church is. In our day I watched people building more modestly and fashioning communities, rather than erecting new buildings.

As I mentioned in the previous chapter, from 2012 to 2016 Church Army's Research Unit examined all the known fresh expressions of church (fxC) in half of the dioceses of the Church of England (1,109 of them). The fxC were strikingly effective in drawing in adults and children who had given up on church and also those who had never tried it. One headline was that, compared with parish churches, fxC were small, young and varied. As team leader I wanted a title for our 230-page report on what these fxC were like, what they were achieving and how they were maturing. Zechariah 4:10 came to me as a gift; it freely admitted the fxC's vulnerability and the danger that they were being wrongly dismissed by some. We called the report *The Day of Small Things*.[13]

I am intrigued that at the close of my full-time working life, it should be summarised by this text from Zechariah 4. For in 1965, on the night of my commitment of my life to Christ, the verse given to me was Zechariah 4:6: '"Not by might nor by power, but by my Spirit," says the Lord Almighty.' I am very content to live by those Zechariah 4 bookends, and I can see how both contribute to living the autumn of life.

A temptation in later years is to think that all we can still do or accomplish is but a molehill of small things. I need to accept that they are not to be despised, which chimes in with well-known aphorisms like lighting a candle in the darkness or throwing back just one starfish. Starting an fxC or fledgling Christian community may indeed look small. However, it was Jesus who affirmed the creative place of small things. He held up the effect of such things as seeds, yeast and salt.

Isaiah 43: the contribution of hope

I have chosen chapter 43 as one among many uplifting, hope-inducing passages in Isaiah 40—66. Its early verses give reasons why fear can be resisted and hope nourished. For when we pass through the water or the fire, God will be with us. The chapter also proffers freedom from captivity at God's expense, because we belong to him and he loves us. So we see that having hope does not preclude us from having to face difficulties, suffer opposition or find ourselves caught up in the consequences of being a people in some kind of exile. Both the wider challenge of living in a post-Christendom exile and the narrower one of living out the autumn of life can be faced.

Isaiah 43:16–19 contains a reminder from God that he has acted decisively in the past to save through the exodus events. Yet the text goes on to invite us not to dwell on the treasures of the past but to perceive the new way that God is disclosing in the desert. But why there? This desert, of Isaiah 43, is not that of the exodus, but rather it is shorthand for the journey back from the exile. Classically, the desert does duty for the bareness of simplicity, the furnace of dependence and the oasis of spirituality. It is the place to need God and where he meets us. As he acts, we shall be his witnesses to the watching world (v. 10) and proclaim in praise what he has done (v. 21).

It is not comfortable living through this new exile, and being a third-ager isn't all roses either. Both involve coping with loss as well as holding on to promise. Part of the hope is that despite, and even within, the post-Christendom exile of the western church, there is the adventure of going with God who is doing a new thing (v. 19). One important 'new thing' in the Old Testament exile was the invention of the synagogue, in the absence of the temple. As I have shown in applying the Zechariah passage, today how we live as the people of God is also being re-imagined, and these fxC have some claim to be 'a new thing' in our post-Christendom context.

The application of hope differs between the exilic and living the autumn of life. The first holds out a genuine departure from the exile and a fresh start back home, whereas for those of us in the autumn of life hope is more about living that season well. Autumn can bring new elements, but we stay there and it is there that we need to hold on to hope, as Isaiah says we can.

Drawing threads together

I've outlined a case that there are several similarities between the history and position of the western church and the Old Testament period around the exile. I've opened up some biblical messages from that period and argued their relevance. I have cited a few books related to this topic, and I appreciate Whitworth's exploration of spirituality and of mission for an exiled church in his chapters 6 and 7. I wonder if he is more like Isaiah in his views and if I am too much of a Jeremiah, but I would want to add more about repentance than he covers.

Another thoughtful and wide-ranging source is Gordon Mursell's *Praying in Exile*, which sees the exile motif in the lives of refugees, migrants, asylum seekers, nomads and whenever we sense we are 'not at home'.[14] He begins the book with his own being sent away to boarding school at the tender age of eight and calls it exile. While all losses in life count – they matter and they have an effect – I am not convinced they are all exilic. Exile is unwanted and enforced, it involves being uprooted and banished, it is without immediate hope of return, it dissolves some past beliefs and, worst of all, exile in the biblical case was deserved and the people brought it upon themselves. In living out the autumn of life, I do not think the losses of older age are truly exilic. There is no need whatever to apologise for being in the autumn of life, but we do need to take care not to deny the reality of ageing and try to inhabit some ageless Neverland. Denial remains an exilic temptation.

There are some aspects of living our autumns that can feel exilic. You have read earlier that I find being taken captive to a digital world has some of that feeling. Other losses such as bereavement or dementia are unwanted indeed; they can be enforced to some extent by age and health. These losses are without realistic hope of a return to summer and spring; certainly they dissolve wishful thinking about perpetual youth, but they are not some sort of deserved punishment. Thus the messages from Haggai about resisting fear, from Zechariah about the value of the small and from Isaiah about hope still speak to us autumnal migrants. These are spiritual responses and attitudes to learn from that period. Yet I am serious in claiming across this chapter that those of us living the autumn of life are doing so with a double whammy. The forbidding backdrop for older Christian people is that the western church is itself in a kind of post-Christendom exile and there, sadly, the additional tough responses of Daniel and Jeremiah do apply.

Let's now look wider and unpack how other parts of scripture explore the autumn of life.

Application questions

🌿 Which of the three different church scenarios (rural, inner urban, suburban) fits your context?

🌿 How does the notion of being in post-Christendom exile correspond to how you see the church today?

🌿 Which of the prophets and their messages do you find you are drawn to, and can you say why?

🌿 How might this chapter change what you pray for?

7

Scripture and the autumnal spiritual journey

Not much should be made of references in scripture to the annual season of autumn. Two such references are found in Psalm 84:5–7 and Joel 2:23. From their Middle Eastern perspective, they saw autumn as a recognised season with the characteristic of bringing much needed rain. This was seen as a sign of God's faithfulness. Today, in view of climate change and the variable weather patterns in the UK, which can bring heavy rain at any season and prompts perennial discussion of the weather, we don't make the same tight meteorological connections. However, we do still believe God has brought into being a remarkably self-adjusting, self-regulating, self-repairing world, which ultimately God sustains.

It may be fair to observe from those Old Testament texts that the autumn rains stocked up reserves of water in cisterns for the year ahead. Similarly, good lessons learnt in the autumn of our lives will assist us to live through it and prepare us for our own wintering. Scripture has much to say about ageing, becoming old, dying and the emotions that accompany these processes.

The backdrop to ageing
is the reality of death

Ian Knox writes that early in scripture, 'it is apparent that growing old, ageing and dying are the normal pattern of life'. That is the condition of all living things. He cites Genesis 3:19, which puts it graphically and emphatically: 'Dust you are and to dust you will return.' I remember reading Tournier's comment that it is not that people die because they get ill, it is that 'they fall ill because they have to die'.[1]

This humble earthy identity is linked to fragility in Psalm 103:14–15. God 'remembers that we are dust' and that humans only flourish 'like a flower of the field'. Our beauty is profoundly transient. Note we are not even likened to a garden flower that might be watered, protected and tended, but compared to a flower out in the open, vulnerable to the sun and wind, to predators and even a trampling human foot. This ephemeral nature of dust, and the transience of grass living and dying in a day, is also portrayed in Psalm 90:3–10. It was paraphrased by Isaac Watts in his hymn 'O God, our help in ages past' and those evocative lines: 'Time, like an ever-rolling stream bears all its sons away.' The book of Ecclesiastes – seldom jolly but often memorable – puts it baldly: 'There is… a time to be born and a time to die' (3:2). And so it is.

I also place John 9:4 within this framework: 'As long as it is day, we must do the works of him who sent me. Night is coming, when no one can work.' Night might refer to opposition, persecution or to failing strength and more advanced old age. If life is one complete day of 24 hours, then for me at 75-years-old I trust that my night is not yet. Trying to write this book may, I hope, be a sign that I can still do some kinds of work. However, I have to admit that within this metaphor, late afternoon or early evening is already upon me. How does doing 'work' fit with that?

A life lived in Christ is essentially and entirely vocational. It begins and ends in the call of God. He is the ultimate source of our birth and our particular and diverse gifts; then come our belonging to him, exercising varying ministries, being servants of God and partners with him throughout our lives.

Early in one of his books, the prophetic American agrarian writer Wendell Berry gladly admits he has had changes of mind to which he keeps returning: 'From "job", the manna of the economists and the politicians, to "vocation" which is the authentic calling to the work that is properly one's own.' Seeing life as vocation is to see it as so much more than doing a job. Tournier concurs, tracing headlines of significant stages in his own life, a process which brought him a sense of unity and meaning to his life. Some years before, he also wrote to assert the totality and width of that vocational view:

> Having a vocation means approaching everything one does in a spirit of vocation, looking upon it as an adventure shared with God. … I serve him by taking an interest in everything.[2]

And it's not just that we work for God, but we also work with him. Recently that partnership was underlined for me by 1 Corinthians 12:6: 'There are different kinds of working, but in all of them and in everyone it is the same God at work.' That partnership is for a lifetime. In that sense we never retire, we just stop being paid for the work that we do. During our autumn of life it may well be that 'different kinds of working' emerge. As I stressed in a former book, *Seven Sacred Spaces*, work is an intrinsic part of being human, because it is part of the image of God in us. Few of us can work with much energy at over 90 years old, though people like David Attenborough and Queen Elizabeth II have been shining examples. Yet, even when night comes and we can do little for ourselves, by the way we treat our family and our carers, we can exercise love, which is perhaps the best sort of work.

While we still live, we are called to some elements of work – to live purposefully in, for and with God. If that is shorn from us, then also an element of human dignity is lost. That is why treating older people as useless or redundant is so demeaning. It is why the best ministries to older people always include a dimension that they are devised and conducted with and by, not just for, older people.

And when our autumn has finally turned to winter, when the day has ceased and night is upon us, when death looks imminent, familiar words are so applicable. Psalm 23:4: 'Even though I walk through the valley of the shadow of death, I fear no evil' (RSV). These words are easy on the ear, comforting to read and important to hold on to. And, I reflect, even walking is a form of work; it's something we do. Dying well will combine a letting go and a walked path.

Scripture names some downsides of ageing

Proverbs 23:22 counsels: 'Listen to your father, who gave you life, and do not despise your mother when she is old.' Older people do fear that they won't be listened to any more. Partly this is because our brains seem to be working slower, so that a key word or term suddenly hides in an inaccessible corner of the labyrinthine mind. We fear we may have told that story once before or are nervous that our views are simply old-fashioned, meaning they are deemed to have passed their sell-by date. We elderly can be a mixed blessing. Grannies come in many guises, as The Pocket Book of Good Grannies illustrates.[3] They vary from the crabby and dowdy, and the glamorous and exciting, to the downright batty and amusingly mistaken. I remember with a mixture of shame and amusement an episode of earlier years. My teenage friends asked their ageing mother to explain why car engines needed oil. 'Oh', she said,' I expect you pour it over them, like gravy.' Hoots of derision unkindly followed, poured over one of the kindest and most hospitable women I have known. Yes, the elderly may fear being scorned or not being listened to; both are ways in which despising happens. Proverbs suggests this is not a new problem.

Psalm 71:9 contains a heartfelt plea: 'Do not cast me away when I am old; do not forsake me when my strength is gone.' 'Don't discard me, don't throw me aside,' are other translations. Nor is this just a passing thought for it is echoed in v. 18: ' Even when I am old and grey, do not forsake me, my God.' Why does the psalmist ask the question? In the surrounding verses the author explains his context; the presence of the attacks of cruel, wicked and accusing enemies and knowing past occasions of many bitter troubles (vv. 4, 10–13, 20). But those could have occurred at any stage of life. Why is the pressure now more intense? It seems to me that these cries represent a common fear. In my old age, will everything change? Will I become useless? Will I be just like a used piece of kitchen towel, of value while I cleared up some mess, but then destined for the bin? Is my value that I still have some ability and strength? Is my identity only determined by my utility? If my utility diminishes so does my value. If I'm no more use, what then – is it the scrapheap? What a very human fear and one that grows with advancing years.

Last summer a talented Swiss theologian in her 40s, with a glittering future before her, was blunt: 'I'm afraid of becoming old,' she said. She related it to fear of dementia and losing her mind. Such comments relate to losing our grip, the decline of our health and creeping dependency. With our better selves we trust that God won't discard us like a used kitchen wipe, yet here the realism of the psalms tells us that such trust, which is also present in Psalm 71, and a very human fear seem to be able to coexist. It's worse because all the features in society that devalue those of us in older age create a spiritual and psychological climate.

This discarding of the elderly becomes the very air we breathe. Do any of you, like me, begin to apologise for being who you are? Do you recognise these sorts of self-deprecating comments: 'Of course, I've been retired for six years so I'm not up to date any more'; 'It may be an old-fashioned view these days, but can I say that…'; 'If it's still relevant, I wonder if…'? Tournier tells of a friend who described himself as 'a poor old chap' and described being 73 as a misfortune, an age which at other times he was at pains to deny being.[4] I think that at heart, when these fears afflict us, we have still further to go in shifting from finding our identity through our achievements to the deeper dynamic of being accepted leading to identity.

The gloomiest passage is Ecclesiastes 12:1–8. Rob Merchant calls it 'stark reality'.[5] Read it one day when you are feeling robust. It bemoans the advent of 'days of trouble' and the advent of years when we say 'I find no pleasure in them' (v. 1). Then sight dims, fear of heights and going into the streets increase, desire no longer stirs, songs fade and 'people go to their eternal home' (v. 5). The teacher cries: 'Remember him – before… the golden bowl is broken… the wheel broken at the well, and the dust returns to the ground it came from' (v. 6). It's all meaningless, is the cry of this depressive.

It's not much of an answer at this point, but I admit I am relieved that such lament is included in scripture, for then I am not excluded. Nor am I alone in those periods of life where questions are easier than answers; when just existing is a heavy burden; when it is easy to ask oneself, 'What's it all been for?'; and when discouraging global features envelop us.

My current list of those concerns includes the climate crisis, the loss of species diversity, the war in Ukraine, the cost-of-living increase, the loss of integrity in public life, the shambles of English politics, the rise of populism, the disproportionate reliance on economics which, from an ecological point of view, is certainly not the bottom line! You can carry on and add your own. They all threaten to undermine or overwhelm us, and at times there is little we individuals can do about it. Yes, my wife and I have done many things to reduce our own carbon footprint, but 80% of the climate crisis is caused by 100 big international companies. All that's without facing up to a century of numerical church decline, including the severance of its message from, and the atrophy of its links to, the everyday life of most people. On top of all this, in one's older age come the temptations to give in to decreasing strength and to give up praying and working for anything better.

In the New Testament we find Paul, as an older man, in his candid correspondence with the Christians in Corinth, likening being human to being a jar of clay , an ordinary and breakable object, that encases 'the light of the knowledge of God's glory displayed in the face of Christ' (2 Corinthians 4:6). This contrast is partly and rightly an expression of spiritual humility, yet it is connected to his recognition that at this stage of life 'outwardly we are wasting away' (v. 16). We'll come to his message of hope despite this reality in later paragraphs. But denial of fragility and decline are no way through.

Eddie Askew writes:

> Some Christians seem to believe that their witness depends on being ever hopeful, optimistic and victorious; and that to confess to moments of despair doubt or unhappiness is somehow to be unfaithful. Yet it doesn't really fit the facts of experience.[6]

I notice how often in the paragraphs above I have written the word 'fear'. Someone once told me the injunctions 'do not fear' or 'do not be afraid' occurs 365 times in scripture. (I have already mentioned this, but thought citing it twice was excusable.) I could have done some tedious concordance work to check that out for numerical accuracy, but what is more to the point is that the frequency tells me this is a very common human problem and we are to resist it. 'Easier said than done,' I reply to myself. Let's see what encouragements there might be for us.

Some biblical encouragements for this autumnal stage of life

Some shouts from the biblical touchline sound rather like words from an energetic and doubtless younger Pilates teacher. 'Do not let your hands hang limp' (Zephaniah 3:16). 'Therefore, strengthen your feeble arms and weak knees' (Hebrews 12:12). Those of us who are still living in houses with steep staircases may either smile or groan.

Nevertheless there is great value in keeping exercising. My wife and I learnt, and most days do, a simple set of Pilates-type stretches that go under a name that can be spelt either ForFit or ForFeit. That double meaning relates to one maxim for living this stage of life – 'Use it or lose it.' Keeping physically fit as an older person not only assists the challenge to keep supple at our age. We now know that pleasurable activities, such as exercise, release endorphins. These hormones help relieve pain, reduce stress and improve our sense of well-being. Our commitment to keeping fit also helps safeguard mental health.

Earlier in his Corinthian correspondence, Paul writes: 'He will also keep you firm to the end, so that you will be blameless… God is faithful, who has called you' (1 Corinthians 1:8–9). Those of us living the autumn of life might hope that our bodies will stay as firm and strong as before. But the text carefully read makes clear this strength is moral and spiritual, as the word 'blameless' indicates, rather than physical strength. As we know, at this age, the fierce challenge of a steep uphill walk or opening a long-sealed marmalade jar tell their own tale. On that upward climb we breathe more heavily and may need to stop for a rest; the obstinate jar is either handed to a younger person, or we dig out the special jar-opening clamp or we cheat and puncture the jar lid thus releasing the vacuum. In the autumn of life, physical prowess diminishes. So let's be sure to seek spiritual strength, knowing God is faithful to that search. Moreover he rewards us as we live in him. Paul, having admitted outward decay, counterbalances that in 2 Corinthians 4:16: 'Yet inwardly we are being renewed day by day.'

There are similar sentiments in Isaiah 46:4: 'Even to your old age and grey hairs I am he, I am he who will sustain you. I have made you and I will carry you; I will sustain you and I will rescue you.' I value the four verbs in that second sentence. His 'making' of us has shaped our past and the times of 'carrying' offer hope for the future. Not only that, we can be 'sustained' in the paths that are good. We can even be 'rescued' from the bad or dangerous ones. We may get weak, we may stand into danger or folly, but they are not the end of the story of God's dealings with us.

Scripture, autumnal fruit and frailty

Don't imagine that the Bible's addressing of older age deals only in remedial advice to ward off the onset of negative factors. Though autumn is a time when the leaves fall off the trees, it is also a season of harvest, of fruit that has come to fruition. Here is expectation of positives that grow. Tina English, writing about the church's ministry among older people, faces down widespread negative views of older age: 'Many people view old age as the winter of life, but I think much of it is the autumn: a time of fruitfulness.'[7] She roots that in Psalm 92:12–14.

I thought the same, and I find in retirement it is particularly encouraging to read Psalm 92:14: 'They will still bear fruit in old age, they will stay fresh and green.' What a lovely thought that, in our elder years, others meeting us can sense a person who is still fresh and green. I guess we won't come across as 'hip and trendy', know the latest slang or be up to date with developments in the digital world. But there can be a light in the eyes, a loving attention to the other person, a readiness to listen and talk, a willingness to continue to learn – in all those ways there is 'life in the old dog yet'.

The context of Psalm 92 makes clear that this blessing comes with conditions. This is the destiny of 'the righteous' and those who 'flourish in the courts of our God... proclaiming, "the Lord is upright; he is my Rock"' (vv. 12–14). How we live and how we relate to God are the roots of a fruitfulness that can be observed in our lives. We meet the same dynamics in the words of Jesus in John 15 about the vine and fruit, with its core message – abide in me. A similar dynamic occurs in Paul's vocabulary about the fruits of the Spirit, who takes up dwelling within us.

The repeated, intertwined themes within this book are that autumn is characterised by both fruit and falling leaves. Both notes are sounded, in passing, in Zechariah 8 and its unpacking of the characteristics of God's return to Jerusalem and its rebuilt temple. Verse 4 comments on the old living safely there: 'Once again men and women of *ripe* old age will sit in the streets of Jerusalem, each of them with *cane* in hand because of their age' (emphasis added). Ripe is a term linked to fruitfulness. How much better to be an older person who is ripe, rather than crusty or crabby. The canes, which they do need to grasp, testify to diminishing powers, and yet thanks to the cane, these elderly still have some mobility, to get out into the streets and sit in the sun and exude ripeness.

This both/and reality – of spiritual significance together with physical weakness – occurs also in 2 Corinthians 4, as we saw earlier, though its application is not just to those of us in our older years. First thing in the morning and stiffly getting out of bed, some of us are reminded that 'wasting away' is going on. When our minds and bodies exhibit signs of vulnerability then 'jars of clay' is a pertinent reminder of our frailty and transience. At the same time, inward renewal can be under way. How strange! Fischer wrote: 'A central paradox accompanies ageing. Interior awareness often becomes richer while physical abilities slowly lessen.'[8] Is this a part of God's power being made perfect in weakness?

I sniff both fruit and frailty in another text: 'To him who is able to keep you from stumbling and to present you before his glorious presence without fault and with great joy' (Jude 24). The first clause is not to be read as a guarantee that we won't ever trip and break a hip or a promise that our future life will not require the aid of a stick or walking frame. Moral and spiritual falling and glory are its concern. Yet I link these two to our perennial frailty and the hope of ultimate fruitfulness. I'm glad too that being described as 'without fault' is not the total sum of the benefits. Mere moral rectitude or legal righteousness is but a Pharisaic accomplishment. The gift of 'great joy' suggests that, beyond moral blamelessness, there will be for us a deeper gratitude, a profound thankfulness, a joy from important relationships, an amazement at all Jesus has both done for us, but also in us and with us.

In that spirit we can read becoming 'without fault' not as indicating an external moral triumph but the arrival of an internal spiritual change. I have always been drawn to the sentiments of 1 John 3:2: 'When Christ appears, we shall be like him, for we shall see him as he is.' Somehow coming into the presence of Christ will transform us. C.S. Lewis likened this change to statues coming to life. In his best-known Narnia story, *The Lion, the Witch and the Wardrobe*, the resurrected Aslan breathes on the creatures turned to cold stone in the courtyard of the White Witch's castle. Colour flows into them and life returns to them. For us, and in us, ultimately frailty will be replaced, not just by fruitfulness, but by fabulous finality. By the gift of the one who on the cross said, 'It is finished' (John 19:30) – meaning accomplished – so too being completed or 'finished' will be true for us. The divine image will be fully restored in resurrected humanity. So how do we engage with these themes? What is our response?

Knowing, trusting, believing and hoping

I've been pondering the differences between these four words and how they play out in living the Christian life, not least in our autumn of life with its fruit and frailty. My present understanding is that the four related words represent different levels of certainty.

Knowing is the most certain of them all. For example, in everyday life, I know that the world is round, that two and two always make four, and even that I am sitting at my PC typing this. This is the world of facts. We also use 'know' to mean direct lived experience. It is this second sense that comes into play when we talk of 'knowing God'. It draws on a Hebrew relational usage of the word 'knowing' that I summarise as being in close, even intimate, relationship with someone else. This 'knowing' is itself a consequence of something else. An example in the Old Testament comes from Exodus 6:2–7. Because of the deliverance by God from slavery in Egypt, the Israelites would know him as 'the Lord your God'. We do well to consciously remember times of God's clear intervention in our lives: events like baptism, a conversion story, if we have one, and for some ordination. We may have memories of a healing, of guidance that was obvious at the time, or which became clear with hindsight.

In the New Testament, 'knowing' is a strong theme in John's gospel. The word 'know' occurs 83 times, whereas in Luke there are but 39 examples, 33 in Matthew and 25 in the shortest gospel, Mark. Scrolling through the Johannine usage shows the word is used to express the summit of the journey to knowledge of who Jesus is. This is true of the Samaritans of Sychar (4:42), following what the woman at the well had told them. It applies to the disciples themselves (6:69; 16:30). At a yet deeper level this knowing is a reflection of the ceaseless knowing between the Father and the Son (8:55; 10:15). So to know Jesus is to know the Father (14:7), of which the consequence is to know both Jesus and eternal life (17:3). There is a level of spiritual certainty transmitted through transformative encounter with Jesus Christ. Classically, evangelicals described this difference of level of meeting and relating as being between knowing about God and actually knowing him.

Trusting comes next. It's less definite than knowledge, for it contains an element of risk and uncertainty. I trust that my wife and children love me. I trust that when I put my foot on the car brake pedal it will slow down and stop. But then, my relations might be pretending and just putting up with me, and the brake fluid might have run out. Trust is action based on belief, and in that sense it is stronger than belief for it puts belief into practice. Baptism services and some other creedal statements begin: 'I believe *and trust* in God the Father Almighty.' The trust amplifies my involvement and it goes further than belief. It both relies upon belief but goes beyond it. Peter believed Jesus was calling him out of the fishing boat, but it was trust that got him out of the boat.

So next in this order comes *believing*. In the Christian tradition believing is more than fancy. A person could say 'I believe that there are little green men called leprechauns', but we rightly dismiss such statements as delusion or so much hot air. The people of God have always been encouraged to believe because of some level of evidence from the past. In the Old Testament this is rooted in the call of the patriarchs, the exodus and then the return from exile. In the New Testament it resides in Jesus' birth, life, ministry, claims, death and resurrection as well as the bestowal of the Spirit. Today, those first-century events are not scientifically or logically provable, but there is reasonable historical evidence for Jesus and his resurrection that could convince an open-minded jury. These two factors – a person and an event – were the heart of the earliest Christian witness. The key events around Jesus are then believed, and they are confirmed in spiritual experience.

Last in my line comes *hoping*. It's a word less strong than belief. As I began writing, a number of people were saying of the men's football World Cup, 'I hope England will win.' That made sense, even if the French team eventually proved it wasn't going to happen. If they had said, 'I believe England will win', they wouldn't have been using that word in the Christian sense; they would just be trying to reassure themselves. And if they had said, 'I know England will win', even then, we would have detected inflated hope, false claims and misuse of language. Hope comes last because it is dependent upon belief. Our belief, and the trust that follows, in the incarnation and resurrection of Jesus is the basis of hope, as Paul teases out in 1 Corinthians 15.

These four words also engage with different aspects of time. True knowledge is the exception. It spans the past, present and future. Two and two making four is timeless, as is the Johannine portrayal of the knowledge between Father and Son. The other three have a focus within time.

Trust is sharpest in the present; it is about how I act in practice. Do I dive into the swimming pool trusting the water will break my fall? Yes, it worked last time, but now is the crunch point and existential question. Similarly, do I trust now that God is guiding me and values me?

Belief, in the Christian sense, as I have already shown, has its roots in the past so that it may operate in the present and be the basis for trust.

Hope is different and looks to the future. It is to a degree uncertain because that future has not yet happened, and it may turn out differently to what we hoped. Hope is also only for this life.

In heaven, hope and belief will be both fulfilled but also redundant. As I read it, when Paul says faith, hope and love remain (1 Corinthians 13:13), he means that is true across this life, for he has just said that tongues, prophecy and 'knowledge' will disappear when perfection comes. We shall find that our trust has been vindicated. Trust is a word connected to enduring, loving relationships. Yet in heaven I guess trust will not need to endure, because it is now fortified in that 'I shall know fully, even as I am fully known' (v. 12) and we shall see Jesus as he is (1 John 3:2). What will last forever is love, for it is in God, comes from God and is now perfected in us.

I also found it significant to realise that belief, hope and trust are not qualities that are listed as fruits of the Spirit in Galatians 5:22–23: 'love, joy, peace, forbearance, kindness, goodness, faithfulness, gentleness and self-control'. Why is there that list of highly desirable attributes and not the three I mentioned just now? My guess is that those listed as fruits of the Spirit are what they say on the tin. They are of the Spirit. They are all qualities that exist in God, and they flow out from him, both in relationship with him and in the mystery that God the Spirit indwells us. Be connected to God and indwelt by him and these qualities will begin to emerge, like blossom as the first stage of growing fruit on a tree. Now, as with that analogy, blossom can be blighted by frost and fruit can be attacked by wasps. That spiritual process and progress is sadly a contested one, but part of the Christian hope is that at our own resurrections the fruiting process will be completed and the image of God fully restored.

Why are these desirable qualities – belief, hope and trust – not in the list of fruits? Because they are responses we make; they are not qualities that God needs or possesses. He knows, therefore, he has no need of belief or hope, nor even of trust that everything might work out well in the end. These qualities belong to another list; they are spiritual muscles that we are to exercise. For them to be growing in our lives, we have some responsibility. There is a consistent biblical call for us to play our part to grow in trust, hope and faith. When stilling the storm, Jesus describes the disciples as 'You of little faith' (Matthew 8:26). Conversely a number of times he says to those who have just been healed: 'Your faith has healed you.'

On trust, consider Jesus' words: 'Don't be troubled. Trust in God. Trust also in me' (John 14:1, CEB). The task to trust is ours; the basis for trust is his. On hope, Paul in Romans 5:3–4 teaches about our involvement: it is through suffering that perseverance comes, which, in turn, produces character, 'and character, hope'. This fact – that arriving at hope can be both sure and also hard work comes out in 1 Timothy 4:9–10: 'This is a trustworthy saying that deserves full acceptance. That is why we labour and strive, because we have put our hope in the living God.' Our part and God's help is also evidenced in Hebrews 10:23: 'Let us hold unswervingly to the hope we profess, for he who promised is faithful.'

In this life we shall have to work at trust, belief and hope. In the next life we shall know. Tournier tells the story of a 90-year-old dying patient with whom he had a deep spiritual bond: 'I found her at peace and serene. She said: "I am ready to go on living, and I am ready to die. At last, I am going to know."'[9]

In our autumns how contented should we be?

The word 'contentment' does not appear very often in scripture, but I found its uses were instructive.

Some instances are not that helpful. Take Job 36:11: 'If they obey and serve him, they will spend the rest of their days in prosperity and their years in contentment.' However, these words are spoken by Elihu, and it is not certain in Job whether God approves of his opinions. It also reflects the Old Testament view that the blessings of God must come in this life, for there was no other. Even then, having obeyed and served God, Job struggled with Elihu's view.

More helpful is the picture drawn by Psalm 131:2: 'I have calmed and quietened myself, I am like a weaned child with its mother; like a weaned child I am content.' It speaks of interpersonal and emotional, rather than physical or material, contentment. Moreover, did you notice that this contentment was learnt over time, not simply received or given?

That necessity of *learning* how to arrive at the state of being content stands out from Paul's comments in Philippians 4:12:

> I know what it is to be in need, and I know what it is to have plenty. I have learned the secret of being content in any and every situation, whether well fed or hungry, whether living in plenty or in want.

How helpful that he calls it a 'secret'. Secrets don't lie around in plain sight. We therefore should not be unduly discouraged if it at times we find that contentment is elusive, not yet discovered or slips from our grasp. I think we can also read this text to infer that only when you have lived through the good and the bad times does the secret show its face. As perverse human beings, it is not difficult to be discontent when all is well. But only when we have lived the bad times do we know if we have unearthed this secret. Bear in mind, too, that the contents of this named contentment are physical, edible and monetary. In a world today of excess, existing curiously together with considerable uncertainty, we do well to ponder and live out that equanimity and learn its secret.

Hebrew 13:5 offers some base for the secret: 'Be content with what you have, because God has said, "Never will I leave you; never will I forsake you."' This 'having' also deals once more with our attitude to possessions and God's provision of them, just as Jesus in the sermon on the mount bids us to turn away from fears about what we will be able to eat or to wear. In connection with material things, living out the view that 'enough is enough' is quite apposite for retirement when, for most, their income falls from when they were employed full-time. But neither of these two helpful passages commends contentment with our present level of spiritual maturity.

Then 1 Timothy 6:6 adds that crucial factor: 'But godliness with contentment is great gain.' I begin by noting that it is gained, it is active, neither passive nor automatic. A further factor is to ask which of these two qualities, godliness or contentment, is the one that is to be gained. The verses that follow underline that the contentment is to do with things. Food and clothing are specifically named. That emphasis is coupled to the perspective that we were born with nothing and take none of our possessions with us at death. Paul goes on further to castigate the love of money as a root of all kinds of evil. He does not say that is true of money itself. Today this verse sits well with the ecological imperative that many of us in the so-called developed world need to take a route to simplicity of life, in which the perspective of contentment would be very helpful. But this verse is no mandate to put one's spiritual feet up or to rest on any spiritual laurels. Indeed, Paul urges the very opposite in verses 11–12, which include a call to pursue righteousness, to fight the good fight of faith and to take hold of eternal life. That takes me to the next question.

Should Christians make spiritual progress and have helpful discontent?

What biblical basis is there for thinking Christians are intended to make spiritual progress and to refuse to let legitimate contentment with what we have in life degenerate into illegitimate spiritual self-satisfaction? Is 'progress' in the Christian life something to aim for – or not?

I have met people who argue against such discontent. I recall the slight annoyance of a friend during a small group meeting at my attempts to express the desire to go deeper, to pursue Christ-likeness, and I was urged to be more content.

In 1986 Roger Pooley and Philip Seddon compiled *The Lord of the Journey*, a book full of thoughtful quotes from down the ages on themes in Christian spirituality. Section 5 takes the topic of progress. It begins by registering suspicion about making 'progress'. Several objections are noted. Is it too like evolutionist notions, in which progress is always onwards and upwards? Is it perfectionist, meaning that it is possible and desirable that we get beyond fallibility, sin and pride? Does it create grades of Christians and threaten the equality across the priesthood of all believers? One could add: does it begin to add 'our own works' to justification by faith alone?[10]

What we do and what God does is taken up by David Cole, otherwise Brother Cassian, in *The BRF Book of 365 Bible Reflections*. He puts the case that the Christian mystics resisted the notion of striving to be 'good Christians', because we are not called to transform ourselves, at which we will fail. Rather we are called to be transformed by the divine work within us. But how? He writes that we become ready to receive transformation 'through contemplation: the practice of stilling our inner being, creating the inner environment for the Divine to work on us, within us'.[11]

I concur that contemplation has a part to play and that any progress we do make is in part due to the work of the Christ and the Spirit. Yet I find a less passive and more active role for us to play across the New Testament. I've tried to find at least one example from each author. Some verses and their images from life have some sense of a healthy discontent leading to a desire to go further; others just evince a positive desire to make progress.

In Matthew 7:24, Jesus likens hearing and obeying Christ's teachings to a person building on the right foundations. To build on something sounds like making progress, and it's an active role.

Luke 13:24 contains even more active words as our part in the journey forward: 'Make every effort to enter through the narrow door.'

John 15:1–16 contains a progression. Jesus speaks first of vine branches with no fruit being cut out, then of pruning branches to be more fruitful, later of those with much fruit and finally fruit that will last. I was entertained that these four images occur in verses 2, 4, 8 and 16, but that mathematical progression is purely accidental. Our role is not in doubt; we are chosen to bear fruit progressively.

Both Paul and the writer of Hebrews use the human analogy of children who need to progress from consuming milk to eating solid food (1 Corinthians 3:1–2; Hebrews 5:11–14). They should be discontent to remain at the milk stage. The latter passage applies this to becoming able to distinguish good from evil or, as we might say, gaining a moral compass. His readers should not be content not to have that ability. Paul prays for his friends 'that your love may abound more and more in knowledge and depth of insight' (Philippians 1:9). Whenever there is a lack of love in his churches, he urges progress.

2 Peter 1:5–8 urges 'make every effort to add to your faith'. The progression of what is listed to be added moves beyond having faith to growing in goodness, knowledge, self-control, perseverance, godliness, kindness and love. These are described as qualities to be possessed 'in increasing measure'. It's quite a list, even without them increasing. Our responsibility for making progress is unmistakeable and extensive.

Jude simply says to build 'yourselves up in your most holy faith' (v. 20). That's down to us, but balanced by verse 24, that God 'is able to keep you from stumbling and to present you before his glorious presence without fault and with great joy'.

If a last word is needed to argue that making progress is expected and normal, let it come from the letters to the seven churches of Revelation. To each young church penetrating critique is made, change for the better is clearly expected, but always coupled with the promises

of gifts of God to assist that progress. It seems to me from that selection that progress as disciples of Jesus is widely expected, considered
normal and there should be healthy discontent if no attempt is made.

There are also verses that expect a transformation, later called by the
Greek Fathers *Theosis*, a term for a process by which we become more
like God, morally and relationally. Ephesians 4:24 refers to 'the new
self, created to be like God in true righteousness and holiness'. How
does this occur? The verse names some qualities God alone brings,
and we can be content that he does so. But the wider context of that
part of the chapter, verses 22–32, contains a mixture of factors. There
is receiving what God alone does, namely that he *creates* the new self,
but also that we are instructed to *put off* the old self. Verses 25–31 spell
out plenty of elements of what that former fallen life looked like. And
we are instructed to *put on* the new self. It's an analogy drawn from
clothing. It reads as though God is its manufacturer and tailor, but we
are the wearers and play our part in dressing that way, wearing what
God provides. Where that process is incomplete, some healthy discontent leading to action is appropriate. Consider 4:32—5:2:

> Be kind and compassionate to one another forgiving each other,
> just as in Christ God forgave you. Follow God's example, therefore,
> as dearly loved children and live a life of love.

Let's relate this expectation of progress to the book's main theme of
living our autumns. I want to explore links between the two sides of
the autumn of life and what I choose to call a *passive* contentment and
an *active* discontentment in how we live out our Christian lives. I see
virtues in both words, 'passive' and 'active'. Neither word is intended in
a negative sense. By passive, I do not mean complacent, but trusting;
by active, I do not mean manic, but purposeful and responsible. The
two sides of autumn are, first, its harvest and beauty and, second, the
falling leaves, diminishing temperature and shortening hours of light.

I suggest that the fruitfulness and harvest of autumn in our lives link
to 'a trusting passivity' in our spirituality. This seems to fit with the

well-known passage of Galatians 5 and its list of the fruit of the Spirit. That image suggests fruiting occurs as a natural, or here one might say supernatural, process. To have the Holy Spirit within us will lead normally to the growth of the nine moral qualities listed as three delightful triads: love, joy and peace; then patience, kindness and goodness; and bringing up the rear faithfulness, gentleness and self-control. What beautiful qualities they are, worthy of any autumnal scene. But, and it's a big but, we probably know in ourselves, or sadly observe in other Christians, that some of these fruits are clearly absent or, if present, rather manky. Why should that be? Could that be that we are blocking or resisting such development of our character and being.

So is trusting passivity enough? I see something similarly complex going on in Jesus' teaching in John 15. Yes, the vine provides the sap that leads to the fruit, just as the Holy Spirit does in our lives. Jesus is unswerving in that assertion: 'No branch can bear fruit by itself… apart from me you can do nothing' (John 15:4–5). Conversely, 'If you remain in me and I in you, you will bear much fruit' (v. 5). Other versions prefer 'abide' to 'remain'. Both words are more passive than active. Even the pruning mentioned in the chapter is done to us, rather than by us. Yet the overall passage does contain a call to action, summarised as obeying Jesus commands, especially to practice a love which at times will need to be sacrificial. That's active language not passive.

I also see links between the falling leaves, a picture not utterly different to the pruning process in John 15, and a healthy kind of active discontent. In the autumn of our lives there is active inner work to do, to process the changes and losses from an identity based around our employed lives and status towards a stripped-back identity centred in who we are. Reverting to the arboreal image, it is a matter of learning and accepting that we are no longer summer trees in full leaf, but rather we are becoming naked autumn trees with what we truly are becoming more visible. Hopefully that will reveal strong trunks and healthy branches, which can also be splendid in their own way. Yet the journey to whom we truly are, when activity and some abilities are stripped away, is very likely to reveal where we still need to grow in grace and virtue. Here healthy discontent may spur us to an active pursuit of holiness and Christlikeness.

I love the modesty of the missionary William Carey (1761–1834), writing to his son about having his life written up. Referring to a possible biographer he wrote: 'If he give me credit for being a plodder he will describe me justly. Anything beyond that will be too much, I can plod.'[12] It seems a maxim of the spiritual journey that those who have made the most progress tend to be those who know how much further there is still to go. Get closer to God and the gap (in all sorts of ways) between us and God may seem to widen. There is also active mental and volitional work to be done as our human faculties diminish. How we process that set of losses well, accepting the change with grace, is work indeed.

In first beginning to write this subsection I became aware of the thought that in the spiritual life we need to honour both passive contentment and active discontentment. I am thinking of biblical passages such as John 14:27 – 'Peace I leave with you; my peace I give to you... Do not let your hearts be troubled and do not be afraid' – and almost its application by Paul: 'Let the peace of Christ rule in your hearts... let the message of Christ dwell among you richly' (Colossians 3:15–16). This dynamic, of 'letting' something from beyond us occur, crops up in the Northumbria Community midday prayer: 'Let the beauty of the Lord our God be upon us.' Letting is active in that we have to decide to do this. It draws on at least a little discontent that I realise I need to do this and that I can't make the results happen myself. And it is passive, for we don't make the result of the letting happen and it involves being content that God can make these differences. A homely illustration of this duality is like deciding to sit out and get a sensible sun tan. I make the active move to get out of the house and am passive before the sun's rays.

In summary, I notice the warnings about the dangers linked to the ideas that we should be making progress. Not least of these perils is either a debilitating sense of failure or a misplaced sense of pride. Nevertheless my trawl through the New Testament leaves me convinced that God does ask progress in the Christian life of us all. It will take a passive trust that, by remaining in the vine and being indwelt by the Spirit, inner transformation does occur and our autumns of life can be fruitful. In the autumn of our lives, the leaves will fall and the naked tree trunk, of who we truly are, will appear; for that trunk to be beautiful it will take the active pursuit of spiritual progress, in which a healthy discontent will have its part.

Application questions

- How did you react to Tournier's comment that it is not that people die because they get ill, it is that 'they fall ill because they have to die'?

- How useful to God do you still think you are? What sense of ongoing vocation do you have?

- How are you finding living with your own fruitfulness *and* frailty?

- Jot down what you think you should be contented with and what place spiritual discontent should have.

8

God and
a question of trust

What can we trust God for?

Emilie Griffin, seeking to make sense of a long life and how to live out
its latter years, writes: 'I think it's all about trust.'[1] I agree with her, yet
I find I have to put the further question: 'Exactly what do we trust God
for?' That, in turn, depends on how we best understand in what way
God interacts with us and his world. What is promised and what is not
included? I can only open up big issues and give the outline of my own
present understanding over whether everything that does happen was
meant to occur. In writing this chapter, I am painfully aware of being a
frail, fallen, feeble human trying to explain how God operates. In prayer
I've confessed the danger of potential arrogance. I hope my readers
may be kind to me in return. I hope this chapter will enable each of
you to place yourself within the options I'll unpack.

By way of an introduction, consider two different and irreconcilable
views that are anchored in two different translations of Romans 8:28.
The NIV has: 'We know that in all things God works for the good of
those who love him, who have been called according to his purpose.'
The alternative translation, found in the 1611 Authorised Version and
the NRSV, is: 'We know that all things work together for good for those
who love God, who are called according to his purpose.' These are
rather different understandings; which of them is nearer the truth?

I remember, as a young man, singing the three-verse song with the first line 'I do not know what lies ahead'. Lines from its ebullient chorus confidently asserted that nothing simply happened, for God had planned absolutely everything. This sentiment was intended to give us confidence and assurance. Beneath it are big questions. Is everything that happens planned and meant to be, because God 'foreknew' and 'predestined' it? Or are those terms, found in Romans 8:29–30, only applicable to God's choice of those called by him to salvation? Or again, are things quite different, that God reacts creatively to the bad things that just happen, seeking to bring good despite them?

Such questions are not details of technical theology. They affect how we live out our faith. Forty years ago, Marion Ashton wrote to help Christians living with inner mental tensions to find what she called in her book 'a mind at ease'. She suggested there were three enemies to an infected mind – fear, frustration and resentment – and these three could be combated respectively by faith, hope and love. Writing about combatting frustration with hope she clearly adopts the viewpoint of the second translation of Romans 8:28:

> Frustration with circumstances is expelled only by real faith in the sovereignty of God and by love which is willing to submit to His will. Faith in the fact that *all* things are working together for good to those that love God. A faith that admits no second causes but which accepts every circumstance as being allowed by him.[2]

That view, and the song I cited, might comfort a convinced Calvinist undergoing frustration. To many others the implications of this view are intolerable. At the micro level, it could be taken to mean that every disaster or tragedy in a person's life is part of God's fore-ordained, predestined intention for them. A softer view, like Ashton's, says: God knew such adverse things would happen but it's not that he planned it that way, rather he was content to *allow* that it be so, knowing the outcome would work out for good for them. This second way of thinking is known as God's permissive will.

I don't easily accept either interpretation of my own father's premature death by drowning at the age of 42, which by being on that beach I watched when I was seven. I still do not know why God didn't prevent that or why he allowed it, but I have learnt to live in peace with the not knowing. However, I can and do thank God that I see many good influences that came alongside our bereaved family and which pretty directly led us all to discover a living relationship with God that went beyond habitual church attendance. Nor has this first view of God, as some eternal and irresistible planner, ever made much sense to me of the death of our good friends' delightful talented daughter at 18 in a head-on car accident many years ago. Nor is her tragic 'untimely death' the only one that I could cite.

At the macro level, the view that 'everything is planned' would have us believe that the Holocaust and every other major piece of ethnic cleansing were predestined by God. For me one of these is not just a piece of unfortunate history. I am half-German and have relatives who fought in Hitler's armies. Another relative, my German cousin Wolfgang, writes as a psychotherapist about the national sense of lasting guilt with which Germany has a convoluted relationship. Staying with him in Berlin last year we walked through the sobering Holocaust memorial, and we walked streets down which Hitler had strutted. In addition, my school had many Jewish pupils and I grew up having Jewish friends. You will understand the existence of the Holocaust is for me no mere academic question of faith. Moving to the second view that 'God allows evil' does reduce that sting of God's direct responsibility, but not the dimension that he foreknew such events and did not intervene sufficiently decisively to stop them. So what God knows and what action God takes are live issues.

Four stances

I want to set out what I see as a spectrum of four different ways in which Christians have seen a connected set of issues. The issues are big because they are about more than the difficult problem of evil. Each stance seeks to give us a view, most of them claiming explicit support from the Bible, of what God is like and how best we understand his dealings with us. The labels of the four stances are: Calvinism, Arminianism, Open Theism and Process Theology. I can but give headlines of each stance. I know too that in some cases later followers developed views of the founding figures beyond what they themselves held. It is really difficult to avoid drawing theological cartoons of each one, and this book isn't the place for detailed pictures of each stance, not least because each 'stance' isn't monochrome and contains a spectrum of outlooks. In addition, people today unknowingly borrow across these four stances and at various points the stances overlap. I only dare to offer this material because learning how best to live by trust in God is so central to what this book is about. I add that the question of God and the problem of evil is not the only factor that motivates me. I want to know God better and how better to live in response of trust to him. So let's begin.

What does God know and what is he like?

The Calvinist holds that God knows everything and is all powerful; he is omniscient and omnipotent. He is perfect, so any change from that would be imperfect. Because he is unchangeable, he is not influenced by events; he neither suffers nor feels pain; he is 'impassable'. He is outside time, predetermining and knowing the future already. Knowing everything, God chose who would become Christians and that choice will be fulfilled. This set of views did not originate with Calvin, but is also found in the thought of Augustine, whom Calvin valued and quoted extensively.

The Arminian concurs with God being all-knowing and eternal, including knowing the future, but says God is influenced by the exercise of human free will, including whether God's grace is accepted or not. Jesus died not just for the chosen few, but for all, though not all accept that gift. The human will has a part to play in determining the future. God is unchangeable but, by his choice, not in absolute control.

Open Theism is less well known so needs more explaining. It is a significant variant from Arminianism, for it holds that God only knows what can be known. That statement needs unpacking in several ways. God does know the past and the present perfectly, and knows the possibilities within the future. But the future is partially settled and partially unsettled. It is not fixed and is genuinely open, hence this stance's label. Here's a thought. The past is past; it no longer exists. All we now have is various expressions of memory and records. We live in the continuing experience of the present. We can anticipate what the future may bring and even plan for that. But maybe the future, like the past, is a concept, not a reality. Because it doesn't yet exist, it can't be known in the same way as the past or present, even for God. As Open Theist writer Clark Pinnock says of God: 'He remembers the past, interacts with the present and anticipates the future.'[3]

Intimately connected to such thoughts, Open Theists believe that God is 'timelessly everlasting'; he always has been and always will be, but he is not 'e-ternal', meaning outside time. Problems with these views are several: does it make 'time' greater than God? What about parts of scripture that do predict factors within the future? Are we putting very human limits on what God can know? It's all deep heady stuff. Yet there is some biblical evidence for this open view of the future. There are passages that portray God as changing his mind or course of action, including God's grief and change of plan for humanity in the story of Noah (Genesis 6:6–8) and his change of mind and outcome after Moses bargains with him following the idolatrous making of the golden calf (Exodus 32:9–14). This is one of two passages that changed the mind of author Dallas Willard to the belief that prayer can change God's mind.[4] Or again, the prophet Jonah is vexed that God changes his mind over the fate of Nineveh (Jonah 4:1–4). Jeremiah was asked to notice the potter starting again with a misshapen pot and God described himself there as reconsidering the good he intended to do (Jeremiah 18:1–10).

What then of predictive passages in scripture? The Old Testament ones are set within the context of covenants between Israel and God. Deuteronomy 7—8 lays out the essential nature of the Mosaic covenant.

God has chosen his people (7:7) out of his faithful love. The people are to keep to its conditions, which will lead to blessing (7:12–13). Conversely, forgetting God and his ways will lead to their destruction (8:19–20). The outcome of covenants is genuinely open and the future not settled. Hence at points later, God, speaking to the prophets, expresses uncertainty over what his disobedient people will do and whether they would return to him and his ways (Jeremiah 3:7; 26:3). Ezekiel 12:3 also has God saying, 'Perhaps they will understand.' In the New Testament, Jesus is not precise about the future fall of Jerusalem and, as we know, fulfilment of his promises of his glorious return have been delayed nearly 2,000 years, as have Paul's hopes (Romans 9—11) for the wholesale saving of Israel. Predictive texts turn out to be more open, less fixed and more conditional than some realise.

Less controversially, Open Theists insist God is a relational being. Biblical images of him such as husband or father to his people illustrate that. Jesus speaking of God as *Abba* epitomises a relational view. God is described as entering genuine relationships, with qualities such as love, patience and compassion. Yes, God is unchangeable, but what is unchanging is his faithful and loving character. He is also affected by his relations with us, which includes his own suffering. God is recorded as grieved over making Saul king (1 Samuel 15:35). Or, as Ephesians 4:30 says, the Spirit can be grieved by us.[5] Jesus weeps over Jerusalem and at the tomb of Lazarus. Both Father and Son do suffer, shown supremely by the cross, and in their ongoing caring relations with us. All this comes from God being relational.

In his relations with us, God has freely chosen to limit his power, and there are things even God cannot do. Some are logical and trivial impossibilities, such as making a square circle. More important, God cannot undo the past, though he can work with its consequences. And most importantly, he cannot make us love him, for that would destroy the nature of love. That's how he has chosen to set up the reality of his world. As C.S. Lewis put it: 'Why did God give them free will? Because free will, though it makes evil possible, is also the only thing that makes possible any love or goodness or joy worth having.'[6]

All three stances described so far believe in God's revelation of himself and seek to be a biblical theology, but they draw on different texts to supply evidence for their conclusions and set aside others that don't fit.

Process Theology has its source in reason and philosophy, developed from the so-called 'process philosophy' of Alfred North Whitehead (1861–1947), most notably by Charles Hartshorne. It was constructed in the face of the considerable problem of evil. In its view God is not all powerful; he does exist within time or he is seen as co-eternal and interdependent with the world and has to react to events in it, hence the word 'process'.

What about evil, free will, the future and the end of time?

Because God is all-knowing and almighty, the Calvinist holds either that evil is part of what has been planned for or that it is allowed, however grim or ghastly that may seem. Human free will and the sovereignty of God are understood as a paradox; they are two contradicting factors, for each of which there is evidence, but how both can be true at once is a mystery. If God has predestined everything that happens, including who will and won't be Christians, do we really have free will? Yet our experience tells us we do have it; moreover God holds us responsible for how we use it. There is confidence that God has completely settled the future. It is predestined. Beyond Romans 8:28, the Calvinist could cite Ephesians 1:11:

> In him we were also chosen, having been predestined according to the plan of him who works out everything in conformity with the purpose of his will.

The Arminian agrees that God 'allows' evil, but it is to be resisted. Free will is held to be genuine and God works with, round and despite it. The future and the end are secure, but how exactly that is delivered is affected by human free will and prayer.

The Open Theist, as unpacked above, sees both free will and love as crucial in the relationship with God. Only freely given love is love. God risks seeking that kind of open partnership with us.[7] Because of this, the world is seen as an arena of spiritual battle, in which there are casualties and in which evil will run its course, but only to the end. The psalmists' prayers of lament and despair are part of that battle, as are the questioning attitudes in the book of Ecclesiastes. The puzzle of the relative inactivity of God in the face of evil remains an issue even for Open Theists. Yet they insist that creation always was an open project, so the future is genuinely open and only partially settled. The predictive passages in scripture are understood to express God's intentions, not that he already exists in that future. God does know what he wants the future to be and knows that his intention will finally prevail.

Process Theology is critical of all such views of God's power, noting his lack of intervention in the widespread suffering, misery and evil in the world. It lacks any biblical hope of certain victory.

Romans 8:28, God's intervention, evangelism and prayer

The Calvinist reads Romans 8:28 as saying everything does work for good. The Arminian and Open Theist take the other translation that 'in everything God is at work' (though at times it can feel like 'despite everything'), and Process Theology almost sees God as the victim of events.

The Calvinist believes God intervenes only as he has already pre-planned, so intercessory prayer never changes God's mind; its purpose is to change ours, to align our wills with God's. That point about alignment of the will is worth prizing, illustrated supremely in Jesus' prayer in Gethsemane. For the Calvinist, evangelism is another paradox. God has decided and knows who will be saved, and his plan for that is irresistible. Some in past centuries even argued evangelism was therefore unnecessary, though contemporary Calvinists see it as biblically commanded and so it should be practised.

In contrast, the Arminian wants us to pray as though God's plans can be furthered. Why else pray 'Your kingdom come, your will be done on earth', they say? Why pray for inspiration or guidance if we have no part to play in shaping the future? Why pray for healing or a person to come to faith, unless God does intervene?

The Open Theist concurs that in all these ways prayer can change things. Somehow, possibilities are modified or opened, as illustrated by Abraham's bargaining prayers for Sodom (Genesis 18) or Moses' for the people (Exodus 32). God can and at times does intervene, though as C.S. Lewis says, in a world created to be stable, miracles 'should be extremely rare'.[8] Conversely lack of faith or prayer can hinder desirable results that could have occurred. Evangelism is needed, but like God dealing with us, is never to be coercive.

The Process Theology approach is set further back and expects no intervention, but commends that praying can bring peace of mind. Evangelism for them is tinged with the stench of proselytising and coercion.

Overlaps and profound differences

The first three stances share orthodoxy in that they believe God reveals himself to us in the three persons of the Trinity. They teach that God and the world are separate and that the birth, life, death and resurrection of Jesus are central and diagnostic. Clearly the three also differ profoundly over issues within those convictions and can deny the tag of orthodoxy to one another. Process Theology differs from these basic views, and indeed rejects these key doctrinal convictions as unbelievable today. It is a so-called 'natural theology' derived from reasoning drawn from human interpretation of what can be observed.

Open Theism and Process Theology do share some instincts. They both believe that God's love is central and humans are free agents. They find the Calvinist position too static, too impersonal and detached.

They agree that God is affected by the world; he is not impassable and does not know everything about the future because of limits he has set himself. Both can welcome the start made by Arminianism, but then go further. The two differ over the basic doctrines named above and as to the authority source on which to base their convictions, biblical revelation or human reason.

Villains or heroes?

These rather black-and-white, summary categories can be simplistic and unfair. A look at what each stance seeks to safeguard may illustrate this.

The Calvinist wants to promote the sole glory, majesty, supremacy and attributes in the perfection of who God is. This stance also distrusts the self-seeking, pride and ambition of human beings, to which the grace of God, in Christ, alone is the antidote.

The Arminian also wants to honour a loving God who is more flexible than that, by whom everything is not predestined. They have a higher view of what part human beings play in responding to God's love with love, exercising faith, in growing in Christlikeness and being active in mission. More mission organisations come from Arminian than Calvinist stock.

Open Theism is a recent arrival to the party. It wants to be faithful to noticing that God is primarily revealed in scripture in relational terms and that scripture expects us to have freedom and creativity. It also claims that the previous views dismiss such relational texts about God by using reason and philosophy, not scripture. It wants the biblical, relational view of God not to be infected by the influence of Greek philosophical thinking, which deals in absolute categories, like being all-knowing, all-powerful, unable to suffer and perfect – here meaning unchangeable in any way whatever. This, they say, is not the relational, creative and wonderful God the Bible testifies to. It believes our lives do make a difference and, in friendship with God, prayer is a dialogue.

The Process Theologian wants to express a faith that relates to people who, looking round the world, don't see much evidence of an intervening God.

What might be the temptations or dangers linked to each of the four stances?

Dangers for the Calvinist position could include a triumphalism which says: 'I'm one of the elect and my salvation is guaranteed.' It can cause offence by an indifference to suffering, saying things to sufferers like, 'It was meant to be,' 'Everything is under control,' or 'God has sent it to you for good.' Thereby this view can sadly portray God as an unfeeling monster. A more subtle factor is that the Calvinist may hold their doctrine, but live differently in practice, praying as though change can occur, fighting evil, taking responsibility for their sins or being positive about human beings.

The Arminian can remain optimistic that the ultimate future is secure, but is less certain about how and when God will bring change. The principal temptation seems to be that the Arminian is vulnerable to overworking, in order to achieve what God wants or commands.

Extending that strand of thought, the Open Theist lives with deep concern, sometimes pessimism, about the present state of the world and can carry a heavy sense of responsibility in the adventure of an open prayerful partnership with God to live purposefully now and bring in the desired future. Admitting life is a tough spiritual and moral fight brings some realism.

The temptation for the believer in Process Theology may be to adopt a form of Deism, a view that teaches God created but then abandoned the world to its own devices. God is but a sympathetic responder, but never an initiator. There may even be the temptation to existential-like despair that God has no control.

What does trust in God mean for me?

Having dipped my toe in the swirling muddy waters of these four stances, I dare to tell the reader what it means for me to trust God in practice, as a person who has found the approach of Open Theism helpful, though still living with unresolved questions. Forgive the alliteration but as I've worked to distil my response, it has turned out to be a set of words all beginning with C.

I primarily trust God for his *character*, which is utterly reliable, lovingly steadfast and remarkably patient. In these attributes he demonstrates himself as unchangeable.

I also trust him within that identity for his *compassion* for whatever I face, perhaps especially when I am faced with failings, feebleness and foibles. The advent of the falling leaves of autumn makes those vulnerabilities a sharper issue. I don't know how many leaves I'll lose, or whether I will make it out of autumn into the dependency of winter, or whether I shall meet death before then. But his compassion will extend to me.

Linked to this, I trust God for his enduring and undying *companionship* through any triumphs or disasters, keeping me humble in any success and helping me ward off despair in my failures. I trust his companionship too for living the humdrum 'everyday' of the present and turning it into something deeper and meaningful.

I trust him for his *cooperation* in navigating the future, both my own and a much wider one which he longs for and works to bring from intention to reality. You have no idea how often in writing this book I have needed his cooperation!

I also trust that he is *constant*. God does not give up on me, because it is true that I am sometimes overwhelmed by this responsibility for sharing with God in living the present and even shaping bits of the future.

And most of all I trust the Father and the Spirit for *Christ*. He is the choice across the Trinity as the divine, best and sufficient way to encounter, understand and experience the reality of God. The stance taken by John's gospel is very helpful in laying down that exalted view of Christ.

As is often the case, I concur with Tournier. He grew up Calvinist but moved beyond narrow expressions of it over the importance of trust and our active, yet surrendered, place within it: 'I know that trusting God is more sure than trusting oneself; I know that trust in God can always carry us forward, impel us resolutely into adventure, despite our mistrust of ourselves.' To live a worthwhile life, he advocates that we 'place the helm of our lives… in God's hands, entrust the direction of our lives to him, confess to him our inability to direct them for ourselves… and so ask him to direct them himself.'[9]

The stance of Open Theism has helped me be more aware of this being directed by God. I am learning to be more open to his prompts, whispers and nudges. They are more frequent than I used to think. For example, I have been prompted to make what proved to be a timely phone call and warned of the imminent dangerous action of a nearby driver. These are consonant with his continuing intervening companionship and desire for cooperation with us. I am grateful for receiving lightbulb moments, such as curiously relevant books I 'happened' to glance at, and for apt messages from others. As a well-versed theological interviewee said: 'God's dealings with us are very curious.' I know I can't prove anything of this, but I sense living with more Spirit-led-incidences. My prayer for guidance and inspiration has been sharpened.

What I also value from both Arminian and Open Theism perspectives is this 'both/and' dynamic. Note the presence of two forces: *both* what we do *and* what God does. The same was going on in the latter half of the previous chapter exploring how contented we should be and whether we are to make progress. As Tournier noted, *we* surrender the helm, *he* directs the course. Yet then *we* sail on into *his* adventure for us. Jesus the compassionate, constant companion and cooperator goes with us. I do trust him for that.

How then are we to respond in the face of loss and tragedy?

It is unlikely that most of us will live through the autumn of our lives without having to face major losses. I am sobered by the fact that a number of my fellow theological college students and fellow Church Army colleagues have died in recent years. Prayer for those widowed that we know is a part of the midday intercessions I share with my wife. Should I trust God that I should be spared all that? Put more bluntly, claiming to trust God for more than he has promised isn't faith; it's folly.

Theological thought and emotional outburst

I am helped that C.S. Lewis wrote two very different books about suffering. *The Problem of Pain* is a wider, longer, careful, rational analysis, published during World War II. It presents his understanding of how things have to be if we believe in a God who wants and has chosen to live in freely given relationships of love with human beings, which necessarily includes the reality of evil and attendant suffering. God thus does not usually intervene to head off intended acts of evil, such as deflecting the assassin's bullet, for it would lead to an essentially unpredictable world without consequences, which would induce chaos and madness. Moreover, pain is a providential alarm signal of disease and of danger in a spoilt world. This book is well known.

Later, in 1961, initially anonymously, he published the narrower, more emotional and shorter book, *A Grief Observed*, describing the long, winding valley of grief following his loss of his wife to a painful drawn-out cancer. There he painfully plods across bereavement's many troughs and ridges: the bolted door of the absence of the presence of God; the sense of being an embarrassment, even a death's head, to everyone else; the redundancy of intended words of comfort, or of religious consolation; questioning whether indeed God is good; that sometimes

God has to bring pain, like the dentist must to fix our teeth; that being bereaved is a permanent marker that isn't undone; whether grief is an endless circle or a spiral, perhaps an upward one? He concludes grief and bereavement are not a state but an imperceptible process, such as with the gradual arrival of daylight that often you only notice after it has begun.[10] The headline I take from this summary is that the content of the first book doesn't answer the white-hot questions of the second one. They operate at different levels. In dealing with our own suffering and grief over the severe loss of falling leaves, we need to know both approaches and choose to listen to the appropriate one.

Emilie Griffin, in her chapter about grief, offers the following practical responses to losses: telling stories of the best of the past; keeping a prayerful journal; keeping past contacts; and not regretting the past.[11] We also now possess the classic analysis of that emotional process, with its five stages of grieving: denial, anger, bargaining, depression and acceptance. In *Autumn Gospel*, Fischer entitles her chapter 6 'Seasons of Mourning'. That choice tells me three things: she too expects mourning is part of the deal in autumn; she knows it takes time; and she knows that it can pass. In the chapter she unpacks her understanding of the grief process – as shock and disbelief, falling apart and connecting again. She adds how this progression can be supported by helpful inner attitudes and externally by others. She concludes:

> Principally that there is no answer to the great questions: illness, death, suffering, vulnerability. There is no answer but faith in Jesus Christ. That is the gratitude that leads to the cross and beyond it, to the crown.[12]

Live with the perplexing mixture

I realise all this book can do is erect a few signposts to where helpful sources such as this can be found. One hint is how to avoid what I'd call a Christian triumphalism or false optimism, yet not fall into some sort of Christian sin-ridden gloom of unending pessimism and despair.

This is not about distrusting God; rather it is seeking clarity over what he says we should trust him for. One heart-rending but helpfully honest example of being forced to face such questions is Pete Grieg's book *God on Mute*. Sometimes it can feel like this: 'Let the one who walks in the dark, who has no light, trust in the name of the Lord and rely on their God' (Isaiah 50:10).

I find it helps to think that life is necessarily a matter of living with a mixture of factors and reactions. I bumped into one expression of this in reading Rowan William's *The Dwelling of the Light*, as he reflected on transfiguration icons. He expresses that in them God clothes Jesus in a light from beyond the created world, itself an insight that this world is open to the hope of God's intervention. Yet the transfiguration is also a prelude to something darker. The Luke 9 transfiguration conversation is about Jesus' 'exodus', and he talks about his coming suffering and death. I add that the three disciples witnessing the transfiguration went quickly the next day from a touch of glory on the mountaintop to the valley of faithless failed healing (Luke 9:28–54). As Williams puts it: 'John's gospel glory culminates in the cross. A huge hope, but also a huge dose of unwelcome reality.'[13]

I remember in one parish that some people's spirituality was inescapably tied to the cross and thus focused on going through suffering. Others were so caught up in the resurrection that they saw everything as positive. I have always suspected we live with the tension that comes from the two. Let's dig a bit deeper.

Different sources, different responses

Some writers see all suffering as being linked to the cross of Christ. For example, Charles de Foucauld writes: 'The senses hold suffering in horror. Faith blesses it as a gift from the hand of Jesus, a bit of the cross which he lets us carry.'[14] Despite this being the view of an impressive recent saint and martyr, I am unconvinced. I think the New Testament only sees self-denial, as in the injunction 'Take up your cross', and persecution as being linked to the cross of Christ. These in some way are said to complete his sufferings (Philippians 3:10) or to participate in them (1 Peter 4:13).

However, there are other kinds of suffering that fall outside this. It includes having an illness, which the New Testament writers can discern as a spiritual attack or receive it as one of those things that occur in a fallen world and which are to be prayed for (James 5:18). Jesus is clear that being in an accident, like the fall of the tower of Siloam, is neither linked to sin or some redemptive meaning (Luke 13:4). Jesus is even fairly matter-of-fact about troubles coming, saying that each day has enough of its own (Matthew 6:34) and 'In this world you will have trouble. But take heart! I have overcome the world' (John 16:33). He never promised his followers an easy life. I was intrigued that a medic, one of my interviewees, said: 'The modern church avoids suffering and wants life easy, on the basis of God being loving and good, whereas suffering is part of life and God will use it, so it should be expected.' She found 1 Peter relevant and helpful.

Accordingly responding to suffering is seen by the New Testament writers as having various positive outcomes. In Romans 5:4, it leads to perseverance, character and hope. In 2 Corinthians 11—12, Paul boasts of a whole variety of sources of suffering, only some for being Christian, others arising from travel, but they all teach him to rest on the power of God. 1 Peter 1:6–7 talks of 'all kinds of trials' as a refining process leading to glory, while 4:15 also knows Christians should not act so as to deserve suffering.

A further complication related to both suffering and trust is that in the Old Testament there is an absence of distinct belief in life after death and so the blessings of God were expected to come during this life. Accordingly bold promises of protection, provision and compensation are given and they are met with praise and confident trust that all these benefits will be delivered in this life. Beware of taking these assurances at face value. The New Testament shows that life is a longer story and more complex.

Additionally there are varied sources of self-inflicted suffering. Examples are wide: from the trivial misplaced blow of the hammer and a resultant sore thumb, through making a bad decision creating a car accident, to serious health problems brought on by habits like smoking or over-eating, let alone from addictions such as gambling, drink or drugs. Is there some connection here to the chilling phrase coming three times in Romans 1: 'God gave them over' (Romans 1:24, 26, 28) to degrading habits of heart and mind? I can't see these later categories as being part of the cross-shaped sufferings of Christ. Beyond discerning what kinds of suffering we are undergoing and thus what to expect and how to respond, what else can we do?

Practising trust, gratitude and joy

I have worked with the four theological stances to explore trust issues connected with suffering and what it is biblical to trust God for. Henri Nouwen, in his classic book *The Return of the Prodigal*, advocates a response to God of living by trust and by gratitude. You may ask what has the parable of the two lost sons to do with living through one's autumn and what we can trust God for? Perhaps nothing directly, except the view of Nouwen that we all have elements of both sons in each one of us, each of whom is lost in different ways. Through life we have to handle the sorts of issues both sons faced.

I guess that in life most of us know times we got lost like the younger son, went off the rails or suffered shame at our past. The challenges of autumn can involve coming to terms with that, as I explored in the section 'Freedom includes "shut the door"' in chapter 2. The tale of the elder son contains losses, as does autumn. He has lost trust in his father; he is hurt and puzzled by how life has worked out. It is almost that his father has been absent and failed him. He struggles to have a sense of gratitude. His outburst in Luke 15:29–30 could be summa-rised as a shout of 'Look, it's not fair!' Well, come to that, is having to live through autumn fair? Did any of us ask for the leaves of our own tree to start falling? What do we make of our past with its springs and summers; have they been what we most deeply desired? If not, what to do about it?

One response arises from Nouwen's description of the reply the elder son receives from the father (Luke 15:31–32), whom we are also to become more like. Nouwen begins by emphasising the joy that characterises God the Father. He sees it in the father in the story, who is able to take joy in his immediate circumstances, like the son's return, even though his life more broadly remains under Roman occupation and there is still the older brother to handle. I can identify with Nouwen, who admits himself too ready to hear the bad news around him, to witness conflict and live expecting friends to tell him of their problems, sadness and difficulties. He admits the need of real discipline:

> It requires choosing for the light even when there is much darkness to frighten me, choosing for life when the forces of death are so visible, and choosing for the truth even when I am surrounded with lies.

Nouwen closes the section by noticing that 'the reward of choosing joy is joy itself… Joy never denies the sadness but transforms it to a fertile soil for more joy.'[15]

I'm grateful to Nouwen for sharpening my desire to choose joy. Now I want to unpack the medicine of gratitude a bit more. I take you to Colossians 3:15–17. I call it 'medicine' because we have to drink it down and because it is restorative; it will do us good.

> Let the peace of Christ rule in your hearts, since as members of one body you were called to peace. And be thankful. Let the message of Christ dwell among you richly as you teach and admonish one another with all wisdom through psalms, hymns and songs from the Spirit, singing to God with gratitude in your hearts. And whatever you do, whether in word of deed, do it all in the name of the Lord Jesus, giving thanks to God the Father through him.

I notice two things. The first is the choice we make to *let* the peace of Christ rule and *let* the word dwell richly. We do the letting, and that decision and its practice may need work by our wills. But it is God who brings the peace and the riches of his word. We drink the medicine, but the medicine brings the restored health. Once again it's this both–and partnership I explored in chapter 7.

The second is that the spirit in which this letting happens is gratitude. In just three verses, giving thanks is urged twice and heartfelt gratitude once. It is always a delight to be with people who are grateful for many aspects of life. They spread sunshine. It's quite the opposite to be alongside the grumpy, complaining and suspicious who bring gloom with them. Paul wants Christians to be so infected with gratitude, such that, whatever they do or say, thankfulness oozes out.

I have found it helpful to practise gratitude, both for the long term or bigger picture, but also as a daily disposition, noticing and then noting details we are thankful for. On holiday in summer 2023, I noticed our German hosts always thanked God at breakfast for a night's sleep and the gift of a further day. It's a good habit. As Griffin says:

> Every night I say a prayer of gratitude for the day that has passed and for still being here… Thankfulness puts us in touch with God's grace. That's the sustaining energy of the spiritual life, holding us up and holding us together in the later years.[16]

Long-term gratitude includes thanks for the important surprises that have occurred in our lives. Some are common to many people. It might be the first meeting with a person who became our spouse or who has been a lifelong friend. It could be the birth of a child, another small beginning but a lifelong relationship. It might be the discovery of a vocation.

For some of us gratitude might also be for a discovery that profoundly changed our minds. I have had two such moments and was reminded of them when I read this in Tournier: 'Whence then come our most original and creative ideas? In general we have no notion.' I concur. The two books that I have already written in later life both had their genesis years before, in an unbidden and surprising thought that erupted without permission in my mind. The first came in 1992, on 1 April of all days. It was this: 'God's church can and should reproduce.' The second surprising thought came during 2009: 'Seven different spaces, and what they are for, are needed for deeper, healthy, sustainable community life in Christ.' I am deeply grateful that these two surprising moments have shaped much of not just my thinking, but also my life. I count them among my crop of late fruits and am grateful to have spotted, gathered and distributed them. I also felt these discoveries came to me and in some sense were bigger than me and have shaped me. Author and critic Carolyn Heilbrun echoes such enduring feelings: 'Traces… are left only by work that has overmastered us, work which we cannot, after we once begin it, imagine not in our life.'[17]

Such is the spirit of the 1897 hymn 'Count your blessings', composed by Johnson Oatman Jr. I recall the first stanza aptly ends 'and it will surprise you what the Lord has done'. Spotting our own surprises brings back that sense of surprise and contributes to having and holding a sense of adventure, all of which we can be grateful for, and it fosters more joyfully trusting, as we traverse the autumn of life, with its mix of fruit and falling leaves.

Application questions

🌿 Which of the two translations of Romans 8:28 have you lived by?

🌿 Having read through the four theological stances, which made most sense to you?

🌿 If you had a friend troubled by 'the problem of evil', what would you want to say to try to help?

🌿 What have been the sources of enduring trust and gratitude in your life?

9

Winter is somewhere round the corner

What and when is the winter of life?

By the winter of life I mean the stage of dependent living, or fourth age. In chapter 1, I explained that the frontier between when summer ends and autumn begins is hard to plot in practice, though a calendar day can be given in theory. That's true of the year's seasons and those of life. So it is today with the border of life's autumn and winter. Geriatrician Lucy Pollock explains that in centuries past humans quite quickly became independent in life and so things continued until a sudden death. Today, with advances in medical and social care, the descent towards dependency and death is a staircase of staggered steps over time. The loss of independence classically begins with a fall, leading to a broken wrist or, worse, a hip. Later on can occur a serious stroke and/or crippling arthritis, yet further on heart failure or some form of dementia. So unfolds the stepped descent towards death.[1]

For most of us that kind of transition, away from independent living to becoming dependent, is gradual and much medical intervention exists to prolong its absence. For some people the arrival of dependency is sudden, brought on either by an accident or a sharp downturn in health, such as only partially recovering from stroke, discovering inoperable cancer or the onset of advancing dementia.

Pollock's book then deals with the wise, humane, medical care of those towards the end of their fourth age. She argues that the big questions of health, life and death are to be faced, not buried by fear of, or prejudice against, the very old or a mistaken love that won't talk about such questions for fear of burdening others. Pollock is realistic about caring and careful medical response to the multifactorial conditions often faced by the very old.

Yet dependency is not the same as incompetency. Many fourth-agers are still alert, bright-eyed and able to tackle many tasks of life. Some stay at home unaided, though conscious of failing faculties, being frail and vulnerable. Some still at home have family and carers coming in to help. For others, sheltered housing or a care home is their address. For this last group decluttering and downsizing are now done. For all these categories, this stage can last for years. Then, having the finance to continue that level of care, and not utterly eat up an inheritance to hand on, may be an issue.

Becoming dependent initially feels negative. Externally, ageism can make the old feel invisible, discarded and condescended to. Internally, there may be shame that I can no longer fend for myself, that I sense my utility has expired, and that I'm a burden and cost to others. Some of that will depend on how I view receiving from others. Longer reflection reminds me I have always been dependent. Firstly on the love of others for my wellbeing, and also on the good earth for food and drink, as well as human supply chains. Nouwen urges 'daring to become dependent'. He calls this ability to receive an art – 'a gesture of humility and love'.[2]

But this book is about autumn, thus it only touches upon winter as a future prospect. It is written convinced that more has been written about winter/fourth age than autumn/third age. So readers need to look elsewhere for wisdom and practical tips on living through winter.

The voices of my third-age friends

To help me get beyond my own feelings and thoughts about the inevitable coming of the winter of life, I invited my 16 interviewees to explore three linked questions about its approach:

22 How do you feel about the future?
23 How long do you think you have left?
24 How well do you feel prepared for either your or your spouse's death?

The questions assumed a person was still in the autumn of life but invited them to look ahead.

Feelings about the future

Ten of the 16 immediately chose upbeat summary words to question 22 about the future, including positive, content, fine, relaxed, excited and confident. A few added a rationale – one saying she was hopeful because God can do more than we ask or think; two others cited the phrase 'a living hope' (1 Peter 1:3); another that God would continue to give her courage to live the next stage of life. Some delved deeper, seeing contentment and gratitude as gifts by which they could accept that diminishing abilities normally occur with ageing. One added that failing to live this way only invited yet more worry and even physical illness. Five others chose not to contemplate their own unknowable future at all and instead focused on the choice to live for now, trusting that the future would take care of itself. A few cited the inspiring example of those ten years older than them who still lived fulfilling lives.

In retrospect, I realised that question 22 was being understood and answered in three different ways and I didn't have the wit to separate them. How do you see the world's future? How do you see your own future? What in your Christian faith affects your view of the future? It was striking that 14 of the 16, without my clarification or prompting, took the first interpretation and expressed profound concern about the planet's climate crisis and its consequences. 'It's worse than the 1962 Cuban missile crisis,' said one. This alarm was compounded by concerns over moral collapse, cultural decay and resultant conflicts, all making agreement about finding ways forward more difficult.

How long do you think you have?

Question 23, about how long they thought they had left on earth, clearly invited people to ponder their own future and fate. Nine people either said they had no idea or they realised they had never thought about it. One added that when she did suddenly think it for the first time six years ago, it put 'the fear of God' into her. By contrast, 'We never know how far ahead death is,' said another interviewee, but he saw it as another adventure. My own diary for 9 August 2022 records a comment from Tilly, my then four-year-old granddaughter. She looked at me with the devastating simplicity of a child and remarked: 'You are old and you will die.' Of course she was right, but I was too rocked back on my heels either to ask how she knew that, how she would react to my death or to make the smart retort, 'You are young, but you will die too.'

Four others took a hint of a likely future from the age reached by their parents, one wanting to outlive his father. Another, whose father was only in his 50s when he died, said the background presence of death was never far away. It reminded me of Tournier and the echoes of my own cast of mind in his, because of the loss of a parent when we were young. He wrote 'I have always lived in this sort of familiarity with death.'[3] Three other people responded with quips such as 'Ten minutes or 15 years' or 'I might go under a bus tomorrow or have 20 years.' I sensed both humour in the impossibility of knowing and disturbing awareness of the uncertainty of life. Others answered in terms of how long they expected to remain useful, itself a measure of life borrowed from a working past. I suspected both a person's overall outlook on life and powerful particular circumstances shaped these varied responses.

How prepared for death are you?

The topic of death leaked across responses to all three questions. Four interviewees named the specific conviction that death itself wasn't the problem, it was the manner of dying and the effect on one's loved ones that was of far more concern. Interviewees were also more troubled by the thought of their spouse's death than their own.

Later I noticed how many interviewees took the phrase 'prepared for death' only to be code for prior practicalities, such as making a will, getting power of attorney and deciding what they wanted at their funeral. Maybe by the end of a two-hour interview session, I failed to have the energy or alertness to draw each person deeper into what they thought about their own dying and death.

A few women were more open, giving intriguing and helpful ways to view death. One saw it as light travelling towards her. That positive sense of an increasing proximity reminded me of Nouwen, who uses the image of a dying person being like a boat sailing away from us till we can't see it: 'Dying is a gradual diminishing and final vanishing over the horizon of life.'[4] He adds that it helps us to be aware that God, on the other shore, sees that boat coming closer and closer. Another saw death as completion, for Christianity is much about dying to self, becoming Christlike, aided by the Holy Spirit and a life of prayer and worship. It was also women who were honest that they sought more personal inner transformation before they felt 'prepared' to die. I concur.

As I have had to live with such questions for months on end, I now realise that in my middle age, I assumed death was something that happened to other people. Maybe taking other people's funerals reinforced such a view. Aged 75, I now realise that death is already slowly happening to me as bits of my body show signs of failure. As Tournier put it: 'The progressive decline of the body which obsesses the old is not the cause of their death; it is the sign of their march towards it.' I am drawing closer to it. I am more aware of my own mortality. The death of friends, especially those younger than me, sharpens this. Tournier concurs: 'Each of us dies a little in the death of those we love and there is a part of our lives which ever afterwards we feel to be incomplete.'[5]

Only my female interviewees acknowledged death as the last enemy. Again, Tournier concurs: 'Death remains a fearful and cruel monster. The Bible says that it will be the last enemy to be overcome (1 Corinthians 15:26).' I find him realistic about anxiety in the face of death coming close:

> The ideal of indifference in the face of death is not Christian... Christian faith... does not involve repressing one's anxiety to appear strong. On the contrary, it means recognising one's weakness, accepting the inward truth about oneself, confessing one's anxiety... and still to believe... The Christian puts his trust... in the grace of God.

I'm intrigued at one of his aphorisms: 'Acceptance of old age is the best preparation for death but also, conversely... acceptance of death is the best preparation for old age.'[6] But I sense I have further to go to truly make both halves of that wisdom my own.

What helps acceptance of old age and death?

Tournier calls acceptance one of the great problems and spends a fifth of *Learning to Grow Old* exploring it. He includes accepting that our lives do include the unfulfilled. Our dreams have proved less than the reality. When we are old, our lives and our careers will have proved both short and incomplete. Even Jesus knew incompleteness: the disappointment with his disciples and friends, let alone being misunderstood by the crowd or the religious authorities. What is it to accept this? Tournier is clear that by acceptance he does not mean fatalism, passivity or resignation. These are motivated by a negative inner attitude that thinks we put up with our falling leaves, our failures and losses, just because we've got to. For him, acceptance is positive, and it says, 'Yes!' What does he advise we say 'yes' to?

> True active personal surrender to necessity is the great task of life… To accept is to say yes to life in its entirety… Life is one way, its law is the same for all, it moves only forwards. One prepares for old age by taking a positive attitude throughout one's life.[7]

In chapter 4, above, I named and unpacked the lifetime lesson of learning to let go. Tournier's championing of acceptance underlines that this attitude is to be embraced not endured, received with gratitude not grumbled at. That sounds simple; maybe it isn't. Tournier explains:

> There are always two movements: first a natural, spontaneous, necessary rebellion against what affects us… But there may be a second movement of acceptance, a sort of reconciliation with ourselves when we perceive that rebellion involves a divorce between our reality and us… It is no easy matter to accept that one is growing old, and no one succeeds in doing it without first overcoming his spontaneous refusal.[8]

I have only begun to walk this complex journey of coming to terms with my own falling leaves and the letting go of various dreams, abilities, responsibilities and opportunities. I am relieved that, like Tournier, I find some books which are determinedly optimistic leave me uneasy. By contrast those that helped him and me accept limits and suffering are those that did not minimise it.

I already see, in theory, that how I accept my autumn and live my winter will depend a lot on how far my identity has been shifted from being based in achievements to identity beyond them. A couple of my female interviewees had similar convictions. One named the journey as from doing to being, the latter unpacked as the gift of 'being' with, for and to others.

Tournier joins this chorus of a necessary shift from doing to being: 'As old age comes, this function, this "doing" gradually ceases to define me. I have to define myself in terms of what I am.'[9] But we need more than psychological acceptance; deeper is spiritual truth. The other woman centred this deeper identity in who she was in Christ. Because of him and us being in him, we are 'a chosen people, a royal priesthood, a holy nation, God's special possession' (1 Peter 2:9). Those are elements of our identity, not a list of our achievements.

The resurrection hope

Another source of acceptance of ageing and death is our view of Christian resurrection. I am grateful that a gift to me, which I never strove for, is that this belief has always been secure, energising and encouraging. It springs from its precedent – the resurrection of Jesus. He was both recognisable as himself and yet transformed. Such continuity and change will be for us, as Richard and Judith Hays point out: 'Note that those who have the Spirit long not for redemption *from* their bodies but rather for redemption *of* their bodies… We expect that the body will not be discarded but rather transformed in the resurrection.' Fischer adds that this new reality is both bodily and social. Heaven is pictured as a banquet, corporate worship and diverse city community.[10]

Another encouragement is the sense that as we move towards death, so too we are nearing home. Five of my interviewees liked this image of nearing home. I could not but note that two of them were well into their 80s and the other three had known serious illness. Home is where one belongs. Tournier sensed this: 'My home is in heaven. And the more I have advanced in age, the more has earthly life seemed to me like an apprenticeship in the love and knowledge of God. What is peculiar to Christianity… is love, faith and hope.'[11] Those last three qualities are relational. Personally, I think being correctly heavenly minded helps us be of earthly use.

I know enough of Jesus' resurrection to look forward in trust. I know so little of heaven that I look forward to the surprises. The last verse of Richard Baxter's hymn 'Lord it belongs not to my care' holds that balance.

My knowledge of that life is small,
the eye of faith is dim;
but 'tis enough that Christ knows all,
and I shall be with Him.

Application questions

- What are your reactions to the thought of becoming dependent?

- What progress have you made to put in place a will, lasting power of attorney and funeral wishes?

- Our attitudes to the process of dying and to the event of death are different. Which are you more reconciled with?

- What hopes of the new heaven and earth do you have?

IO

The art of living the autumn of life

Keeping your balance

Living the autumn of life is a dynamic balancing act, not a static one. An example of dynamic balance is riding a bike. As we cycle along, we make little adjustments to the steering as we go. On the bike and in life we will wobble and even swerve. It's not for nothing I said it was a balancing *act*. Living, not merely existing, is a live show of which the script is still being written. There are days when I am content in this stage of life and think I am managing it quite well. I can scan my past with gratitude, see the present as opportunity for adventure and view the future with hope. There are other days when regret for the past, inadequacy in the present and fear for the future all gang up on me. One day during writing I needed to be reminded of something I wrote years ago: 'All true holiness is characterised by falling and getting up again – perhaps a thousand times.'[1]

Chapters 1–4 remind me that I need to take delight in the fruits and freedoms of retirement *and* I have to notice and admit which leaves are falling, continuing to learn to let go. In short, this balancing act is negotiating with both fulfilment and loss. Tournier calls this *learning* to grow old. It is learnt, not automatic, not least as so little in our working lives prepared us for autumn. Nor is this completely learnt; the learning continues, which is part of what makes living this stage an adventure. Of course, adventures contain risk and even cost, but I have found 'adventure' is a word I need to hold on to, not least as the leaves continue to fall.

What factors contribute to this art?

I have long pondered factors that Tournier and Knox think influence the manner in which we live out our autumn years. I have bounced them off other older people. I found four factors, which can be graded in significance.

As this book's opening pages argued, least diagnostic is chronological age itself. As is sometimes said, 'You are as old as you feel.' That comment takes us to a more important factor.

Our health and energy levels are more important than sheer age. You can be 90 and very fit, or 60 and living with chronic pain or a degenerative disease. Among my third-age friends it is a common complaint to notice how tired we are, say, at the close of a long day interacting with delightful grandchildren or after taking significant exercise. A geriatric joke is that gatherings of people in the autumn of life involve listening to an organ recital – which organ in the body is playing up now!

Health and energy are one aspect of a third wider term, our circumstances. These include being poor or wealthy, married or single, and what our genes and upbringing have dealt us. These circumstances change when meeting tragedy or the loss of faculties, both of which, Knox says, lead to sensing our further ageing. Such circumstances can press upon us more sharply than the general state of our health.

But it was an older friend, Mary, from a previous parish, who across the years has lived through good times as well as illnesses, losses and tragedies. She put in words what she saw as the most important factor, which interacts with all the others. She called it 'outlook'. I think authors I have been tracking would agree, though they might use the synonym 'attitude'. It's what Tournier's first chapter in *The Adventure of Living* is about. Knox both names attitude himself and concludes from his qualitative interviews that people's verbal responses were fundamentally shaped by that factor.[2] Our basic attitude to life sounds as though it is the most diagnostic factor in how well we will live the autumn of life.

Then a question pops up. If my attitude is less than serenely positive, can that be changed, and if so, how? My own exploration of that question was what led to my writing chapters 7–8. Our outlook can and should be shaped by scripture's take on fruit and frailty and shaped by any theology derived from the Bible. So I explored the differences between knowing, trusting, believing and hoping. I argued scripture values living with both contentment in our outer circumstances and a healthy spiritual discontent that seeks becoming more Christlike. I especially explored what it means to trust God in the face of suffering and evil, and what Open Theism can offer.

I also asked my interviewees two wider but connected questions: what helped them spiritually in their autumn of life; and were there spiritual practices or aspects of theology that no longer worked for them?

Factors that helped

Twelve out of the 16 specifically mentioned their life of prayer. This echoed an aspect of chapter 2 naming freedom and time to pray more. What helped them pray varied. Four respondents related to God through being in nature. Three cited the spiritual benefit of listening to choral music. Three found themselves drawn into contemplative prayer, one discovering this as a coming home to whom she was, another stressing just being with God, and a third called it 'sharing with the God who accompanies me'. Styles of prayer varied across liturgical, extemporary, prayer in tongues, meditation, praying and processing while driving, and being silent.

Another four interviewees cited being part of congregational worship, but six others said that was no longer true for them. As one put it: 'I am seeking the life of Jesus beyond the paraphernalia of church.' Another described herself as 'weary of the effort to keep the wheels turning'. Three found themselves more critical of the church than they used to be, and only went out of guilt and duty. These latter views echo negative sentiments aired in chapter 5 about third-agers' experiences of church.

Half of the interviewees named exposure to scripture. This included daily Bible reading, exploring it more deeply in groups, reading through the whole Bible or in big chunks, and preparing for sermons. A few widened this attentiveness to a speaking God through the practice of devotional reading. A further factor named by several was being inspired by the faith of others. Examples were provided by children, spouses, peers, parents and heroes of faith. Two people named fasting and another two took an annual retreat.

Practices and theology that no longer worked

What spiritual practices or aspects of theology no longer worked for the interviewees? More comments were made about theology than practices. There, the most obvious commonality was that tight, closed or narrow approaches, whether labelled Catholic or Evangelical, had been set aside as inadequate. Here's a selection of such comments:

My theology is more messy.
I'm happy to live with mess and mystery.
My theology is more open; it's less arrogant or judgmental.
I'm more and more distraught by the Old Testament and God slaughtering other nations.
I'm less happy with off-the-peg answers.
I'm frustrated at neat answers.
I now see a bigger picture.

*I see my past Evangelicalism as misogynist, cerebral and lacking
    the experience of God.*
I'm less governed by an emphasis on confession, guilt and fear.

One person suggested a helpful diagnostic feature; she had explored
many theologies as markers on her journey, hoping some of them had
become integral, but insisting if any of these did not have Jesus at the
centre they would go off-beam and self-destruct. All these comments,
though sharp, were seen to be signs of progress and helped them in
the autumn of life.

But beyond this sense of widening out and discerning what endured,
a couple of people bravely admitted that they now struggled with
fundamental questions, such as the very existence of God, whether
Christianity was the only way, how does one explain bad things that
happen, what is worship and does God need it. They also sensed that
usually church was not a place where such questioning could be welcomed and sensed relief in the few places they found it.

Attitudes and practices that help me

The following elements arise from my conviction that what is really
going on in this process during the autumn of life is summed up by
2 Corinthians 3:18: 'And we all, who with unveiled faces contemplate the
Lord's glory, are being transformed into his image with ever-increasing
glory, which comes from the Lord, who is the Spirit.' And I see that
process as the response to two deceptively simple words of Jesus:
'Follow me.'

Gratitude and trust

As we follow Jesus, we can be gradually transformed by gratitude for
the fruit of our lives, for the leaves that remain and even, on our better
days, for the leaves there used to be. Psalm 92:1-2 gives me a practical

prayer of gratitude, praising God for his love in the morning of the day ahead and for his faithfulness at night when another day is done.

Trust needs to be employed more over adverse changing circumstances and what our own falling leaves mean. Chapter 4 on letting go and chapter 8 on trusting God have tried to address that. A memory that has helped me comes from the life of my college tutor Julian Charley. He was godly, humble, caring, joyful and wise. If sometimes things went wrong or were difficult, his smiling quip was: 'It's a great life if you don't weaken.' I saw him face suffering with a trusting spirit of gratitude and humour. Emilie Griffin's third chapter 'Stretching towards happiness' echoes these qualities; she commends laughing in the face of the worst in life, then deliberately choosing life and practising being thankful.[3]

Numbering our days

Through praying the Northumbria Community midday office, I came face-to-face daily with the pertinent request 'Teach us, dear Lord, to number our days that we may apply our hearts unto wisdom.' It prompts me to use my time more carefully, to accept that my days are a finite resource. These attitudes practise the gift of noticing. This numbering is noticing the now and consciously valuing it.

There's more. Numbering something brings order, it discloses patterns, and it sharpens perspectives. In all these ways numbering my days helps me see it is true that they have meaning. This view is significantly different to the colloquial phrase 'His days were numbered', which smacks of fatalism and portrays humans as but pawns in life. This prayer invites me to take responsibility and make the most of my days, while knowing that at some point death will approach. The fruit will have been gathered and leaves will have fallen. And that's okay.

From achievement to identity

One key transition to make is letting go of finding my meaning and significance in life through my achievements. What needs to emerge and grow is finding that meaning in who I am – my identity as a person who is in Christ and is a child of God. The biblical material of chapters 7 and 9 drew out some contours of that release and relationship. That transition was illustrated in chapter 2 and especially the section 'The fruit of character'. I suggested a core aspect of what is going on in the autumn of life is the removal of the tree's leaves and the bare tree being seen naked, in its glory and scars. What it is, at its heart, will now be seen.

This self-acceptance and acceptance by God are well put by two comments. Carolyn Heilbrun wrote about a fellow 70-year-old who, when asked 'Why is it good to be old?', replied: 'Because I am more myself than I have ever been.'[4] Interviewee Michael aptly said to me: 'I am the age I need to be for the purposes of God.' He contrasted the way society tends to think of a retired person as of little use, whereas with God he was valued as he was.

The greatest of these is love

Given that it is the view of 1 Corinthians 13, I should have expected that the exercise of love would prove crucial. Tournier writes of a whole positive attitude to life as learning 'to grow in love, because to be interested is to love, love persons and love things'. He adds: 'The love of truth is the source of all harmony with oneself.' Fischer, in a paragraph on a woman seeking simplicity and essentials, writes: 'She is concentrating on the basics, which have to do with love.' In another chapter she tells of a grandmother seeking compassion for herself: 'What I want to do before I die is to learn how to love.' Similarly Griffin tells of a grieving widow recalling a recently dying husband who valued the saying of John of the Cross: 'In the evening of life only love matters.'[5] Loving life, loving others, loving ourselves, all emanate from knowing we are loved by God.

What makes a difference? A secular view

In an article entitled 'The secret to a long and healthy life', Louise Addison highlights research across the world focused on so-called 'blue zones', in which people have low rates of chronic illnesses and live longer. This reveals that those who have this longer and healthier life do the following things: exercise, live with purpose, take time out, only eat till they are 80% full, have a plant-based diet, drink moderately and have a community to belong to.[6]

I see there good practical advice, yet I seek deeper values behind sentiments like 'live with a purpose' and 'have a community to belong to'. This book has tried to spell out such values for living a better autumn of life. Fischer cites courage and hope as two gifts of the Spirit at this stage of life.[7] I want to combine them with two other virtues: gratitude and trust. Perhaps the combination looks like this. We practise gratitude for autumn's fruits and freedoms, and courage for entering its adventures, including noticing and accepting our falling leaves. We practise trust and hope, amid the vicissitudes of our autumn and the advent of winter. This includes cooperating with God over his transformation of our characters. That last factor will become all the more obvious, as the naked tree emerges and we are seen shorn of past competencies.

A spiritual headstone

How each of us lives out the autumn of our lives will indelibly determine the memory of us we leave behind. This legacy will last, every bit as much as words inscribed on a headstone. To borrow an image from Fischer: this fills up 'the ancestral well from which all [family] members drink'.[8]

I end with a quote from Paul Tournier, my most frequent teacher as I grow older through my own autumn of life and share with you my discoveries and frailties on this adventure. Let him have the last word:

> It is for us old people to build our own lives, lives that are worthwhile, interesting, and worthy of respect, and so to arouse fresh hope in the young that they can look forward to a happy old age.[9]

Application questions

🍂 Which aspects of the art of living the autumn of life are securely in place for you?

🍂 Which aspects do you now realise need working at?

🍂 How far down the road from achievement to identity would you say you are?

🍂 Note any other aspects that this book revealed which were new to you and need applying.

Appendix 1

26 questions to 16 interviewees

---

1 In what year and at what age did you retire? How old are you now?
2 How do you see this present stage of your life? What phrases best describe it for you?
3 Does any image come to mind of what this stage is like?
   a Do any of these resonate: autumn, evening, an emptying sweet jar, moving from the front seat to the back seat, entering a foreign land, nearing home?
4 How have you found life since stopping employed work?
   a What adjustments did you make to your lifestyle?
5 How does the reality of your retirement compare with what you expected?
6 Is there anything you miss from when you were employed?
7 Since retiring, what have been the highlights?
8 What adventures have opened up or come along?
9 What do you see as your gifts and are they still being used?
10 How well do you think church provides for people at your stage/age?
11 What Christian music (hymns and songs) do you find spiritually life-giving?
12 How often does your church sing these items?
13 What have been the biggest difficulties or challenges at this stage of life?
14 What loss of faculties have you noticed and how do you cope with that?

15 How has your health been, say in the last 10–15 years?
16 What kind of illnesses do you fear most? Are there other significant fears?
17 In what ways has your relationship with your children (or any nephews and nieces) changed during this autumn period of life?
18 How do you feel about decluttering?
19 Have you downsized? What was that like for you?
20 What have you found helps you spiritually during this overall stage of life?
21 Are there any past spiritual practices or aspects of theology that no longer work for you?
22 How do you feel about the future?
23 How long do you think you have left?
24 How well prepared do you feel for either your own or your spouse's death?
25 Do you have a bucket list? What has been on it, what's ticked off and what's left?
26 What else would you like to tell me, which has not been included in these questions?

Appendix 2

The spiritual development process of a meet-up

Do any of these questions ring bells for you?

- Have you noticed that many Christians get stuck in their spiritual development?
- Have you wondered why home groups also reach a similar plateau?
- Have you sometimes wanted to take deeper steps yourself in following Jesus?

So what is a meet-up for?

A meet-up helps you to more closely follow Jesus and encourages the development of Christian character. It isn't *discussing* a book. It is a deliberately slow way of reading and being accountable for *applying* what you read.

1 A meet-up is best thought of as a process, not a programme or a course. It is about learning to be attentive to fellow members and to the Holy Spirit.

2   Engaging with a book, such as this one, or some other resource via a meet-up is the process of facilitating personal, communal and spiritual *transformation* as a Christian. It is not mainly about acquiring or sharing *information*. However, some new knowledge can help to disclose what God may be saying to each person.

3   The learning process is not like 'formal education', such as doing a course. It is more like learning through 'socialisation' as the members interact with one another, aided by the host. Also it involves 'non-formal learning or apprenticeship'.[1] Through it, *skills* of Christian personal and communal spiritual life can be acquired, and these start to become *habitual* through practice.

How do meet-ups actually work?

1   Participants need to be aware that the meet-up process is unlike most small groups in church life. To help make that distinction, they are not called 'groups' but 'meet-ups'.

2   The meet-up size is smaller (five to six people). This gives time for the vital mutual listening and careful responses. Larger groups easily become unapplied discussions or turn into a lecture.

3   There is no 'leader', only a 'host', who models and enables this mutual learning and support.

4   Engaging with new content occurs slowly. Only one chapter is read each month by participants between the meet-ups. This slow pace seeks to avoid trying to learn too much too soon, as otherwise further new information hinders the sustaining of recently acquired spiritual habits. All new spiritual habits need time to put down roots.

5   People are responsible for doing that slow reading at home beforehand, assisted by the questions at the end of each chapter.

From this, they write a short account (four minutes) of this journey. In the meet-up, they read out what they have prepared. Other meet-up members, in turn, then respond briefly with encouragements and insights into what that person has shared.

6 Two key values in meet-ups are honesty and confidentiality.

7 Each member takes responsibility for what they are putting into practice. This might include lessons they are learning, mistakes made and creative discoveries found.

8 For all these reasons, meet-ups are a month apart and they last for 90 minutes. The overall process can include breaks for the summer holidays and for major festivals like Christmas. This gives people time to assimilate and put their learning into practice.

This whole approach also draws on the much older early church process called *catechesis*. This lasted a period of years, which included teaching the Christian faith but was more about acquiring and demonstrating a Christian character, lifestyle and habits.[2]

Further reading

On autumn

Tina English, *A Great Place to Grow Old: Reimagining ministry among older people* (Darton, Longman and Todd, 2021)

Kathleen Fischer, *Autumn Gospel: Women in the second half of life* (Paulist Press, 1995)

Emilie Griffin, *Green Leaves for Later Years: The spiritual path of wisdom* (IVP Books, 2012)

Katherine May, *Wintering: The power of rest and retreat in difficult times* (Rider, 2020)

Rob Merchant, *Pioneering The Third Age: The church in an ageing population* (Paternoster, 2003)

Paul Tournier, *Learning to Grow Old* (SCM Press, 2012)

Paul Tournier, *The Adventure of Living* (SCM Press, 2012)

On post-Christendom exile

Steve Aisthorpe, *Rewilding the Church* (St Andrews Press, 2020)

Patrick Whitworth, *Prepare for Exile: A new spirituality and mission for the church* (SPCK, 2008)

Alan Kreider, *The Patient Ferment of the Early Church: The improbable rise of Christianity in the Roman Empire* (Baker Academic, 2016)

Internet sources

afterworknet.com – a website aimed at third-agers
faithinlaterlife.org – resources for third- and fourth-agers

Notes

Introduction

1 One example of ministry focused on the dependent elderly is BRF Ministries' Anna Chaplaincy: see **annachaplaincy.org.uk**
2 Katherine May, *Wintering: The power of rest and retreat in difficult times* (Rider, 2020) pp. 265-266.
3 Paul Tournier, *Learning to Grow Old* (SCM Press, 2012), p. 214; *The Adventure of Living* (SCM Press, 2012), p. 56.
4 Tina English, *A Great Place to Grow Old: Reimaging ministry among older people* (Darton, Longman and Todd, 2021), p. 16; Kathleen Fischer, *Autumn Gospel: Women in the second half of life* (Paulist Press, 1995), p. 1.
5 Tournier, *Learning to Grow Old*, pp. 9, 10–11.
6 Richard Rohr, *Falling Upward: A spirituality for the two halves of life* (SPCK, 2012), pp. vii, xiii.

Chapter 1

1 Michael Mitton, *Seasoned By Seasons: Flourishing in life's experiences* (BRF, 2017), p. 16.
2 Tournier, *Learning to Grow Old*, p. 131.
3 George Lings, *Reproducing Churches* (BRF, 2017), pp. 40–42.
4 Simon Barnes, *How To Be a Bad Birdwatcher: To the greater glory of life* (Short Books, 2004), p.165.
5 Fischer, *Autumn Gospel*, p. 76.
6 **photocrowd.com/photo-competitions/ageing-bigger-picture-documentary-photo-contest-374/overview**, accessed 13 May 2024.
7 Tournier, *Learning to Grow Old*, pp. 68, 198.
8 Fischer, *Autumn Gospel*, p. 160; Tournier, *Learning to Grow Old*, p. 69.

9   Fischer, *Autumn Gospel*, p. 161.
10 Carolyn G. Heilbrun, *The Last Gift of Time: Life beyond sixty* (Ballantine Books, 1998), p. 122.
11 George Lings, *Seven Sacred Spaces: Portals to deeper community life in Christ* (BRF, 2020).

Chapter 2

1   The Irish Jesuits, *Sacred Space: The Prayer book 2022* (Messenger Publications, 2021), p. 148, and repeated p. 294.
2   **sunlife.co.uk/articles-guides**, accessed 13 May 2024.
3   'People aged 65 to 79 "happiest of all", study suggests', BBC, 2 February 2016, **bbc.co.uk/news/uk-35471624**, accessed 13 May 2024.
4   Iris Moore-Sparkes, *A Grain of Sand* (Church in the Market Place Publications), pp. vi–vii, 59.
5   Emilie Griffin, *Green Leaves for Later Years: The spiritual path of wisdom* (IVP, 2012), pp. 71–72, citing P.D. James, *Time To Be in Earnest* (Knopf, 2000), pp. 240, 37; Fischer *Autumn Gospel*, pp. 124, 125–31.
6   Lings, *Seven Sacred Spaces*, pp 56–58.
7   Myra Chave-Jones, *Coping with Depression*, (Lion, 1981), p. 22: 'A person bereaved in childhood is likely to be at risk to depression in later life.'
8   Tournier, *The Adventure of Living*, p. 188.
9   Tournier, *The Adventure of Living*, p. 185.
10 Dallas Willard, *The Divine Conspiracy: Rediscovering our hidden life in God* (Fount, 1998), p. 71; Fischer, *Autumn Gospel*, p. 131.
11 Rob Merchant, *Pioneering The Third Age: The church in an ageing population* (Paternoster, 2003), p. 138.
12 Tournier, *The Adventure of Living*, p. 36.
13 Tournier, *The Adventure of Living*, p. 39.
14 Tournier, *The Adventure of Living*, pp. 41, 42.
15 Tournier, *The Adventure of Living*, p. 63.
16 Tournier, *The Adventure of Living*, pp. 92–93, 56–57.
17 Merchant, *Pioneering The Third Age*, p. 51, 58; Tournier, *Learning to Grow Old*, p. 123; Ian Knox, *Older People and the Church* (T&T Clark, 2002), pp. 186–205.
18 Tournier, *Learning to Grow Old*, p. 198.

19 Fischer, *Autumn Gospel*, pp. 66–82.
20 Griffin, *Green Leaves for Later Years*, p. 18.
21 The original version is found in Dawna Markova, *I Will Not Die an Unlived Life: Reclaiming purpose and passion* (Conari Press, 2000), p. 1.
22 Tournier, *Learning to Grow Old*, pp. 100, 118, 130.
23 Lucy Pollock, *The Book About Getting Older* (Penguin, 2022), p. 51.
24 Brian D. Mclaren, *Naked Spirituality: A life with God in twelve simple words* (Hodder and Stoughton, 2010). He calls the four stages simplicity, complexity, perplexity and harmony.
25 Tournier, *Learning to Grow Old*, pp. 204–205.
26 Knox, *Older People and the Church*, p. 32.
27 Tournier, *Learning to Grow Old*, p. 34.
28 OO/HO is the most common choice, in which a tender locomotive would be some 10 inches/25 cm long. N gauge is smaller and the same loco would be barely 4 inches/ 10 cm long.

Chapter 3

1 Fischer, *Autumn Gospel*, p. 86; Mitton, *Seasoned By Seasons*, pp. 22–23.
2 Fischer, *Autumn Gospel*, p. 91.
3 Griffin, *Green Leaves for Later Years*, pp. 63–73.
4 May, *Wintering*, p. 78; Fischer, *Autumn Gospel*, p. 132.
5 Fischer, *Autumn Gospel*, p. 32.
6 Willard, *The Divine Conspiracy*, p. 224.
7 Griffin, *Green Leaves for Later Years*, pp. 101–03; Mitton, *Seasoned By Seasons*, p. 20; Tournier, *The Adventure of Living*, p. 110.

Chapter 4

1 Mitton, *Seasoned by Seasons*, p. 16.
2 Tournier, *The Adventure of Living*, p. 239; Fischer, *Autumn Gospel*, p. 28.
3 Tournier, *Learning to Grow Old*, pp. 177, 178.
4 Henri J.M. Nouwen, *Bread for the Journey* (Darton, Longman and Todd, 1997), p. 81.
5 Fischer, *Autumn Gospel*, p. 35.

6   Tournier, *Learning to Grow Old*, p. 142.
7   Fischer, *Autumn Gospel*, p. 30.
8   Fischer, *Autumn Gospel*, p. 40.
9   Fischer, *Autumn Gospel*, p. 33.
10 Patricia Jung, in Stanley Hauerwas, Carole Bailey Stoneking, Keith G. Meador and David Cloutier (eds), *Growing Old in Christ* (Eerdmans, 2003), p. 114.
11 Tournier, *Learning to Grow Old*, p. 1 (my italics).
12 Mitton, *Seasoned By Seasons*, p. 17.
13 Fischer, *Autumn Gospel*, p. 37.
14 Fischer, *Autumn Gospel*, p. 29.
15 Tournier, *The Adventure of Living*, p. 166.

Chapter 5

1   Tournier, *Learning to Grow Old*, pp. 36, 40, 52.
2   Tournier, *Learning to Grow Old*, pp. 43, 55, 64, 62.
3   Tournier, *Learning to Grow Old*, pp. 65, 90–91, 76.
4   Tournier, *Learning to Grow Old*, pp. 1–2.
5   Tournier, *Learning to Grow Old*, p. 78
6   Tournier, *Learning to Grow Old*, p. 118.
7   Tournier, *Learning to Grow Old*, p. 187.
8   Knox, *Older People and the Church*, p. 1, citing Tourner, *Learning to Grow Old*, p. 36 (my italics).
9   Merchant, *Pioneering the Third Age*, p. 3. He goes on to show average age varies not only by gender, but by social class and levels of poverty on pp. 9–11.
10 Knox, *Older People and the Church*, pp. 11, 4, 13; Merchant, *Pioneering the Third Age*, pp. 29, 162–65.
11 Knox, *Older People and the Church*, p. 13; Merchant, *Pioneering the Third Age*, pp. 6, 24–26.
12 Merchant, *Pioneering the Third Age*, pp. 7, 17, respectively.
13 Knox, *Older People and the Church*, pp. 43, 20, 24.
14 Knox, *Older People and the Church*, pp. 111–12, 116.
15 Knox, *Older People and the Church*, p. 119–20; Merchant, *Pioneering the Third Age*, p. 141. The old were called 'the problem' and 'yesterday's church'.
16 Knox, *Older People and the Church*, pp. 127–8; Merchant, *Pioneering the Third Age*, pp. 130–31.

17 Knox, *Older People and the Church*, pp. 149, 153–58, 159–61.
18 Knox, *Older People and the Church*, pp. 171–82.
19 Knox, *Older People and the Church*, pp. 261, 262–63.
20 English, *A Great Place to Grow Old*, p. 14.
21 May, *Wintering*, p. 60.
22 *The State of Ageing 2022: Summary* (Centre for Ageing Better, 2022), pp. 1–4, 15.
23 David Metz and Michael Underwood, *Older, Richer, Fitter: Identifying the consumer needs of Britain's ageing population* (Age Concern, 2005), pp. 77–78.
24 Chris Harrington concurs: *Reaching the Saga Generation: Fresh expressions of church for ageing baby boomers*, Grove evangelism booklet 83 (Grove Books, 2008), p. 7. The Sheffield Diocesan Resource Group for Seniors wrote a fine paper in 2019 on ministry to older people, but even the title included the word dementia. Its contents page reads like thoughtful practical provision for fourth-agers. Fourth age is the major focus for national bodies like Age Concern, The Centre for Ageing Better and Embracing Age.
25 English, *A Great Place To Grow Old* pp 122.
26 'Third age discipleship', Methodist Church report MC/13/40 (2013), p. 3, para 10.
27 'Third age discipleship', p. 4, para 16.
28 J. Cox, *Going on Growing* (Church of England Board of Education, 2012), p. 27, para 88.
29 Merchant, *Pioneering the Third Age*, p. 30.
30 Cox, *Going on Growing*, p. 27, para 90.
31 English, *A Great Place to Grow Old*, pp. 28–29.
32 Tournier, *The Adventure of Living*, p. 41.
33 J. Harris, *Older People and the Church* edited by Albert Jewell (Methodist Church, 2001), p. 97.
34 Bishop James of Stepney (chair), *Ageing: A report from the Board for Social Responsibility* (Church House Publishing, 1990), p. 121.
35 English, *A Great Place to Grow Old*, p. 29.
36 English, *A Great Place to Grow Old*, pp. 29–30.
37 Harrington, *Reaching the Saga Generation*, pp. 5, 14–23.
38 Harrington, *Reaching the Saga Generation*, pp. 17–18 give ten points to be aware of.
39 Cox, *Going on Growing*, p. 30, para 101.
40 'Third age discipleship', p. 6, para 25, ss 23–30 explore this learning style more.

41   Philip Richter and Leslie Francis, *Gone But Not Forgotten: Church leaving and returning* (Darton, Longman and Todd, 1998), and *Gone for Good? Church leaving and returning in the 21st century* (Epworth, 2007); Alan Jamieson, *A Churchless Faith: Faith journeys beyond the churches* (SPCK, 2002); and Steve Aisthorpe, *The Invisible Church: Learning from the experiences of churchless Christians* (Saint Andrew Press, 2016).

Chapter 6

1   Anna Norman-Walker, 'Festival churches: a step towards sustainable rural ministry into the future', *Ecclesiology Today*, no. 49–50 (2014).

2   Patrick Whitworth, *Prepare for Exile: A new spirituality and mission for the church* (SPCK, 2008), p. 34.

3   Michael Riddell, *Threshold of the Future: Reforming the church in the post-Christian west* (SPCK, 1998), p. 1.

4   Whitworth, *Prepare for Exile*, p. 19.

5   Steve Aisthorpe, *Rewilding the Church*, (Saint Andrew Press, 2020).

6   Robert Warren, *Building Missionary Congregations*, Board of Mission Occasional Paper No. 4 (Church House Publishing, 1995).

7   Lings, *Seven Sacred Spaces*, ch. 13.

8   David Watson, *Discipleship* (Hodder & Stoughton, 1981), p. 16.

9   Whitworth, *Prepare for Exile*, pp. 22–29.

10   From Canticle for use on a Wednesday mornings, *A New Zealand Prayer Book – He Karakia Mihinare o Aotearoa*, p. 74. Used by permission.

11   Alan Kreider, *The Patient Ferment of the Early Church: The improbable rise of Christianity in the Roman Empire* (Baker Academic, 2016).

12   Taken from the 1979 edition of the NIV.

13   George Lings, *The Day of Small Things: an analysis of fresh expressions of church in 21 dioceses of the Church of England* (Church Army, 2016). For a 36-page summary of how fxC develop, who attends them and how they can be sustained, see George Lings, *Encountering The Day of Small Things* (Church Army, 2017). Both reports, along with several others, can be downloaded at **churcharmy.org/our-work/research/publications/#fresh-expressions-of-church-reports**.

14   Gordon Mursell, *Praying in Exile* (Darton, Longman and Todd, 2005).

Chapter 7

1   Knox, *Older People and The Church*, p. 129; Tournier, *Learning to Grow Old*, p. 164.
2   Wendell Berry, *The Art of Loading Brush: New agrarian writings* (Counterpoint, 2017), p. 6; Tournier, *Learning to Grow Old*, p. 214; *The Adventure of Living*, p. 209.
3   Jane Fearnley-Whittingstall, *The Pocket Book of Good Grannies* (Short Books, 2011).
4   Tournier, *Learning to Grow Old*, p. 183.
5   Merchant, *Pioneering the Third Age* p. 68.
6   Eddie Askew, *A Silence and a Shouting* (The Leprosy Mission International, 1982; reprinted 2001), p. 58.
7   English, *A Great Place to Grow Old*, p. 38.
8   Fischer, *Autumn Gospel*, p. 86.
9   Tournier, *Learning to Grow Old*, p, 240-241.
10   Roger Pooley and Philip Seddon (eds), *Lord of the Journey: A reader in Christian spirituality* (HarperCollins, 1986), p. 274.
11   David Cole (Brother Cassian), 'From simple stillness to shining greatness', in Olivia Warburton and Karen Laister (eds), *The BRF Book of 365 Bible Reflections* (BRF, 2021), p. 268.
12   Pooley and Seddon, *Lord of the Journey*, p. 281, citing a letter used by a 1926 biography.

Chapter 8

1   Griffin, *Green Leaves for Later Years*, p. 25.
2   Marion Ashton, *A Mind at Ease* (tenth edition, Overcomer Literature Trust, 1979), p. 28.
3   Clark H. Pinnock, *Most Moved Mover: A theology of God's openness* (Baker Academic, 2001), p. 32.
4   Willard, *The Divine Conspiracy*, pp. 269–70. The other passage was the prayer of Hezekiah in 2 Kings 19:8–37.
5   Far from being unmoved, God is very moved. Hence the title chosen by Pinnock, *Most Moved Mover*.
6   C.S. Lewis, *Mere Christianity* (Fontana Books, 1955), p. 49.
7   Hence the title by John Sanders, *The God Who Risks* (IVP, 1998).
8   C.S. Lewis, *The Problem of Pain* (Fount, 1977), p. 22, cited by Pete Grieg, *God on Mute: Engaging the silence of unanswered prayer*

(David C. Cook, 2007) p. 145, in a chapter discussing reasons for unanswered prayer.

9   Tournier, *The Adventure of Living*, pp. 114, 193.
10 C.S. Lewis, *A Grief Observed* (Faber and Faber, 1961), pp. 9, 11–13, 19, 24–25, 26–28, 35–36, 43, 46, 47, 49.
11 Griffin, *Green Leaves for Later Years*, pp. 63–73.
12 Fischer, *Autumn Gospel*, p. 57.
13 Rowan Williams, *The Dwelling of the Light* (Canterbury Press, 2003), p. 15.
14 Quoted, but unreferenced, in *Celtic Daily Prayer* (Harper Collins, 2000), Finan Readings, 20 April, p. 655. A quote with a similar view is taken from Henri Nouwen cited in the Finan Readings, 2 June, p. 684.
15 Henri J. M. Nouwen, *The Return of the Prodigal Son: A story of homecoming* (Darton, Longman and Todd, 1994), pp. 115–16.
16 Griffin, *Green Leaves for later Years*, p. 40.
17 Tournier, *The Adventure of Living*, p. 193; Lings, *Reproducing Churches*, p. 11; Lings, *Seven Sacred Spaces* (the seven are Cell, Chapel, Chapter, Cloister, Garden, Refectory, Scriptorium); Heilbrun, *The Last Gift of Time*, p. 51.

Chapter 9

1   Pollock, *The Book about Getting Older*, pp. 31–33.
2   Nouwen, *Bread for the Journey*, p. 112.
3   Tournier, *Learning to Grow Old*, p. 225.
4   Nouwen, *Bread for the Journey*, p. 104.
5   Tournier, *Learning to Grow Old*, p. 175, 172.
6   Tournier, *Learning to Grow Old*, pp. 222–23, 218. Tournier comments that the ideal of indifference in the face of death is instead an Epicurean and Stoic view.
7   Tournier, *Learning to Grow Old*, p. 178.
8   Tournier, *Learning to Grow Old*, p. 185.
9   Tournier, *Learning to Grow Old*, pp. 210–11.
10 Richard and Judith Hays, in Hauerwas et al. (eds), *Growing Old in Christ*, p. 15; Fischer, *Autumn Gospel*, pp. 95–99.
11 Tournier, *Learning to Grow Old*, p. 227.

Chapter 10

1 Lings, *Seven Sacred Spaces*, p. 93.
2 Knox, *Older People and the Church*, pp. 37, 38, 157.
3 Griffin, *Green Leaves for Later Years*, pp. 42–62.
4 Heilbrun, *The Last Gift of Time*, p. 6.
5 Tournier, *Learning to Grow Old*, pp. 113, 182; Fischer, *Autumn Gospel*, pp. 32, 126; Griffin, *Green Leaves for Later Years*, p. 71.
6 Louise Addison, 'The secret to a long and healthy life', *Dinnington Village Magazine*, January 2022.
7 Fischer, *Autumn Gospel*, pp. 36–38.
8 Fischer, *Autumn Gospel*, p. 156. My addition in brackets.
9 Tournier, *Learning to Grow Old*, p. 146.

Appendix

1 Lings, *Seven Sacred Spaces*, pp. 169–71 unpacks the relationships of these three types of learning, and which Jesus used.
2 A source to understand this practice is Kreider, *The Patient Ferment of the Early Church*, ch. 6.

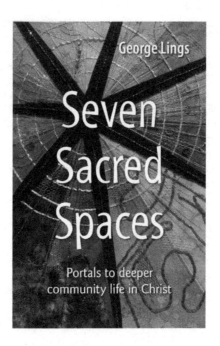

Too often people's understanding of and engagement with 'church' is reduced to corporate worship, when it is so much more. George Lings identifies seven characteristic elements in Christian communities through the ages, which when held in balance enable a richer expression of disciple ship, mission and community – cell, chapel, chapter, cloister, garden, refectory and scriptorium. Through this lens George Lings explores how these seven elements relate to our individual and communal walk with God, hold good for church and family life, and appear in wider society.

Seven Sacred Spaces
Portals to deeper community life in Christ
George Lings
978 0 85746 934 2 £10.99

brfonline.org.uk

Grandparenting brings new life and joy and also the opportunity to walk spiritually alongside our grandchildren. In this book, Becky Sedgwick explores how grandparents can actively encourage and equip their grandchildren to meet and know God, offering tools and skills for the journey. Whatever your circumstances, God has positioned you to be a unique voice speaking into your grandchildren's lives, helping to nurture them into the reality of a relationship with the God who loves them.

Grandparenting for Faith
Sharing God with the children you love the most
Becky Sedgwick
978 1 80039 204 5 £9.99

brfonline.org.uk

Ministries

Inspiring people of all ages to grow in Christian faith

BRF Ministries is the home of Anna Chaplaincy, Living Faith, Messy Church and Parenting for Faith

As a charity, our work would not be possible without fundraising and gifts in wills.
To find out more and to donate,
visit brf.org.uk/give or call +44 (0)1235 462305